**OTHER TITLES IN THE
HEART OF OAK SEA CLASSICS SERIES INCLUDE:**

The Wing-and-Wing by James Fenimore Cooper

Doctor Dogbody's Leg by James Norman Hall

Mr Midshipman Easy by Frederick Marryat

Peter Simple by Frederick Marryat

The Black Ship by Dudley Pope

LORD COCHRANE

Seaman, Radical, Liberator

COCHRANE IN 1807 (*from a portrait by Stroehling*)

CHRISTOPHER LLOYD

Lord Cochrane
Seaman, Radical, Liberator

A Life of Thomas, Lord Cochrane,
10th Earl of Dundonald

HEART OF OAK SEA CLASSICS

Dean King, Series Editor

Foreword by
Dean King

Introduction by
John B. Hattendorf

AN OWL BOOK

HENRY HOLT AND COMPANY   NEW YORK

Henry Holt and Company, Inc.
Publishers since 1866
115 West 18th Street
New York, New York 10011

Henry Holt ® is a registered
trademark of Henry Holt and Company, Inc.

Published in Canada by Fitzhenry & Whiteside Ltd.,
195 Allstate Parkway, Markham, Ontario L3R 4T8.

Library of Congress Cataloging-in-Publication Data
Lloyd, Christopher, 1906–
Lord Cochrane: seaman, radical, liberator: a life of Thomas,
Lord Cochrane, 10th Earl of Dundonald / Christopher Lloyd; foreword
by Dean King; introduction by John Hattendorf. — 1st Holt ed.
p. cm.—(Heart of oak sea classics series)
Originally published: London: Longmans, Green, 1947.
Includes bibliographical references (p.   ) and index.
ISBN 0-8050-5986-5 (hardcover : alk. paper).
ISBN 0-8050-5569-X (pbk. : alk. paper)
1. Dundonald, Thomas Cochrane, Earl of, 1775–1860. 2. Great
Britain—History, Naval—19th century. 3. Admirals—Great
Britain—Biography. I. Title. II. Series.
DA88.1.D9L6 1998
359'.0092—dc21
[B]   98-6484

Henry Holt books are available for special promotions and
premiums. For details contact: Director, Special Markets.

This edition of *A Life of Thomas Lord Cochrane*, First Edition,
is published by arrangement with Addison Wesley Longman,
Limited, London.

First published in 1947 by Longmans, Green and Co. Ltd.

First Owl Books Edition 1998

Designed by Kate Nichols

Printed in the United States of America
All first editions are printed on acid-free paper. ∞

1 3 5 7 9 10 8 6 4 2

HEART OF OAK

Come cheer up, my lads, 'tis to glory we steer,
To add something new to this wonderful Year:
To honour we call you, not press you like slaves,
For who are so free as the sons of the waves?

CHORUS:
Heart of Oak are our ships,
Heart of Oak are our men,
We always are ready,
Steady, boys, steady,
We'll fight and we'll conquer again and again.

We ne'er see our foes but we wish them to stay;
They never see us but they wish us away:
If they run, why we follow, and run them on shore,
For if they won't fight us, we cannot do more.

Heart of Oak, etc.

They swear they'll invade us, these terrible foes,
They'll frighten our women, and children, and beaux;
But should their flat-bottoms in darkness get o'er,
Still Britons they'll find to receive them on shore.

Heart of Oak, etc.

We'll still make them run and we'll still make them sweat,
In spite of the Devil, and Brussels Gazette:
Then cheer up, my lads, with one voice let us sing
Our soldiers, our sailors, our statesman, and King.

Heart of Oak, etc.

—DAVID GARRICK

Source: C. H. Firth, *Naval Songs and Ballads*. Publications of the Navy Records Society, vol. XXXIII (London, 1908), p. 220.

CONTENTS

FOREWORD BY DEAN KING ix

INTRODUCTION BY JOHN B. HATTENDORF xi

SUGGESTIONS FOR FURTHER READING xvi

PART I. THE SEA WOLF

I. THE CAPTAIN OF THE *SPEEDY* 7

II. THE CRUISE OF THE *SPEEDY* 16

III. THE FIRST QUARREL 26

IV. THE GOLDEN *PALLAS* 33

V. THE CRUISE OF THE IMPERIEUSE 38

VI. THE BATTLE IN THE AIX ROADS 54

VII. THE COURT MARTIAL 68

PART II. CRUSADER IN PARLIAMENT

I. THE CAUSE OF REFORM 83

II. PRIZE COURTS AND SECRET PLANS 98

III. THE STOCK EXCHANGE TRIAL 115

IV. IN THE WILDERNESS 127

PART III. CRUSADER AT LARGE

I. THE LIBERATION OF CHILE AND PERU   141
II. IN THE SERVICE OF BRAZIL   157
III. THE GREEK WAR OF INDEPENDENCE   168
IV. IN HIS OWN CAUSE   184
V. LAST YEARS   195

BIBLIOGRAPHY   205
INDEX   211
ABOUT THE EDITORS   215

FOREWORD

I T IS HARD to imagine any more literarily inspirational historical figures than Horatio Nelson and Thomas Cochrane, the 10th
earl of Dundonald. Admiral Nelson, of course, has been canon-
ized as a savior of England. He was bold, innovative, intensely loyal
to his men, and he pursued the enemy as relentlessly as any military
leader in history.

Nelson, even when described by the most circumspect historian,
hovers somewhere in the realm of the superhuman. Certain that his
country depended upon him for its survival, he sacrificed his life to
achieve his goal—the defeat of Napoleon's fleet. And, in modern-day
parlance, Nelson departed at the top of his game.

As Lloyd so skillfully describes in *Lord Cochrane: Seaman, Radical,
Liberator*, Lord Thomas Cochrane, like Nelson, possessed indomitable
courage, creative genius in battle, an almost savage hunger to engage
the enemy, and the natural ability to motivate his men—who in turn
genuinely loved him. While Nelson was the master of fleet action, involving line-of-battle ships, Cochrane was the master of single-ship
action, involving frigates and unrated vessels.

Naturally, part of what makes these larger-than-life men so interesting to us today is their larger-than-life flaws. According to Sir

Arthur Wellesley, later Duke of Wellington, when he first met Nelson (who did not know whom he was addressing) Nelson's conversation was "so vain and so silly as to surprise and almost disgust me." Nelson wore decorations, like a peacock wears feathers, even in battle, where it made him an obvious target of sharpshooters, eventually costing him his life.

A fiery and outspoken Scot, Cochrane was almost equally self-destructive. He regularly berated the political and naval establishments and criticized his superiors, much to his own detriment. Furious at his superior, Admiral Lord Gambier, for lacking aggression at the Battle of Aix Roads, Cochrane tainted the victory by publicly decrying Gambier, doing so at a time when good news was badly needed at home. Despite his heroism at sea, Cochrane was laid low by his radical politics, as well as by a financial scandal. He was a tragic hero in the classical sense, one whose flaws were apparent to everyone but himself.

However, as this biography shows, Cochrane's basic integrity was undeniable. He stood by his convictions and fought back from adversity time and again, and so his life continues to fascinate us for reasons beyond his brilliance in battle. Having inspired Patrick O'Brian's great Aubrey-Maturin series as well as a slew of other fictional accounts, the life of Cochrane—not nearly so well chronicled in history books as Nelson's—continues to stir readers today, especially as told in Christopher Lloyd's taut biography.

MY SINCEREST THANKS to John B. Hattendorf, who—as an alumnus of Kenyon College, which owes much to the generous benefaction of the evangelical Episcopalian Admiral Lord Gambier—courageously overcame this inherent conflict of interest to introduce here Lord Cochrane's biography. Professor Hattendorf's examination of Christopher Lloyd's distinguished career as a naval historian and his presentation of the scholarly backdrop to *Lord Cochrane: Seaman, Radical, Liberator* are extremely helpful to anyone interested in naval history or literature.

—Dean King

INTRODUCTION

FEW NAVAL OFFICERS have been so talented and had so tumultuous a career as Thomas Cochrane, the tenth earl of Dundonald. A brilliant inventor and tactician, he won gallant victories, received the highest decorations for valor, and held major commands in the navies of five different countries: Britain, Chile, Peru, Brazil, and Greece. Yet in his turbulent career, he was also discredited, imprisoned for fraud, financially ruined, stripped of his rank, degraded from his knighthood, expelled as a member of Parliament, and repeatedly involved in litigation and legal squabbles. Despite this, his honors and position were eventually restored to him and, as one of Britain's great seamen, he was buried, with honors, in Westminster Abbey.

Not surprisingly, the biography of such a man is, itself, controversial. The first books published about him were both defensive and contentious. For many years, the main texts written about him were the three volumes of autobiography that he published between 1859 and 1861 and the equally defensive volumes of biography, covering the latter period of his life, written by his son, the eleventh earl of Dundonald. In his bitter autobiography, Cochrane's aggressive self-justification and venom for his antagonists overshadow his remarkable success as a master of seamanship, as an inspiring leader, and as a great naval commander.

Fortunately for Cochrane, however, one of the men whom he had greatly inspired at sea was none other than the future novelist Frederick Marryat, who joined Cochrane's ship as a fourteen-year-old midshipman in 1806. At the time, the thirty-one-year-old Cochrane commanded the *Imperieuse*, a frigate he led into many successful actions. Marryat remained with Cochrane, a strict but fair disciplinarian who took great interest in the welfare of his men, through the Battle of Aix Roads in April 1809. Like most of Cochrane's junior officers and seamen, Marryat came to virtually worship the fearless Scot.

Cochrane played a role in literature well before his autobiography appeared, through Marryat's famous sea novels. Many of Marryat's scenes were based on events during his years under Cochrane's command, and Marryat modeled on Cochrane his fictional captain in *Frank Mildmay*, Captain M—— in *The King's Own*, Captain Savage in *Peter Simple,* and Captain Wilson in *Mr. Midshipman Easy*, all published between 1829 and 1836. In these works, Marryat depicted Cochrane in idealistic terms as the dashing and inspiring leader that he was, and it was this aspect of the captain's personality that would be immortalized in fiction rather than his quarrelsome public persona.

Marryat's wildly popular novels ignited a literary genre that continues to this day: historical fiction about the Royal Navy fighting Napoleon (1793–1815), much of which is inspired by the real-life achievements of naval officers. In these works, Cochrane's exploits are second only to Lord Nelson's. No doubt many of the events recounted in this book by Lloyd will sound somewhat familiar to the readers of the fictional genre by writers such as Dudley Pope, C. Northcote Parkinson, Kenneth Maynard, and, most notably, C. S. Forester and Patrick O'Brian.

For many years, there was a great disparity between Cochrane's reputation among readers and writers of historical fiction and the view that historians took of him. The first work to begin to correct the historical view was Sir John Knox Laughton's ten-page biographical sketch, written in 1883 for the *Dictionary of National Biography*. This was followed in 1896 by a short volume entitled *Dundonald* in Macmillan's Men of Action series. In *Dundonald*, Sir John Fortescue, who would later become famous for his multi-volume *History of the*

British Army, added to the bridge between the fictive and the historical Cochrane.

In the century that followed, a number of writers produced biographies and historical works relating to Cochrane's career. Among them, Christopher Lloyd's 1947 biography, *Lord Cochrane: Seaman, Radical, Liberator* stands out as the first attempt to publish an impartial and authoritative study about Cochrane that would have popular appeal. As an author, Charles Christopher Lloyd was particularly well suited to this task.

Born in Bangalore, India, on September 2, 1906, Lloyd was educated at Marlborough School in Wiltshire and Lincoln College, Oxford, where he took a first in history. His first academic appointment was at Bishop's University in Quebec, where he lectured in history from 1930 to 1934. Returning to England, he took up an appointment at the Britannia Royal Naval College at Dartmouth. While lecturing in history to naval cadets in 1939, he published *Captain Marryat and the Old Navy*, a biographical study that linked Marryat's naval and literary career with Cochrane's. Lloyd remained at Dartmouth through the Second World War and developed a deep interest in using history to inspire young naval officers. In his decade there, he also saw many of his former pupils die in the war. Thus, it was with the profoundest of feelings that he would dedicate his study of Cochrane to "the Cadets who were in my tutor set at Dartmouth and to the memory of those who were killed in action."

In 1945, Lloyd moved on to the Royal Naval College at Greenwich where he was lecturer in history to mid-career naval officers. In 1947, he published *Lord Cochrane*, a natural sequel to his biography of Marryat, and one that built directly on exploring the interrelationship of literature and history. In 1949, he published *The Navy and the African Slave Trade*.

In 1962, Lloyd succeeded Michael Lewis as the college's Professor of History. Remaining in that position until he reached the age of sixty in 1966, he also devoted great effort to many of Britain's prominent organizations of naval and maritime history, including the National Maritime Museum, the Navy Records Society—of which he served as publications secretary from 1949 to 1962—and the Society for Nautical Research, where, from 1970 to 1979, he edited *The Mariner's Mirror*, one of the most scholarly of maritime journals. Lloyd remained a tireless writer and editor throughout his long career and almost up until his death on March 31, 1986, at the age of seventy-nine.

Among Lloyd's most important scholarly works are the editions he edited for the Navy Records Society. These include two volumes of *Papers of Lord Keith* (1950, 1955), *Naval Miscellany* (1952), *A Memoir of James Trevenen* (with R. C. Anderson in 1959), and *The Health of Seamen* (1965).

In his narrative writing, Lloyd was particularly noted for his focus on individuals, his understanding of the ways of sailing ships, and his intimate knowledge of the many abstruse technicalities involved in naval life afloat, all of which he explained in a manner that was easily understood. His biography of Lord Cochrane shows this in great measure, as do his works *Medicine and the Navy in the Period 1714–1815* (1961), which he edited with Jack L. S. Coulter, and *The British Seaman 1200–1860: A Social Survey* (1968).

Many of Lloyd's other works concentrated on the great battles and leaders. Among his biographical studies were *William Dampier* (1966) and *Mr. Barrow of the Admiralty: A Life of Sir John Barrow, 1764–1848* (1970). These were paralleled by studies of battles, for example, *The Capture of Quebec, 1759* (1959), *St. Vincent & Camperdown* (1963), *The Nile Campaign: Nelson and Napoleon in Egypt* (1973), and his popular *Atlas of Maritime History* (1976). Throughout, Lloyd balanced his technical knowledge and accurate research with a devotion to promoting the romantic side of naval history and to capitalizing on its inspirational value in teaching professional naval officers. His clear and vivid writing style, matched by his choice of maps and illustrations, made his volumes on naval history very popular, not only for officers of the Royal Navy but to the public at large.

Lloyd was at his best and was most successful when writing about traditional naval actions at sea, particularly in bringing to bear the insights and reactions of individual seamen and officers. His study of Lord Cochrane is an excellent example of his literary skill in dealing with a romantic naval figure. When the volume first appeared, it was generally welcomed, but some academic critics had mild reservations. Professor Theodore Ropp of Duke University, then the leading scholar of military history in the United States, commented in the pages of the *American Historical Review:*

Though the story of the soldier of fortune in the nineteenth century remains to be written, this short volume is an excellent footnote to the separate histories of the Royal Navy, parliamentary reform, and Latin American and Greek independence. It is an excellent case study of one of the more turbulent characters of the romantic age, and a useful reminder that the English radicals, who now appear so tame and unexciting, were real fighters. (LIII, 1947–48, pp. 531–32)

The reviewer in *The Times Literary Supplement* noted, Lloyd's "portrait of Cochrane differs from Fortescue's as much as the charming drawing by Adam Busk differs from the painting by Ramsay . . . of about the same period; but like Fortescue, Mr. Lloyd shows the man of action only" ("A Great Captain," *TLS*, 46, 1947, p. 388). That is to say, while Fortescue treats this fighting seaman with cold formality, Lloyd paints a vivid and distinctive portrait.

From the scholarly point of view, the book's weakness lies in focusing only on English-language materials for Cochrane's career abroad. More recently, others have made some progress in this area, particularly on his period in Latin America. Details on these books may be found in the Suggestions for Further Reading below.

Among the several studies available, Christopher Lloyd's 1947 biography, *Lord Cochrane: Seaman, Radical, Liberator* remains, in the opinion of the editors of this series, the most engaging introduction to Cochrane's life. Because Lloyd was also a Marryat scholar, this is especially true for those interested in the relationship between naval history and historical fiction.

—John B. Hattendorf

SUGGESTIONS FOR
FURTHER READING

A guide to scholarship relating to Cochrane since the publication of Christopher Lloyd's biography in 1947.

Billingsley, Edward Baxter. *In Defense of Neutral Rights: The United States Navy and the Wars of Independence in Chile and Peru* (Chapel Hill, 1967). Provides some details on the U.S. Navy's relations with Cochrane.

Cochrane, Michael. "Cochrane: Basque Roads, 1809," in Eric Grove, ed., *Great Battles of the Royal Navy as Commemorated in the Gunroom, Britannia Royal Naval College, Dartmouth* (London, 1994). The most recent re-examination of the action at Aix Roads, by Cochrane's great-great grandson, a lieutenant-commander in the Royal Navy.

Garín Jiménez, Jorge, ed. *Vicealmirante Lord Thomas Alexander Cochrane* (Santiago, 1993–95). Three volumes of documents from the Chilean National Archives, published by the Chilean Navy's Historical Office.

Graham, Gerald S., and R. A. Humphreys. *The Navy and South America, 1807–1823: Correspondence of the Commanders-in-Chief on the South American Station.* Navy Records Society, volume 104 (London, 1962). Official Correspondence from British admirals during the period Cochrane was in South America.

Grimble, Ian. *The Sea Wolf: The Life of Admiral Cochrane* (London, 1978). Uses Dundonald family papers not available to previous biographers.

Lloyd, Christopher. *Captain Marryat and the Old Navy* (London, 1939). A view of Cochrane from Marryat's personal and literary viewpoint.

Thomas, Donald. *Cochrane: Britannia's Last Sea-King* (New York, 1978). Uses some British Library and Public Record Office manuscripts which complement those used by other authors.

Tute, Warren. *Cochrane: A Life of Admiral the Earl of Dundonald* (London, 1965). With special interest in his political ideas, the author uses Dundonald family papers and artifacts previously unavailable.

Vale, Brian. *Independence or Death: British Sailors and Brazilian Independence, 1822–1825* (London, 1996). An important study based on original research, placing Cochrane's Brazilian activities in perspective.

—J.B.H.

LORD COCHRANE

Seaman, Radical, Liberator

To the Cadets who were in my tutor
set at Dartmouth

*"who in these declining times have yet in
your brave bosoms the sparks of that
sprightly fire of your courageous ancestors,
and to this hour retain the seeds of their
magnanimity and greatness"*

(*Drayton, 1627*)

AND

TO THE MEMORY OF THOSE WHO WERE
KILLED IN ACTION

PART I

The Sea Wolf

CHAPTER I

The Captain of the Speedy

THE CAPTAIN of the *Speedy* pushed open the skylight of his tiny cabin, propped a mirror on the edge of that part of the quarter-deck which served for a dressing-table, and began to shave. It was unfortunate that a man well over six feet tall should be appointed to the command of a sloop in which it was impossible for him to stand upright in his cabin; and since the table clamped to the floor occupied nearly all its space, it was equally difficult for him to sit down.

However, she was his first command, and the coast of Spain lay like a summer cloud on the horizon. An independent command, even if it was only that of a converted coasting brig of 158 tons, gave him, for the first time in his life, the opportunity of doing what he liked without the necessity of consulting those with whose advice he was almost certain to disagree.

In 1800 Lord Thomas Cochrane was twenty-five years old. A tall, red-haired Scotsman, traditionally descended from a band of Scandinavian sea-rovers, he was gifted with exceptional physical strength, high courage and an ingenious turn of mind; but he was cursed with an inexhaustible capacity for harbouring a grievance. Proud as only an impoverished Scottish nobleman can be, he detested the necessity, dictated by the nature of his profession, of having to truckle to senior officers whose attainments he frequently despised and whose politics he invariably detested. He was too outspoken an egoist to enjoy wardroom life, and of too active a temperament to submit to the boredom of a blockading fleet. Since so much of a naval officer's life, in those days as in these, was spent in some such humdrum way, Cochrane's career in the Navy was bound to be brief and stormy. When the opportunity for action offered, he rose to heights unequalled even in that age of daring enterprise; but his unruly temperament made it impossible for him to earn the higher prize for selfless devotion to duty, however dull, of which the patient endurance of Collingwood is the supreme example. Indeed, Cochrane was born in opposition, and it was unfortunate from the point of view of a successful career that he had chosen so highly disciplined a profession as that of a naval officer.

"THE COCHRANES," it was commonly said in Scotland, "have long been noted for an original and dashing turn of mind, which was sometimes called genius, sometimes eccentricity." Thomas's father, the ninth earl of Dundonald, was as typical of this family trait as he was himself. It is time justice was done to the achievements of this eccentric old gentleman. His researches into the by-products of coal brought him neither reward in his own day nor posthumous fame in ours. Inventors are notoriously bad business men, and his son lived to deplore the dissipation of energy with which his father's inquisitive mind turned from one line of research to another, every line offering enormous possibilities which have been exploited in our day, but none of which were commercially successful in his own. Such men usually reap their reward after their deaths, but the value of Dundonald's work is not yet sufficiently appreciated. In the opinion of Sir John Dalrymple, Watts's legal adviser, "I consider very well what I say, when I say that from a Naval Nation Lord Dundonald deserves a Statue of Gold."

As a young man he had seen service in the Navy, but a single voyage to the tropics was enough to convince him that it was no career for an intelligent aristocrat. One thing, however, struck him during that cruise to the coast of Guinea, and that was the extraordinary inefficiency of contemporary methods of combating the depredations of the *teredo navalis*, or naval worm. This was before the practice of coppering the bottoms of ships was introduced, a practice which went far to rendering his first invention useless. When he succeeded to the Earldom in 1778 he inherited little more than the title and the entailed estates of Culross Abbey on the shore of the Firth of Forth. However, he found here an abundant supply of coal, which it was easy to mine. It appeared to him that "by working these coals which are on the Sea side properly, and carrying on a Salt Work, very great benefit in all probability would arise." From coal, he soon discovered, any number of by-products, particularly tar, could be extracted.

In a maritime nation the problem of obtaining sufficient tar to coat the bottoms of ships is obviously a matter of the most urgent importance. In olden days good Stockholm tar was a byword in the British Navy, but at the beginning of the eighteenth century the Baltic countries forced up the price of this, their chief monopoly. In consequence an alternative source of supply was sought in the forests of the American colonies, but the bounties necessary to encourage its manufacture there made the cost equally prohibitive. There remained the possibility of extracting it from coal deposits in the mother country. It was to this problem Dundonald addressed himself, and his experiments rapidly met with such success that the kilns of the British Tar Company were to be seen all over that part of Scotland. In this he was associated for some time with his cousin, John Loudon Macadam. After consultation with eminent scientists Dundonald was able to extend his patent for coal-tar to 1807. His *Account of the Qualities and Uses of Coal Tar and Coal Varnish* (1785) enumerates coke, lamp black, ammonia, as well as tar, as among the most useful by-products. It looked as if his coal mine would prove to be a gold mine, but the misfortunes which dogged the finances of the Dundonald family wrecked his prospects. In some mysterious way, money seemed to turn to water in the hands of both father and son. It is not long before we find Macadam suing him over the Muirkirk tar works, and the Admiralty refusing to use his varnish preservative. The latter's reason, given to a fellow researcher, was just of the type which made his son fight the administrative abuses of the old Navy so venomously in later years: "The principal reason is that it succeeds too well; the ships not requiring such frequent repair." Not till 1822 did the Admiralty commission the Royal Society to enquire into a more efficient preservative, and then Sir Humphry Davy's favourable report on Dundonald's work came too late to retrieve the family fortunes. When he was put on the pension list of the Literary

Fund the next year, the earl's position is described as one of "destitution and distress."

Besides tar and varnish Dundonald stumbled on the invention of gas lighting. Here again, it was Murdoch and Winsor who ushered in the Age of Gas. Murdoch never acknowledged any acquaintance with Dundonald's work (though he did not, indeed, claim to be the discoverer of the illuminating properties of coal gas); but we know that the earl discussed this very matter with Watt at a date when Murdoch was in the latter's employment. Thomas describes his father's accidental discovery as follows: "Having noticed the inflammable nature of a vapour arising during the distillation of tar, the earl fitted a gun-barrel to the eduction pipe leading from the condenser. On applying fire to the muzzle, a vivid light blazed forth."

It would take us too far afield to describe other instances of the earl's inventive genius. Ammonia, agricultural chemistry, the salting of herrings, were all subjects to which he made important contributions both in print and in actual experiment. But the result of his father's devotion to science was that the only thing he could give his son when the latter went to sea was a gold watch; an uncle had to pay for his clothes. As an old man he played little part in his son's life until, indeed, he became so eccentric that his behaviour was a cause of embarrassment to him. He borrowed extensively from him, quarrelled violently, took to drink, and died in Paris at the age of eighty-three, mad, penniless and alone.

By frittering away the scanty remains of the family fortune he was able to leave his eldest son nothing more tangible than the title and a ruined castle in Renfrewshire. None the less it was from him that Thomas inherited that scientific bent which led him to devote so much of his life to research and invention, in many cases along the lines laid down by his father. In his secret plans for smoke-screens and chemical warfare, in his ingenious propaganda methods, his mosquito ships, his innumerable experiments with steamships, rotary engines, convoy lamps, screws and explosives, the tenth earl of Dundonald was indeed his father's son.

His mother died before the school bills began to come in, and with her died Thomas's chief hope of joining the Navy, a hope which he appears to have entertained from his earliest years. She was herself the daughter of a distinguished frigate captain, and it was this naval inheritance, together with his pastime of sailing the Firth of Forth with sheets from his bed for sails, that was responsible for her son's early love for the sea. Disillusioned by his own brief experience, the ninth earl held that the Army was the profession of the Cochranes. So, after an uneasy succession of tutors whose salaries were paid by their grandmother, the two eldest boys, Thomas and Basil, were sent to London, commissions having been bought for them in His Majesty's 104th Regiment of the Horse Guards. "I have just seen the young gentlemen off by the coach," writes the family agent; "it is true that they have not had very much education, but they are strong and fine to look at and very sensible and will get on anywhere."

Self-reliance, indeed, was the only lesson Lord Cochrane had so far learned. Throughout his life he was the brilliant amateur, in war, in politics, in the field of scientific invention. He realised early that only by his own efforts could he achieve that place in the world's esteem to which he felt his gifts and his lineage entitled him. A granite streak of obstinacy enabled him to gain what he set out to achieve, in spite of the formidable obstacle of an insubordinate temperament. "Ambition," says Bacon, "is like choler; which is an humour that maketh men active, earnest, full of alacrity and stirring, if it be not stopped. But if it be stopped, and cannot have its way, it becometh adust, and thereby malign and venomous." That in itself is a sufficiently accurate summary of Cochrane's career. Perhaps if he had enjoyed the advantages of a more normal education he might have turned out a "sounder" character. If so, his record would have been a dull one. Along with the self-assertive egotism which made him so many enemies, he would also have lost the generous, quixotic enthusiasm which spurred him to so many brilliant exploits in so many parts of the world. His temperament led him to prefer crusading in the cause of liberty to devoting himself to the narrow path of professional duty.

To be forced into the Army was bad enough; it was worse to be compelled to wear the uniform which his eccentric father had designed for him. His long hair was plastered back with candle-grease and flour, his legs enclosed in tight-fitting breeches and leggings, and, since his father was an ardent Whig, a horrible mustard-coloured waistcoat was thrust upon him. A humiliating encounter with some street urchins near Charing Cross sent him home weeping with renewed requests to be allowed to go to sea. His father gave him a sound cuffing and sent him to M. Chauvet's military academy in Kensington Square.

Unknown to the earl, his uncle, Sir Alexander Cochrane, had already entered the boy's name on the books of no less than four of His Majesty's ships-of-war—a practice of "false muster" common enough earlier in the century, but now dying out on account of the scandals it provoked. Thus it happened that at the age of seventeen Thomas Cochrane had the unusual advantage of being both a midshipman of the *Vesuvius, Caroline, Sophie* and *Hind* frigates and an officer in the Guards. His father's inability to pay the fees at M. Chauvet's academy decided the matter. Even then £100 had to be borrowed from a relative in order to fit him out for the Navy. On 27 June 1793 he joined his uncle's frigate, the *Hind*, at Sheerness.

The usual mode of entry into the Navy was for a boy to join his first ship at the age of thirteen as a captain's servant or first class volunteer, and to work himself up in the course of a few years to the rank of midshipman. Hence when Lord Cochrane was introduced to his "sea daddy," Jack Larmour (one of the few instances of a seaman promoted from the fo'castle to the quarter-deck), the latter looked askance at this exceptional midshipman of nearly eighteen years of age and over six feet tall.

"This Lord Cochrane's chest?" he grumbled as he was interrupted in the work of setting up the ship's rigging. "Does Lord Cochrane think he is going to bring a cabin aboard? The service is going to the devil! Get it up on the main deck!" His lordship having gone below to the midshipmen's berth on the orlop deck, orders were given for the end to be sawn off to make it manageable in the limited accommodation of a 28-gun frigate. From below Cochrane could hear the sound of sawing, accompanied by sundry uncomplimentary remarks on midshipmen in general and himself in particular.

But the boy's keenness, his delight in learning what most young noblemen would regard as the unpleasantly dull arts of navigation and seamanship, his quick intelligence and practical ability soon changed honest Jack's mind. Of course he continued to maintain as he had maintained for the past score years (and as his like still complain) that "he had never heard of such a thing as a perfect midshipman," but he only had to masthead the boy once, and he came to feel an affection and an admiration for his pupil which was generously returned. Cochrane was very far from being a humble person, but whenever he came across anyone who had something to teach him he showed a fine humility in his anxiety to learn. It was only with supine admirals and corrupt politicians that he got really angry.

Britain had been at war with Revolutionary France for less than a year when he joined the Navy. Young Cochrane felt that he had every chance of seeing some fighting, but his hopes were dashed when, instead of being sent to the scene of action, the *Hind* was ordered to cruise off the coast of Norway. For the next twelve months he enjoyed exploring the fiords and learning, as few have ever learned, the art of seamanship. When the ship returned to port and he was transferred to his uncle's new frigate, the *Thetis*, he was not content, as most boys would have been, to go on leave; discarding the rig of an officer, he helped Larmour as an ordinary seaman to set up the rigging, splice and knot, make bends and hitches, manage the boats, furl the sails and work the anchor.

The *Thetis* was ordered even farther from the seat of war. She was sent as a fishery protection vessel to cruise off the Banks of Newfoundland. For five long years Cochrane was on the North American station in one ship or another, hearing by the packets of the great naval victories in European waters and of the rising star of the young Napoleon, while he himself was condemned to a pointless existence of pig-sticking and hard drinking, the usual routine of a naval officer in peace-time. Nevertheless, as a result of the excellent training he had received at the hands of Jack Larmour, he rose rapidly in his profession; indeed he passed for lieutenant after only eighteen months' service, long before he had even served the regulation time afloat.

Although he spent so much time in later life attacking the abuses of patronage, he himself benefited not a little from the fact that he was of noble birth. It was probably this that led to his appointment to the flagship on the American station, and when at last he returned to England it was to this he owed the favour conferred on him by Admiral Keith in taking him into his flagship as a supernumerary. When they arrived at Gibraltar at the end of 1798 Lord St. Vincent, then in command of the Mediterranean fleet, received him kindly and confirmed his appointment to the *Barfleur*, Keith's flagship in the blockade of Cadiz. Such was his introduction to the stern old man with whom he was soon to quarrel so disastrously.

It was not long before he gave fresh proof that he was unfitted for wardroom life. He was too tactless, too impatient of etiquette, too wise in his own conceit, to get on with men he saw no reason to admire.

He had been on shore duck-shooting near Tetuan, and had got his uniform into a filthy state. On returning to his ship he went below to shift instead of reporting himself as soon as he came on board. The officer of the watch was a certain Lieutenant Beaver, a Pantisocratic crank who had actually succeeded in establishing one of his communistic colonies on the coast of Sierra Leone in the days before the war. He was an irritable sort of fellow who thought no small beer of himself. That evening he came into the wardroom and demanded why Lord Cochrane had not reported himself. Such conduct, he complained, made him appear "exceedingly ridiculous." Cochrane gave his reason, adding that he really could not help it if Lieutenant Beaver appeared ridiculous. The first lieutenant flew into a rage and forbade him to leave the ship. "Lieutenant Beaver," replied Cochrane, "we will, if you please, talk of this in another place." When Beaver demanded what he meant by those words, "his lordship turned his face aft and whistled."

Beaver immediately reported this act of insubordination to the captain. The latter was reluctant to make much of a wardroom quarrel, but Beaver was clearly within his rights and a court martial was held a few days later at which Keith presided. The miserable business made the admiral exceedingly angry. "Here are all the flag officers and captains called together," he complained, "at a time when the wind is coming fair, and the ship ought to be under way. I think I am made the most ridiculous person of the whole!" He dismissed the case with some sensible advice: "Lord Cochrane, I am directed by the Court to say that officers should not reply sharply to their superior officer, and a first lieutenant's situation should be supported by everyone; a ship is but a small place where six or seven hundred persons are collected together and officers should in every part of it avoid any flippancy."

A small matter. But an administrator like St. Vincent was not the man to overlook anything in the past record of the officers he promoted. A few years later when Cochrane demanded the promotion he deserved it was chiefly this episode which proved his undoing.

Service in the Mediterranean when Nelson was not in command was no more exciting than on the American station. For nearly two years Cochrane served in a ship of the line and never saw an action. Like many others he was disgusted when the French under Bruix slipped through the meshes of the British blockade and home again to Brest without being intercepted. Of course he blamed St. Vincent for it, but actually Keith was the more responsible. At Palermo he met Nelson for the only time in his life. Even to such a critical eye as

Cochrane's Nelson was the ideal commander, for the latter had that offensive spirit which he regarded as of the first importance in an admiral. "Never mind manoeuvres, always go at them," Nelson told him. No words can better describe Cochrane's own methods whenever he had the opportunity to command, always providing that we remember how meticulous were the preparations both men invariably made before an attack.

Soon after this Keith sent him in command of a prize to Minorca. She was the *Genereux*, one of the two ships of the line which escaped from the Battle of the Nile. The voyage was a stormy one and he was only able to bring his big ship safely into port after he and his young brother Archibald had forced the crew to do their duty by themselves leading the way aloft in a gale. Keith was evidently impressed by the way he had handled the ship, and even more by the admirable initiative shown in a gallant attempt to cut out a privateer near Algeciras. In April 1800 he recommended him for promotion and at the same time appointed him to the command of the sloop *Speedy*, lying in Port Mahon harbour.

CHAPTER II

~~

The Cruise of the Speedy

A BURLESQUE on a vessel of war" was Cochrane's description of his new ship. Though she appears in the Navy List as a sloop of war, she was really nothing but a converted coasting brig of 158 tons, mounting an armament of only fourteen 4-pound guns, "a species of gun little larger than a blunderbuss." Indeed, he claims to have walked the deck with a broadside of her shot in his pocket. He tried to get the authorities to mount two 12-pounders, but it was clear that the discharge of even these moderate-sized guns would dangerously strain the timbers of his little ship; so decided that what he lost in gun-power he would make up in speed. His task would be to harry the coasting trade, and a fast sailingship would achieve his aims almost as well as a heavier-armed vessel. With this aim in view he rigged a spare fore-topgallant yard from the *Genereux* as the *Speedy*'s mainyard.

Under her new rig the *Speedy* carried a dangerous stretch of canvas. She would need skilful handling if she was to avoid mishaps. She also carried far too large a crew—eighty-four men and six officers. But even this crowd had its compensations. Every vessel captured needed a prize crew to take her to the nearest friendly port, and if his cruise

was as successful as he meant it to be, at least a score of his men would
be out of the ship at any given time. For the last eighteen months the
Speedy had been commanded by Sir Jahleel Brenton, who had seen in
her, as he put it, "a service of much animation and even of enjoy-
ment." A first-rate officer, he had trained the ship's company now under Cochrane's command in their special duties of boarding and
cutting-out expeditions. Her first lieutenant, Parker, had already
shown himself a brave and energetic officer; Guthrie, the ship's doctor, became a life-long friend; and with his brother Archibald as senior
midshipman he took over the command of a happy ship.

His first orders were to join Keith's blockading squadron off
Genoa, where a starving French army under Massena was threatened
by the Austrians. The *Speedy* remained attached to this, the main
Mediterranean fleet, until Napoleon's victory at Marengo rendered
the blockade useless. She was then ordered to cruise off the south-
east coast of Spain to harass the coasting trade.

It was a task altogether after Cochrane's heart, and it is astonish-
ing how his genius blossomed as soon as he was given an independent command. Up to this date his story is the story of a thousand
other naval officers. He had never yet had the opportunity of showing his talents, and his seamanship had merely been a matter of carrying out the orders of his superiors as efficiently as possible. Now
he was able to handle a ship in his own way. He solved the tactical
problem by concentrating on speed, since he could not have weight
of metal. Moreover, with the intuition of a born fighter, he realised
the value of surprise in attacks on merchant vessels ill disciplined
for naval warfare. It was no good, he decided, attacking in the full
light of day; the local vessels which would be his prey knew the
coast far better than he did, and they would run for protection of
some fort or inlet at the first appearance of a hostile warship. He
therefore determined to watch the enemy's movements from far out
to sea and then close inshore to attack in the cold light of dawn. But
speed and surprise did not alone suffice; careful preparation before
any sort of an attack was made would ensure the minimum risk of
life among his men. When we consider what a rash impetuous man
he was in politics, such care is all the more noteworthy in Cochrane
the seaman. In all his operations as a frigate captain he never took a
risk unless his plans were well laid and there was a good chance of
success.

As soon as the *Speedy* left the fleet the list of her captures begins:

"June 16.—Captured a tartan off Elba. Sent her to Leghorn in charge
of an officer and four men.
"June 22.—Off Bastia. Chased a French privateer with a prize in
tow. The Frenchman abandoned the prize, a Sardinian vessel
laden with oil and wood, and we took possession. Made all sail in
chase of the privateer; but on our commencing to fire she ran un-
der the fort of Caprea, where we did not think proper to pursue
her."

So the log continues for the next thirteen months. Every type of
craft fell to her commander's daring and ingenuity—privateers of
every size and build, lateen-rigged feluccas, tartans, xebecs and what
he intriguingly calls "bombards." Nearly fifty vessels were captured,
together with over five hundred prisoners, during the cruise of the
Speedy in 1800 and 1801 without the loss of a dozen men. By December the little ship was the terror of the coasting trade between Cartagena and Barcelona. Large privateers and even frigates were sent to
put a stop to her depredations, with the result that her commander
experienced increasing difficulty in maintaining his average of three
or four prizes a week. Apart from those sunk or driven on shore,
every prize needed a crew to take her to port, and though there was
little sickness in such an active life, slight wounds had their effect in
depleting his numbers. Furthermore, the small storage capacity for
water necessitated frequent calls on the enemy's coast, and in every
bay a surprise might await the raider. Nor was it easy at a time when
privateers swarmed the seas to distinguish an ineffective merchant
vessel from a dangerous enemy. The *Speedy* herself was frequently
disguised, and she had the flags of all nations in her locker, to be
used as occasion demanded, for the etiquette of sea warfare permitted any ruse to gain an advantage.

One day shortly before the end of the year he sighted what he
supposed to be a large merchant vessel of the xebec type. However,
as he ranged up alongside, gunports suddenly opened in her sides
and the evil glint of a line of muzzles proved that she was one of the
ships sent to stop his activities. But he was prepared for just such an
emergency. In a trice the Danish colours were hoisted to the peak,
and to make things doubly sure the yellow quarantine flag was run
up to the foremast. A pseudo-Danish quartermaster, prompted by the

captain, had his story ready when the ship's boat reached her side. Pointing to the quarantine flag, he explained in guttural Spanish that the ship had but two days ago cleared a port on the Barbary Coast where plague was raging. That was enough to make the Spaniards pull back to their ship in terrified haste.

The *Speedy*'s crew was by this time bursting with self-confidence. They felt that they could tackle bigger problems than those set by coasting vessels, and some of the officers expressed their regret that they had not been allowed to attack the privateer. "Next time you shall have your chance," replied Cochrane.

On the evening of May 5 a large frigate, *El Gamo* as she proved to be, was sighted off Barcelona. Every preparation was made for the *Speedy*'s first and only big fight. To appreciate her captain's situation in this almost unparalleled feat of arms we should remember that for the *Speedy* to attack *El Gamo* was as if a small sloop were to attack a large destroyer of the "Battle" or "Tribal" class. Her armament was useless at a range of more than a hundred yards, and her total broadside weighed no more than 28 pounds. The weight of the Spaniard's broadside was 190 pounds, as she mounted twenty-two 12-pounders on her main deck, eight 8-pounders and two 24-pound carronades (a short-range gun firing a murderous charge of grape) on her upper deck. Her captain, Don Francesco de Torres, commanded a crew of 319 men compared with his rival's 54, so far had the latter's crew been depleted. Had Cochrane known these facts he would have hesitated to attack. As it was, the frigate looked big enough to destroy the *Speedy* with a single broadside. But he knew his men and he knew something of the poor quality of Spanish crews.

At half-past nine the next morning *El Gamo* hoisted the Spanish colours. The *Speedy* countered by hoisting the American flag to obtain time to get on the right tack. Then, as her captain put the helm over, down came the American flag and up ran her ensign. The Spaniard greeted him with an ineffective salvo at long range. Knowing that his popguns were useless at that distance, Cochrane ordered his gun-crews to reserve their fire until, running under the Spaniard's lee, he closed to grapple, locking his yards with those of the enemy. By so doing the enemy's guns could not be sufficiently depressed to do much damage. As soon as he felt the shock of the collision he gave the signal to fire. A broadside of his heaviest metal tore into the frigate's hull. Locked in this deadly embrace, the enemy's upper deck was a good ten feet above the *Speedy*'s, so the Spanish captain gave the order to board. But somehow Cochrane heard him and pushed off from the side while enemy boarders were still being turned up from below. As soon as they were collected the *Speedy*'s gun-crews, having double-shotted their guns, swept the decks with a devastating broadside; by the greatest good fortune both the Spanish captain and the boatswain were among those killed.

So the fight continued for close on an hour, the *Speedy* now closing to silence the Spaniard's fire, now standing away to rake her decks, worrying the frigate like a terrier. Two of the British had been killed and four wounded. Though Cochrane was certain that the Spaniards must have lost a far greater number, he knew that a chance shot might dismast him at any moment. He concluded that his only hope of silencing the frigate was to board her.

That was not easy from a vessel lying so low in the water. His quick mind thought of a brilliant ruse. He himself, with Lieutenant Parker, would lead the main party over the side into the waist. His brother, with a handful of agile seamen, cutlass in mouth, their faces blackened with soot to strike terror into the hearts of their superstitious foes, was to climb up by the chains on to the forecastle of the frigate and take the Spaniards in the flank at the same moment as the captain attacked them in the waist.

Giving the helm to the doctor, Cochrane shouted the order to board. His own six-foot figure was the first up the side, followed by the gallant Parker, who was wounded by a shot from a musket and a slash across the thigh as he climbed through the boarding-nets. No sooner had the main party come to grips with the enemy in the waist than a fearsome horde of black-faced cheering devils emerged from the smoke of the forecastle guns. Seeing the Spanish colours still flying, Cochrane ordered one of his men to cut them down. When they saw the flag fluttering down they thought that someone had surrendered the ship and they stopped fighting. At the same moment Cochrane mounted the side to shout to the *Speedy* for reinforcements fifty strong, though he knew perfectly well that he had left a bare dozen men behind. Without waiting for this magnificent threat to materialise, a Spanish officer stepped forward to surrender the ship.

When it was all over it was found that *El Gamo* had lost her captain and fourteen men killed and forty-one wounded—a casualty list amounting to more than the total complement of the *Speedy*. Of Cochrane's men three were killed and seventeen wounded, Lieutenant Parker seriously. When the wounded had been cared for as far as the primitive medical facilities of the period permitted, the prisoners were driven below decks, guns were pointed down the hatchways to keep them quiet, and Midshipman the Hon. Archibald Cochrane with a prize crew of thirty sailed her off to Port Mahon, whither the *Speedy* followed a few days later.

The capture of *El Gamo* was a turning-point in Cochrane's career. It convinced him that he had the ability to perform greater things, thereby encouraging his naturally strong self-confidence to the point of egotism. As a result of it he became involved in a quarrel with the Admiralty from which he emerged a man with a grievance. On the other hand, had not the cruise of the *Speedy* been crowned with such a signal success, Cochrane's name might never have figured in the naval history of Great Britain. That action set his feet upon the first rung of the ladder of his fame as a seaman.

What happened when Cochrane himself was not in supreme command can be seen from an event which took place a month later. The *Speedy* was again upon her cruising ground off the south-easterly coast of Spain, but this time in company with a tender under Archibald Cochrane, which had been fitted out as a 6-gun privateer. In the first week in June they fell in with the 18-gun brig *Kangaroo*, commanded by Captain Christopher Pulling, a senior officer to Cochrane. For a day or two they cruised down the coast until they were off the harbour of Oropesa, where a Spanish convoy of ten merchantmen, guarded by a xebec and three gunboats, was lying. Cochrane suggested his usual surprise attack soon after midnight, but Pulling's methods were more conventional. He insisted on waiting till next morning. Cochrane reluctantly agreed.

The result was a tough fight at the expense of considerable loss, though significantly not to the *Speedy* herself. At noon on June 9 the three British ships stood in, the tender guarding the left flank, the *Speedy* in the centre to attack the guardships, and the *Kangaroo* with her heavier armament engaging a 12-gun battery overlooking the harbour on the right. For over four hours a ferocious cannonade ensued, which inflicted little damage on either side. Then, at half-past three a 12-gun felucca and other gunboats appeared out to sea on their port beam. Cochrane decided to close to the attack before these reinforcements could come into action; Pulling agreed and anchored closer inshore to silence the fort. The *Speedy* soon put the xebec out of action, but in so doing she almost exhausted her ammunition. Cochrane persuaded Pulling to agree to man the boats of both ships to cut out the merchantmen, Foulerton, the first lieutenant of the *Kangaroo*, and Warburton (in Parker's absence) of the *Speedy*, together with three midshipmen, being placed in command. They managed to cut out three brigs laden with wine, rice and wheat, but that was not enough for Cochrane. Though Foulerton had been killed by musketry fire from the shore, he decided to make another dash in the boats in the gathering dusk. He did not succeed in capturing any more of the enemy's vessels, but he forced the remainder to run on shore for safety's sake.

Pulling's despatch mentions the loss of three officers and eight men in the *Kangaroo*, the only damage done to the crew of the *Speedy* being the severe bruises and burns suffered by her captain. He handsomely acknowledges the credit due to "so able and gallant an Officer as his Lordship," a tribute which Keith endorses in his despatches by stressing "the continued meritorious conduct of Lord Cochrane." But a loss of eleven men killed was not a record of which the captain of the *Speedy* could be proud.

The raid was the last of the *Speedy*'s efforts. On his return to Minorca her captain was disgusted to learn that he was to convoy a packet carrying despatches to Gibraltar. This was the sort of service a small ship like the *Speedy* would normally be employed upon, but after such an extraordinarily successful cruise no wonder Cochrane thought it beneath his dignity.

On the way south he could not resist burning a large oil-carrying merchantman he encountered off Malaga. But the flames from the wreck proved his undoing. Unknown to the British, three big line-of-battle ships under Admiral Linois had escaped from Toulon to join the Spaniards blockaded at Cadiz. The flaming wreck attracted the Frenchman's attention, and he hove to to make enquiries. Cochrane himself saw the vast bulk of the French ships hull down on the horizon that evening, but he supposed them to be galleons from the Indies. His mind inflated with ideas of plunder, he proposed to attack them next morning, and so, during the hours of darkness he drifted down upon his doom.

When dawn broke on July 3 he realised his mistake: he was within range of three powerful ships, two eighty-fours and one seventy-four. The wind had dropped and he was trapped. In a desperate attempt to creep out of range he ordered out the sweeps, but a thunderous broadside from the *Desaix* brought his rigging crashing about his head. He ordered studding-sails to be set; he threw the stores overboard; he did everything possible to lighten the ship. Finally, putting up his helm, he tried to run the gauntlet between the enemy's ships, but in the prevailing light airs he could get no way on his little ship. For hours he strove by every art of seamanship to elude his gigantic pursuers, until a shot from the *Desaix*'s bow chasers dismasted him. The *Speedy* drifted helplessly towards the enemy. Soon she was within the range of musketry and at any moment the little craft could be sunk by a round shot. There was nothing for it but surrender.

Captain Pallière stood at the top of the gangway as his prisoner came up the side of the *Desaix*. Cochrane bowed and began to unbuckle his sword. "No," said the Frenchman, "I will not accept the sword of an officer who has for so many hours struggled against impossibility. I beg of you to continue to wear your sword, though you are my prisoner." Cochrane thanked him, adding that he had not expected to encounter a French squadron in those waters. Pallière laughed, concealing his destination with the remark that they had heard of the *Speedy*'s depredations and had been keeping a special look-out for her.

As he sat in the captain's cabin Cochrane consoled himself by wondering what would happen when they approached Gibraltar. Surely a few British battleships would be lying in the bay. But as they weathered Europa Point he saw nothing at all but the *Calpe* gun-brig. Seeing that he was in no immediate danger, Linois decided to refit at Algeciras before he continued round to Cadiz. However, the *Calpe* got a message through to Sir James Saumarez off Cadiz, who turned east with his six seventy-fours to attack the French.

Cochrane was talking with Pallière in the cabin when he caught sight of the pendants of the British squadron over Cabrita Point. Saumarez's squadron ships sailed majestically into the bay, the *Venerable* leading. Pallière examined the British through his telescope; as he handed the glass to his guest he asked, "Will they attack, or will they anchor off Gilbraltar?"

"Certainly they will attack, and before nightfall both French and British will anchor off Gilbraltar, where of course it will give me great pleasure to repay your hospitality and that of your officers."

"None the less," smiled the other, "it shall not spoil our breakfast." But the crash of a round shot through the cabin windows put an end to further compliments. Pallière decided that his presence was required on deck, and Cochrane was left alone in the cabin to get an admirable view of the ensuing action through the broken glass of the stern windows.

The British were in line ahead, outnumbering the French by two to one. But Linois had a strong defensive position in shallow water with newly reinforced coastal batteries to guard the end of his line. Cochrane saw the French making desperate efforts to warp their ships closer inshore. So did the captain of the *Hannibal,* now the leading British ship, and he unwisely tried to stand in between the French and the shore. By so doing he ran aground right under the guns of the northern fort, where he was soon after captured. At the same time light airs made it impossible for Saumarez to come to grips with the enemy, and Cochrane was not surprised when the action was broken off soon after midday, the British having lost one ship and 121 men killed.

The paths of Brenton and Cochrane now crossed for the second time. His predecessor in the *Speedy* was at the moment captain of Saumarez's flagship, and he must have been surprised to recognise his old ship lying behind the French line. The day after the battle he was sent over to arrange an exchange of prisoners. At first Linois demurred, since he was awaiting instructions from Paris, but ultimately he agreed to release the officers of the *Hannibal* on parole, together with Cochrane and the officers of the *Speedy.*

Cochrane returned to Gibraltar to find his fellow countrymen crestfallen at what the French papers were already calling a great naval victory. Being on parole he had nothing better to do than watch what the next move would be. Four big French ships lay on one side of the bay, and five battered British ships lay on the other. For a week neither squadron moved. Then one morning the Spanish fleet, including two 112's, the biggest ships afloat, came round to join the French, and Linois at once put to sea in command of ten ships, excluding the captured *Hannibal* and attendant frigates.

Saumarez had his opportunity of fighting in the open, though he was now in his turn outnumbered by two to one and dockyard repairs were still going on. That evening he also left his anchorage in pursuit. The inhabitants of Gibraltar turned out with much the same expectancy as had the inhabitants of Montevideo when they saw the *Graf Spee* put to sea, to watch the British sail out towards the setting sun with the signal for General Chase flying and the bands playing "Come cheer up my lads, 'tis to glory we steer."

As night fell flashes of gunfire showed that the fleets were in action. The next day Cochrane cheered in company with a thousand others as the British squadron returned after a brilliant night action off Cape Trafalgar; the *Hannibal* and a Spanish line-of-battle ship were brought home in triumph, and the two 112-gun ships had been sunk by their own fire, having mistaken each other's identity in the confusion of the night. The question of the exchange of prisoners was at once reopened and Cochrane himself was exchanged for the captain of the Spanish prize. At the end of July 1801 he was able to return to England after an absence of nearly three years. He had made his name, and he naturally expected his immediate promotion to the rank of post captain.

CHAPTER III

The First Quarrel

JOHN JERVIS, Earl St. Vincent, nicknamed "Old Jarvie" more in fear than in love, was the most unpopular admiral in the Navy. Crippled with gout and leaning on a stick, he looked fierce and he was fierce; at the same time he was one of the best administrators who has ever controlled the destinies of the service.

His rough tongue and inflexible discipline were well known in every fleet: "on occasions of inefficient or unseamanlike conduct, or when retarded by laziness or factiousness, a torrent of impetuous reproof in unmeasured language would violently rush from his unguarded lips." When the testy old man became first lord in February 1801 he set himself to root out the twin evils of patronage and corruption with his customary iron determination. After only two years in office an insurrection of jobbers forced him to resign, for his endeavours had naturally stirred up a hornets' nest of enemies; but the prospect of defeat did not deter him from doing what he conceived to be his duty during the short term he was in office. "Frippery and gimcrack," "flippant and pert" behaviour were, in his opinion, chiefly due to "the great influence of the nobility in the Navy." A self-made man himself, and proud of it, he was always determined to "promote the son of an old deserving officer than any noble in the land." The many brilliant exploits at sea during the past few years had created such congestion in the Navy List that St. Vincent insisted on promotion by seniority, and very occasionally by merit, to be the only rule. In that heyday of patronage he was of course besieged with applications from those who were expected to wield influence in the interest of their protégés. All such applications St. Vincent brushed aside in his usual brusque manner, leaving a trail of disgruntled patrons behind him who were eager to seize the first opportunity to drive him from office.

Such was the dangerous man with whom young Cochrane chose to quarrel at the start of a promising career. The pity of it was that both men were really on the same side in their crusade on inefficiency. What Cochrane was later to say publicly in Parliament, St. Vincent had already written in private. "The Civil Branch of the Navy is rotten to the very core," he told the first lord in 1797. Five years later when he himself held that post, he wrote to a fellow officer: "I am sorry to tell you that Chatham Dockyard appears by what we have seen to-day a viler sink of corruption than my imagination ever formed. Portsmouth was bad enough, but this beggars all description." That was just the language Cochrane was to use, yet in his opinion the parlous condition of the dockyards and hospitals, the crazy, ill-found ships that were sent to sail the seas, were due to St. Vincent's ill-timed economies during his years in office. He came to regard St. Vincent as just another member of the old corrupt gang, while the latter regarded him as a pert sprig of the nobility who did not know his place in the service. Both were wrong in their estimate of each other, but the sad thing is that their quarrel, which left Cochrane for the rest of his life with a sense of grievance, need never have occurred. That it did occur was chiefly Cochrane's fault. He had, indeed, a genuine if minor grievance; but the manner in which he tried to rectify it was a model of tactless, even insubordinate, behaviour.

He returned to England late in the summer of 1801. By all the rules of the service his promotion to the rank of post captain dated from the action entitling him to it, in this case the capture of the Spanish frigate in May. Unfortunately the despatch describing the event took three months to reach London, before which date garbled versions of the action were current and the news of the capture of the *Speedy* had already been received. The result was that it was not till August 8 that he was notified of his promotion, and even then his name appeared at the bottom of the list, several of his juniors who had merely assisted at the Battle of Algeciras having been promoted over his head. The consequent loss of three months' seniority was a serious matter at a time when five hundred captains were competing for promotion.

Cochrane was anything but a modest man. Full of pride at his own achievements, he was intensely chagrined at this belated and inadequate recognition of his services. Sinister influence, he felt, must be at work; corruption, jealousy, favouritism and what not. He imagined that perhaps his out-spoken remarks about the indignity of having to convoy a mail packet, or his criticism of St. Vincent for having let Bruix slip through the Mediterranean Fleet, had come to the ears of the first lord.

The real reason for the delay was quite otherwise. Quite apart from the question of seniority, St. Vincent never promoted a man whose record he had not examined. He must have pondered over Cochrane's court martial aboard the *Barfleur* on a charge of flippancy towards a senior officer. Moreover a man who prided himself on the independence of his judgment was not going to have his mind made up for him by letters from senior captains and earls canvassing their claims for their sons and nephews. And this is exactly what Cochrane's relations had been doing. Lord Keith, his commanding officer, had already recommended him for promotion when he forwarded the despatch describing the capture of the *El Gamo*. Foolishly, but entirely in accordance with the practice of the times, his uncle, Sir Alexander Cochrane, had written twice hoping that "your lordship will excuse me trespassing in favour of my nephew, who is now twenty-five years old, a time of life that promotion can only be of great use," and pointing out that the capture of the Spanish frigate was "an act hardly equalled in this war of naval miracles."

Replying to this letter St. Vincent stated quite civilly that he had "the pleasure to acquaint you that a commission has been signed this day (August 8) appointing Lord Cochrane a post captain, which would have been done sooner had we received the account of his gallant action, before that of his capture."

A few days after the list appeared the earl of Dundonald sent an even more foolish protest against the position of his son's name at the bottom of the list. "My lord, we must make Lord Cochrane post captain," remarked one of St. Vincent's staff in consequence of this barrage of requests. "Sir, the first lord knows no 'must'," was the snub he received in reply.

St. Vincent's answers are sufficient proof of the justice of the delay, though a man of more humanity might have acted a little more generously. To Lord Keith he wrote on September 4: "The list of Post Captains and Comamnders so far exceeds that of ships and sloops, I cannot, consistently with what is due to the public and to the incredible number of meritorious persons of those classes upon half-pay, promote except upon very extraordinary occasions, such as that of Lord Cochrane and Captain Dundas." To the earl of Dundonald he replied on September 24: "The first account of that brilliant action reached the Admiralty very early in the month of August, previously to which intelligence had been received of the capture of the *Speedy*, by which Lord Cochrane was made prisoner; and until his exchange was effected and the necessary enquiry into the causes and circumstances of the loss of that sloop had taken place, it was impossible for the Board to mark its approbation of His Lordship's conduct. Lord Cochrane was promoted to the rank of post captain on the 8th of August, the day on which his sentence of acquittal for the loss of the *Speedy* was received, which was all that could be done under the circumstances."

Though St. Vincent succeeded in being polite under circumstances of extreme provocation, young Cochrane chose this moment to exacerbate his feelings still further by a typically rash and generous action. He begged him to promote Lieutenant Parker, who had performed such gallant service in the *Speedy*. No reply being vouchsafed him, he wrote again, only to be informed that "it was unusual to promote two officers for such a service—besides which, the small number of men killed on board the *Speedy* did not warrant the application."

The last sentence infuriated him. Having taken the utmost care to minimise the butcher's bill in every action he undertook, he was to receive no thanks for so skilfully achieving the most difficult part of his duty. He sat down and wrote a letter which for arrant insubordination can have few equals. "His Lordship's reasons for not promoting Lieut. Parker are in opposition to his Lordship's own promotion to an earldom, as well as that of his flag captain to knighthood: for in that battle from which his Lordship derived his title there was only one man killed on board his own flagship, so that there were more casualties in my sloop than in his line-of-battle ship."

The sting of Cochrane's point was all the more galling because it was widely said that the battle off Cape St. Vincent was won, not by the commander-in-chief, but by the entirely independent action of a junior captain—Nelson.

He followed up this letter with a regular bombardment of requests on Parker's behalf. Though sharply informed by the secretary of the admiralty "that it is not regular for officers to correspond with the Board," he continued his applications as before. Whereupon the secretary closed the correspondence by saying he had "nothing in command from their Lordships to communicate to you." Of course nothing was done, and Parker died a ruined man, leaving a wife and three daughters in penury. Cochrane's well meant efforts had not merely wrecked his lieutenant's prospects; they had also jeopardised his own career. He realised this only too well later on: "To argue with a First Lord is no doubt an imprudent thing for a naval officer to attempt and my remonstrance in this instance had such an effect as to get my name placed in the black list of the Admiralty, never again to be erased. . . . There was clearly some sinister influence at work, of the real cause for which I am to this day ignorant."

That he was out of employment was not entirely due to St. Vincent's prejudice against him, as he seemed to think. It was the year of the Peace of Amiens, and few fresh ships were being commissioned. With no immediate prospects in view he attended lectures at the University of Edinburgh, where Lord Palmerston was one of his classmates, a method of spending his leave which could only have occurred to an officer of his independent and inquisitive cast of mind.

With the renewal of war in 1803 he again applied for a ship, once more repeating the fatal tactics of enlisting the aid of influence. To the request of the Marquis of Douglas in May, St. Vincent replied laconically that he could not appoint him to a frigate with so many senior captains still without ships, but that he hoped to find him a suitable ship soon. In July he was still promising the earl of Dundonald that "Lord Cochrane will be employed, but the precise moment cannot be ascertained." It was becoming obvious to Cochrane that he was not going to be employed again if St. Vincent had his way. His uncle appealed to Admiral Markham, another member of the Board: "Do, my good friend, send Lord Cochrane afloat. I do not care what ship is given him so she is not a block, as I trust if ever he has an opportunity he will not be behindhand with his brother officers."

Nothing came of it, not even a "block." So Cochrane decided to take matters into his own hands by visiting the dockyards to see what ships were actually fitting out. Having done so, he boldly interviewed the first lord.

He met with a frigid reception. No vessel was available, stated the old man, glaring at the young cub who had caused him so much trouble. Cochrane replied that, since he himself had just come from the dockyards, he knew that could not be the case, and he began to enumerate a list of possible ships. St. Vincent refused to listen: this ship was too large for him, that one was not fit for service, the next already promised to a senior officer, and so on. In that case, replied Cochrane as he rose to go, "as the Board is evidently of the opinion that my services are not required, it will be better for me to go back to the College of Edinburgh and pursue my studies with a view to occupying myself in some other employment." St. Vincent looked at him keenly, hesitated for a moment, and said, "Well, you shall have a ship. Go down to Plymouth, and there await the orders of the Admiralty."

Old Jarvie was a cruel man to have as an enemy. Posting down to Plymouth in high spirits, Cochrane discovered that the ship to which he was appointed was the *Arab,* a converted collier which he saw at a glance would sail like a haystack, a "block" if ever there was one. In Steele's Navy List she appears as a sixth-rate of twenty guns, captured in 1798; but according to her new commander she was of no more use than a Thames barge as a vessel of war.

He found himself attached to the channel squadron under Keith. First of all he was sent in his "penal hulk" to reconnoitre the harbour of Boulogne, but as the *Arab* would not work to windward and proved unmanageable in an onshore wind, she was withdrawn to be sent to the Orkneys as a fishery protection vessel. During the whole of the winter her commander never set eyes on a fishing vessel of any description. It became only too clear that this degrading command was a "dreary punishment" for having offended the first lord. Nor did the latter ever forget the trouble he had been put to by Cochrane's pertinacity. "The Cochranes are not to be trusted out of sight," he wrote three years later. "They are all mad, romantic, money-getting, and not truth-telling." To which a letter from Keith in 1804 may be added to explain why the *Arab* was sent up to the Orkneys: "You will find that Captain (Alexander) Cochrane is a crack-headed, unsafe man, and was one with the others who endeavoured to stir up dissensions in the fleet; and I am sorry to find his nephew is falling into the same error—wrong-headed, violent and proud."

By the end of that year St. Vincent was himself in trouble. His personal enquiry into naval abuses had stirred up such a stink that vested interests, under the unworthy leadership of Pitt, drove him from office. When Cochrane brought the *Arab* home to Plymouth in December 1804 he found that Lord Melville had replaced his old enemy. Not that he had much use for Melville, who was as corrupt and inefficient as St. Vincent was honest and firm, but from the point of view of his own future the change made all the difference. Melville was amenable to influence, and the duke of Hamilton (as Cochrane learned thirty years later) immediately approached him, with the result that the young man found to his joy that he was appointed to a fine new frigate of thirty-eight guns.

After three years' idleness and insubordination, which had given him a bad name with his superiors, the clouds lift, and a brilliant new chapter in his career opens. So it was to be all through his life—unworthy squabbles, precipitated by his own egotism and followed by endless recrimination, alternating with episodes of unparalleled audacity and success.

~~

CHAPTER IV

The Golden Pallas

A S A RAIDING CRUISER such as he intended her to be, the *Pallas* was all that could be desired. A new fir-built frigate of 667 tons, she was armed with twenty-six 12-pounders on her main deck, and twelve 24-pound carronades on her quarter-deck and forecastle. The only difficulty was to collect a crew of 215 men. Cochrane always held that seamen joined a ship chiefly for prize money. They therefore took into consideration the prize record of a captain on her last cruise, and Cochrane's record in the *Arab* was not impressive. For the first and last time in his career he had recourse to the press gang, a method of recruitment which, by its very nature, forced the dregs of the population into a service they detested. None the less a contemporary officer states that he manned his ship "with a celerity peculiar to himself, at a time when seamen for other ships could rarely be procured." He appears to have embroiled himself with the city authorities in the process. Among the Borough records of Plymouth there exists a demand issued by the Corporation that he should attend the Guildhall to answer charges of violently assaulting two constables. Cochrane, safe on board the *Pallas* in the Hamoaze, paid no attention. On January 1 a summons was issued, followed by a warrant for his arrest. His absence from England on duty during the summer interrupted the proceedings, but in September we find him in his turn bringing an action against the mayor for assault whilst employed in the impress service on His Majesty's behalf. Judgment being given for the defendants, the episode closes with a lawyer's bill for costs to the tune of £380 18s 10d. Whatever the methods employed, he was fortunate in getting hold of a good first lieutenant, David Mapleton, and a number of other fine officers, and, as a result of his own outstanding talent for inspiring devotion and enthusiasm in his men, the *Pallas* was soon one of the finest frigates in the service.

He was given an independent commission to cruise off the Azores, the happy hunting-ground of raiders from Elizabethan times onwards. In the hands of a man like Cochrane a single cruise could make the fortunes of captain and crew. Rich prizes from the Spanish-American trade were soon falling into his hands, as the Plymouth newspapers show:

> "*March 7.—Came in a rich Spanish prize from Rio de la Plata, with diamonds, ingots of gold and silver, and valuable cargo captured by the* Pallas. *Another Spanish ship,* La Fortuna, *from Vera Cruz, laden with mahogany, logwood, and 432,000 dollars, captured by the* Pallas, *is not yet arrived.*
>
> "*March 23.—Came in and went up the harbour a most beautiful Spanish Letter of Marque, of 14 guns, said to be very rich and valuable, prize to the* Pallas.*"

La Fortuna carried specie worth £150,000. On her capture her captain and the only passenger came on board the *Pallas* in tears because they had lost all their savings after twenty years' residence in South America. Cochrane's generous nature was touched. After talking the matter over with his officers he turned the men up to ask them if they approved his giving back five thousand dollars to each of the Spaniards. "Aye, aye, my Lord," replied the crew, "with all our hearts." It is obvious from many other such incidents in his career that Cochrane was by no means the close-fisted man his enemies averred him to be.

In April he returned to Plymouth, sailing up the Sound with three five-foot candlesticks lashed to his masts in true Elizabethan fashion. She was well called the "Golden *Pallas.*" In a three months' cruise her captain is said to have amassed £75,000 in prize money, of which the port admiral, Sir William Young (Marryat's Sir Hurricane Humbug and later a dangerous enemy to Cochrane) took half by virtue of the prize regulations then in force.

The year of Trafalgar was uneventful as far as the *Pallas* was concerned, because she was next employed on tedious convoy duty in the North Atlantic. But as Lord Barham's letters prove, the destruction of the enemy's merchant marine was still the prime object of the Admiralty, and it was to this welcome task that she returned at the beginning of 1806.

She was now attached to the squadron of Admiral Thornborough operating in the Bay of Biscay. Before leaving England Cochrane had the foresight to fit out at his own expense a double-banked 18-oared galley, knowing that such a craft would be invaluable in cutting-out expeditions when the absence of wind rendered his prey immobile.

He had not been long off the Bordeaux coast when the opportunity was given him to attack bigger vessels than the wine-laden *chasse-marées* he encountered daily. Lying off the mouth of the Garonne on April 5 he learned from one of his prizes that some big French corvettes were lying twenty miles up the river. The news that these guardships were protected by shore batteries did not deter him from sailing up the estuary, accounted one of the most difficult to navigate on that coast, to the attack.

Using the tactics he had found so effective in the *Speedy*, he ordered the galley under Lieutenant Haswell to creep up on the nearest corvette in the darkness. After a brief resistance she was carried by boarding, proving to be the *Tapageuse* of fourteen guns and ninety-five men. No sooner had Haswell hoisted the British colours to notify his captain of his success than two guardships were observed to be approaching. Cochrane realised that the prize would be easily overcome unless he could warn off the approaching ships by some stratagem. He ordered his men to furl the sails of the frigate in such a way that they could be let fall in a moment, hoping that the sight of this cloud of canvas would persuade the enemy that they were in the presence of a swift and powerful vessel. The trick succeeded to perfection. As the guardships went about in retreat the *Pallas* pursued them under full sail. She was soon well up on them, and after firing a few shots both ran themselves aground. Cochrane then turned to take the *Tapageuse* out to sea. His despatch suggests that all this was done on the same day, but Haswell's log shows that it was not till two days later that the *Pallas* was able to rejoin her prize, because a strange sail was sighted on the next day and had to be beaten off before the *Tapageuse* could be retrieved.

Thornborough forwarded Cochrane's despatch to St. Vincent, now in command of the Channel Fleet, with warm praise of "the intrepidity and good conduct displayed by Lord Cochrane, his officers and men in the execution of a very hazardous enterprise in the Garonne, a river the most difficult perhaps in its navigation of any on the coast." "The gallant and successful exertions of the *Pallas*," wrote the commander-in-chief in reply, "reflect very high honour on her captain, officers and crew, and call for my warmest approbation." Unappreciative of the old admiral's laconic style, Cochrane chose to regard this as "cold, reluctant praise, no doubt intended as a wet blanket on the whole affair."

Most of the summer was spent in reconnoitring the well fortified approaches to Rochefort, the great French naval arsenal. The experience of the shoals and tides gained during these months in the Basque Roads was to prove of the utmost importance when he came to fight the biggest action of his career at the same spot three years later. In a despatch suggesting the possibility of sending a military expedition to land on the Isle of Aix as had been done in 1757 he makes a curious prophecy of this very battle: "All the enemy's vessels may be driven (upon the Isle of Oleron) by sending fire vessels to the eastwards of Isle d'Aix."

Fireships were an old method of warfare. It was during this cruise that he anticipated modern methods in a highly original way which shows his understanding of the art of war. The Admiralty had sent him packets of leaflets to be distributed among the crews of captured vessels. Cochrane realised that this would have little effect on enemy morale, but by an ingenious device he sent the leaflets inland, where they would be far more useful. A number of small kites were constructed to which slow matches were attached in such a way that they burned through the string tied to the leaflets, thus dispersing them over the whole of the countryside. More than a century elapsed before Lord Northcliffe adopted similar methods by using balloons instead of kites; the effectiveness of such propaganda methods was fully appreciated by the political warfare department in the late war.

The cruise of the Golden *Pallas* ended in May with a remarkable success against French warships. A big new frigate of 1,100 tons, twice the size of the *Pallas*, had been annoying Thornborough's ships for some time past. In company with the 16-gun sloop *Kingfisher*, the

Pallas fell in with this "large black frigate" (the *Minerve* as she proved to be) off the entrance to Aix Roads. Seeing the puny size of her opponents, the Frenchmen made all sail to the attack, while the shore batteries opened up at long range. Cochrane worked his ship against a full breeze to get to windward of the enemy, tacking to and fro to avoid the shoals and answering the *Minerve* shot for shot. Suddenly ranging up alongside her, he fired two terrific broadsides. The enemy's fire slackened for a moment, so he told the master to lay her aboard. The man did so a little too eagerly. Instead of striking her opponent with a glancing blow, the *Pallas* ran the *Minerve* on board with a rending crash which drove her own guns into the ports and wrecked her yards and fore rigging; even the bower anchor, "with which I intended to hook him," was carried away by the shock of the collision. Locked together, the crew of the *Pallas* double-shotted their guns and fired such a broadside into the enemy's hull that she shuddered from stem to stern. The enemy's crew were driven below by a hail of musketry; only her captain remained on deck where, standing on a gun, he politely raised his hat as a compliment to his opponent's daring.

Now was the moment to board. But just as he was about to give the order, Cochrane saw two other frigates bearing down to the assistance of the enemy. There was nothing for it but to sheer off and retreat. Unfortunately the *Pallas* was now almost a wreck. Her captain tried in vain to get way on her, but her fore and top sails were hanging in shreds and her spritsail yard broken by the force of the collision. With the two fresh frigates almost within range, it was only by superb seamanship that he managed to take her out to join the *Kingfisher*, which was coming up before the wind to take her in tow. It was the *Kingfisher*'s captain, George Seymour, who in the same *Pallas* rendered Cochrane equally invaluable assistance at the battle in the Aix Roads three years later.

Six years later Cochrane discovered his gallant opponent in the *Minerve* a prisoner in a stable of Dartmoor prison. He obtained more comfortable quarters for him, at the same time telling the government from the floor of the House of Commons what he thought of their treatment of a French gentleman who had the misfortune to become a prisoner of war.

A week after the action the *Pallas* limped back to Plymouth to be paid off for repairs.

CHAPTER V

The Cruise of the Imperieuse

CCOCHRANE was appointed to the command of the *Imperieuse* frigate on 23 August 1806. He continued in command of her until the summer of 1809. It was during that period that he earned his place in British naval history. He proved himself a commander of exceptional qualities of courage and initiative, a seaman who could handle a ship with consummate skill, a tactician with sufficient imagination in the art of war to utilise novel and ingenious weapons, a strategist of insight, and a first-rate military engineer. More than this, his brilliant career during those three golden years was the source of inspiration to generations of naval officers yet unborn.

The reason for this was the happy chance of his connection with Frederick Marryat. It was probably through his relations in the West Indies that he met Marryat's father—his uncle, Sir Alexander Cochrane, was now in command of that station, and that shifty relative (of whom we shall hear more), Cochrane Johnstone, was for a time an administrator there. Joseph Marryat was a rich West Indies merchant, and he had a scapegrace son who longed to go to sea. Cochrane agreed to take him into his ship as a first class volunteer, when he sailed in the autumn of 1806.

The impact of such a colourful and resourceful captain as Cochrane at the age of thirty-one on the mind of an impressionable boy of fourteen was ineffaceable. Cochrane was gifted with exactly those qualities—courage, physical strength, good looks, an easy and striking manner—which most appeal to a boy in search of a hero. Just as the schoolboy idealises a popular master, and in later life remembers his schooldays with far more vividness than he does the intervening period, so Marryat idealised Cochrane, and recalled the incidents of the cruises of the *Imperieuse* so well that when he came to write his books about the sea those episodes formed the core of his material. Indeed it may be said that he wrote best when he had those incidents in mind. Look at Stroehling's portrait of Cochrane at this time, the dramatic pose against the smoke-shrouded rigging, and imagine the effect of such a romantic figure on the boy going to sea for the first time. Read the bare bones of the episodes of those cruises in the flat style of Cochrane's *Autobiography of a Seaman,* and compare their imaginative reconstruction in Marryat's first novel, *Frank Mildmay.* His masterpiece, *Peter Simple,* is really a rich comic elaboration of scenes and characters recollected from that period.

Here is Captain Savage as he appears in the latter book, and who will deny that it is a portrait of Cochrane?

> "A sailor every inch of him. He knew a ship from stem to stern, understood the character of seamen and gained their confidence. He was besides a good mechanic, a carpenter, a rope-maker, sail-maker, and cooper. He could hand reef and steer, knot and splice: but he was no orator. He was good tempered, honest and unsophisticated, with a large proportion of common sense and free with his officers."

Of course the young Marryat could not understand the complexities of his captain's character. He only saw the man in action, the man at his best. He knew nothing of the political wrangles, the cupidity, the instability and jealousy, the unwholesome capacity for harbouring a grievance which made up the whole man. But the art of the novelist ensured that it was the good, not the evil, which outlived the man. As Conrad wrote at the end of the age of sail, Marryat's work marks "the beginning of an inspiring tradition." The old Navy lives in his pages, and the memory of Cochrane forms the heart of such characters as Captain Savage, the captain of Mildmay's first ship, and Captain M——— of *The King's Own.* Such books drew Conrad to the sea, as he himself admits; and not only Conrad the Pole, but Von Hipper the German. The latter's mother disapproved of her son's longing for a life at sea, and presented him with a set of Marryat's books to deter him by showing him what a barbaric life it really was. The result, of course, was the reverse of what she intended. So Marryat and Cochrane between them have drawn to the sea, not only generations of British naval officers, but the greatest sea writer in our language and the finest admiral the German navy has produced.

One aspect of Cochrane as a commander of men is singled out in Marryat's fragmentary autobiography: "I never knew any one so careful of the lives of his ship's company as Lord Cochrane, or any one who calculated so closely the risks attending any expedition. Many of the most brilliant achievements were performed without the loss of a single life, so well did he calculate the chances; and half the merit he deserves for what he did accomplish has never been awarded him, merely because, in the official despatches, there has not been a long list of killed and wounded, to please the appetite of the English public."

In order that we may not suppose that Marryat alone was spellbound by his captain's personality, it is worth adding the independent testimony of Sir Jahleel Brenton, whose *Spartan* joined the *Imperieuse* in the Mediterranean: "Bold and adventurous as Lord Cochrane was, no unnecessary exposure of life was ever permitted under his command. Every circumstance was anticipated, every caution against surprise was taken, every provision of success was made; and in this way he was enabled to accomplish the most daring enterprises with comparatively little danger, and still less actual loss." His brother, E. P. Brenton, in his contemporary naval history, tells us exactly how:

> "No officer ever attempted or succeeded in more arduous enterprises with so little loss. Before he fired a shot, he reconnoitred in person, took soundings and bearings, passed whole nights in the boats, his head line and spy glass incessantly at work. Another fixed principle of this officer was, never to allow his boats to be unprotected by his ship, if it were possible to lay her within range of the object of attack. With the wind on shore he would veer one of his boats in by

a bass hawser (an Indian rope made of grass, which is so light as to float on the surface of the water): by this means he established a communication with the ship, and in case of a reverse, the boats were hove off by the capstan, while the people in them had only to attend to the use of their weapons."

The *Imperieuse* was a 38-gun frigate of 1,046 tons, nearly twice the size of the *Pallas*. Originally the 40-gun *Medea* captured from Spain in 1804 in an attack on a treasure fleet, she was the fastest ship of her class in the Navy. She carried twenty-six 12- or 18-pounders on her main deck; twelve 24-pound carronades on her forecastle and poop (a murderous short-range weapon); and two long 8-pounders, with a range of over a mile, as bow and stern chasers. By constant exercise at what were then called the great and small guns, Cochrane trained her crew to an accuracy and fine discipline in conserving their fire and concerting their broadsides which was remarkable in the post-Trafalgar epoch, a period when snowwhite decks, gleaming brasswork and record time in climbing up and down the rigging were apt to be more admired than efficiency in fighting a ship. That of course is true only of the big ships in the blockading squadrons; frigates (e.g., the fine gunnery record of the *Shannon* under Broke) led a more active life which enabled them to maintain a high standard of efficiency.

Frigate service was, as we have seen, always preferable to the full slave-driven existence on board a ship of the line. The crew of the *Pallas*, already a well disciplined body, therefore willingly turned over to the *Imperieuse*; and for the extra hands needed for a bigger ship, all Cochrane had to do was to post a notice on the dockyard walls:

WANTED. *Stout, able-bodied men who can run a mile without stopping with a sackful of Spanish dollars on their backs.*

The Muster Book of the *Imperieuse* for 22 September, 1806, shows that her complement was 284 men, including a ship's company of 160, 35 marines under Lieutenant John Hoare, and as fine a body of officers as could be found. The first lieutenant on this cruise was Sam Brown, second lieutenant David Mapleton, third lieutenant Richard Harrison. The purser was Mr. Marsden; the ship's doctor

Guthrie of the *Speedy*, whose assistant, Mr. Gilbert, appears to have preferred joining landing-parties to performing operations on the mess table in the midshipmen's berth. Mr. Burney, the chief gunner, Mr. Lodovick, the carpenter, Thomas Knight, the boatswain are frequently mentioned in the captain's despatches. Of the midshipmen on the second cruise the most important were Houston Stewart, a future admiral, and Henry Cobbett (the nephew of Cochrane's political friend), a bully and a fighter, who later served with his old captain on the coasts of South America. Marryat suffered much from his behaviour, which seems to have been mitigated in some degree by the master's mate, the Hon. William Napier, a particularly fine character and a member of that distinguished family which included his cousins the historian and the commander-in-chief in the Crimean War; he himself became our first ambassador in China. "A giant amongst us pigmies," writes Marryat, "one of the best navigators in the service, he devoted his time and talents to those who wished to learn. At the same time as he laughed and played with us as children he ensured respect; and although much feared, he was loved much more ... Well do I recollect the powerful frame of Napier, with his claymore, bounding in advance of his men and cheering them on to victory."

Such men and such a ship could work miracles; and they did, in spite of officialdom. They went to sea on November 16 miserably ill-equipped for the Bay in the season of south-west gales. In spite of expostulations, Sir William Young, whose share in the *Pallas* prize money still rankled with Cochrane, determined that the ship must put to sea, though her rigging was only half set up, her guns unsecured, casks of provisions encumbered the decks, and two lighters had to put to sea on either side of her. "Damn his eyes!" the port admiral exclaimed as he watched the receding figure on the quarter-deck, "there he goes at last! I was afraid the fellow would have grounded on his beef bones before we should have got him out!" As a matter of fact it was partly Cochrane's own fault. He had just been elected a member of Parliament for Honiton, and political business prevented him from attending to the fitting out of his new ship.

The result was nearly a disaster. Whilst hove to off Ushant in order to set up the rigging properly, a gale blew up. On their third day at sea the captain's log reads:

"November 19th.——Fresh breezes and cloudy. 5:15 A.M. ship struck and beat over a shoal. Clewed up and came to. Struck top gallant masts."

In the confusion of leaving port some iron too near the binnacle had attracted the needle of the compass. The ship was out of her course, and struck a rock between Ushant and the Main. With the exception of tearing off her false keel, she suffered no serious damage. But, exclaims Marryat, recounting his initiation to the terrors of the sea, "how nearly were the lives of a fine ship's company, and of Lord Cochrane and his officers, sacrificed to the despotism of an admiral who *would* be obeyed!"

The ship reached her destination when she joined the blockading squadron in the Basque Roads off Rochefort. She was detached to do much the same work in harrying the coastal shipping—or rather what shipping that dared to move at night, for few ships on that coast could be encountered in the daytime—as had been done the previous year by the *Pallas*. Fully experienced in this type of warfare in this particular area, Cochrane's list of prizes mounted rapidly: eight gunboats and over fifty sail of merchantmen were taken within four months, besides half a dozen coastal batteries destroyed. It would be confusing to follow these activities in detail. A paragraph from Marryat's autobiography gives a fine general picture of those memorable months:

"The cruises of the *Imperieuse* were periods of continual excitement, from the hour in which she hove up her anchor till she dropped it again in port; the day that passed without a shot being fired in anger was with us a blank day; the boats were hardly secured on the booms than they were cast loose and out again; the yard and stay tackles were for ever hoisting up and lowering down. The expedition with which parties were formed for service; the rapidity of the frigate's movements day and night; the hasty sleep, snatched at all hours; the waking up at the report of the guns, which seemed the only key note to the hearts of those on board; the beautiful precision of our fire, obtained by constant practice; the coolness and courage of our captain, inoculating the whole of the ship's company; . . . when memory sweeps along those years of excitement, even now my pulse beats more quickly with the reminiscence."

The ship returned to Plymouth on 11 February 1807. After a summer in port, during which time her captain (as we shall see) was elected Member for Westminster in the new Parliament, and had already made his Radical politics a nuisance to the torpid government of the day, the *Imperieuse* sailed on her second cruise on September 12. This time her destination was Valetta, whither she convoyed fifteen vessels to relieve the garrison at Malta. The only important change in her crew was a new first lieutenant, Edward Caulfield. Though Cochrane's ship was now destined for a long spell of foreign service, he did not wish to be encumbered with unnecessary officers appointed, as often as not, for political or personal reasons; he preferred to make the midshipmen he himself had trained undertake the duties of lieutenants and mates.

Having safely delivered his convoy, he set out in search of his admiral, Collingwood. The task of the commander-in-chief in the Mediterranean at this date was one of the most arduous a naval officer has ever been called upon to perform. He was not merely in command of the blockading fleet which imprisoned the French in Toulon Harbour for close on ten years; he did not only have to control the activities of scores of frigates, brigs and sloops, which coursed over the waters of the Mediterranean as commerce destroyers, messengers or reconnaissance ships; he had to be a diplomatist as well as an admiral, and something of an economist as well. At a period when it took weeks for news to reach London, and months for an official decision to be transmitted to a commander on a distant station, such officers had important decisions to make on their own judgment. Thus Collingwood had to pacify the treacherous little court of the Neapolitan Bourbons exiled at Palermo; he had to watch out for any hostile developments on the part of the Sultan, such as Napoleon was perpetually instigating; he had to do his best to quell the pirates of the Levant and the Barbary Coast; he had to arrange for the transfer of garrisons at our bases in Sicily, Malta, Minorca and Gibraltar. Events were moving fast in the Iberian peninsula and on the shores of the Adriatic at that date, and he could never be certain which territory was friendly and which was not. As he sat, month by month, at his desk in the stern cabin of his flagship he thought of his home in the north of England, where the trees he had planted and the daughters he had bred were growing up without a sight of him. He was so indispensable out there that leave was again and again denied him, until the multifarious duties imposed upon him literally killed him. Of all the admirals with whom Cochrane came into contact, Collingwood is the one for whom he has nothing but praise.

By the time the *Imperieuse* reached the Mediterranean the international situation was about as depressing as it was in 1941. Before the end of 1807 the entire coastline from St. Petersburg to Lisbon was under the direct or indirect control of Napoleon. That control, which culminated with the occupation of Spain by 100,000 men early in 1808, was not to last long; but at the moment it looked as if Napoleon's Continental System would succeed in bleeding Britain white. All ports were closed to British merchants, and the total of our export trade fell catastrophically. However, it made matters simpler for commerce destroyers like Cochrane to know that every sail not flying the British flag could be taken in prize. A certain amount of coastwise traffic still continued as small ships darted from port to port under cover of night, in constant apprehension of being sighted by a British sloop or frigate. The only big merchantmen that sailed the seas were there by licence under the Orders in Council of January 1807. The Chancellor of the Exchequer defined the principle behind these Orders as follows: "That trade in British produce and manufactures . . . is to be protected as much as possible. For this purpose all the countries where French influence prevails to exclude the British flag shall have no trade but to and from this country and its allies." To this end an elaborate licensing system, legalised smuggling in fact, was instituted to ensure that British products did in fact penetrate some parts of Napoleon's dominions. After a time the few remaining neutrals, such as the Americans, unwillingly complied with this burdensome system; but in 1808 Collingwood could write of the Mediterranean that there was "nothing but ourselves: it is lamentable to see what a desert the waters are become."

It was the work of frigate captains like Cochrane and Brenton, Maxwell and Hoste, to ensure that this was so. Their admiral was duly grateful to them: "The activity and zeal of those gallant young men keep up my spirits, and make me equal to bear the disagreeables that happen from the contentions of some other ships. Those who do all the service give no trouble; those who give the trouble are good for nothing."

The complications of the licence system made the start of

Cochrane's cruise somewhat inauspicious. On his way north after leaving Malta he caught up with a large poleacre-rigged vessel, which, to judge from the guns glinting from her ports, was a privateer of sorts. He guessed her nationality to be Genoese, so he despatched Napier with three boats to enquire her business. When the boats were about two cables' length away from her she hoisted British colours. This did not allay Napier's suspicions, so he demanded permission to board. He was refused, and a bloody scuffle took place (it is described with gusto in the 29th chapter of *Midshipman Easy*), in which two of the *Imperieuse*'s men were killed and Napier and others wounded. "I never at any time saw Lord Cochrane so much dejected as he was for many days after this affair," writes Marryat. The vessel was taken back to Malta as a prize, where she was found to be the *King George*, for whose capture as a pirate £500 reward had been offered. However, some influential persons connected with the Court of Admiralty there had an interest in her, with the result that her captor was fined 500 double sequins for interfering with a British vessel. This was Cochrane's first contact with that notorious body, whose behaviour he was later to examine with startling results.

Equally unfortunate was his brief experience in command of the small Corfu squadron. He overtook thirteen merchantmen in the Adriatic armed with illicit passes issued by his predecessor on that station. Again he made the mistake of taking them back to Malta, with the result that, in consequence of representations made against his behaviour, he was himself superseded.

The fresh instructions Collingwood gave him after this unfortunate episode were far more satisfactory to a person of his temperament. He was told to harass the French and Spanish coasts as opportunity served; "consequently I determined to make every exertion to merit his lordship's approval." For the next few months he cruised up and down between Cartagena and Marseilles, harassing the coastwise traffic, cutting out all types of vessels from bays and harbours, destroying batteries and signal stations. The French made use of semaphore stations to transmit news overland. In more than one instance Cochrane succeeded in capturing the code book, and, by deliberately leaving torn pages all over the place, in fooling the enemy into the belief that the code itself had been destroyed. The effect was just as he hoped, and the inshore ships of Collingwood's fleet were able to read the enemy's signals for some time to come.

We cannot pause to describe all the exciting episodes of that cruise—the nightly landings and assaults, the surprise of enemy strong-points, the cutting out of vessels at dawn, when the boarding party swarmed up the sides of a trader lying at anchor, roused the sleepy crew and brought the vessel out in triumph as a prize. Usually a lieutenant, assisted by one or two midshipmen, was in charge; but an anecdote which found its way into one of the volumes of the *Naval Chronicle* (that enormous scrapheap of miscellaneous information about this period) shows how the captain was always at hand to help. An attack on a battery had failed, and the boats pulled back disconsolately for the ship. Cochrane met Milton the coxswain at the gangway.

"Well, Jack, do you think it impossible to blow up the battery?"

"No, my lord, 'tis not impossible—we can do it if you will go."

Cochrane thrust a pistol into his pocket and jumped into the stern sheets of the cutter, to lead the party in a second and successful attack.

On the morning of 1 June 1808, the *Imperieuse* fell in with the *Trident*, which carried surprising news. The Spanish people, particularly in the south, had spontaneously risen against the forces of occupation. Britain had promised armed assistance. Portugal and Spain were now at war with France. Cochrane hastened south to meet Collingwood at Cadiz for fresh instructions. Instead of the easy task of capturing Spanish vessels and bombarding a poorly defended coast, his duty now was to cut the line of French communications along the coasts of Valencia and Catalonia. The idea appealed to Cochrane, who knew how closely the road from Perpignan to Barcelona followed the coast, hemmed in by the mountains of the interior, where Spanish *guerrileros* now swarmed. In fact he was convinced that a larger force, based on Port Mahon in Minorca, could make that road totally impassable. But such a force was not at Collingwood's disposal at the moment, so Cochrane hastened back to do what he could with the *Imperieuse* and the few other ships in that area.

He arrived off the coast of Catalonia just about the time that Wellesley landed at Oporto to begin the Peninsular War. After years of defensive war, Britain had gone over to the attack. "Bonaparte is stepping, or rather striding on to universal empire," a disgruntled diarist had noted the previous year. "We really seem to be in a sort of lethargic dream from which we can only be awakened by a tremendous shock." The Spanish Revolt administered the shock, and the lion roused himself to make use of the opportunity.

In the course of blocking roads, blowing up forts and bridges, animating the Spanish resistance movement in true commando style, Cochrane learnt something of the cruelties of this type of warfare. It was war as Goya depicts it; not the honourable professional trade known to sailors, but a war of bloody ambushes, tortured prisoners, garrotted bodies hanging from trees, women and children starving in gutted villages. "I was indignant at seeing the wanton devastation committed by a military power, pretending to high notions of civilisation, and on that account spared no pains to instruct the persecuted inhabitants how to turn the tables on their spoilers; making—as throughout life I have ever done—common cause with the oppressed." Whenever a body of French troops was compelled to surrender, it was with Cochrane and not with the blood-thirsty Spanish levies that the commandant tried to negotiate. But Cochrane never lost the opportunity of lecturing such officers on the barbarities committed by their troops. Time and again he marched his prisoners down to the boats between lines of screaming civilians, whom the marines had to repel with the butts of their muskets.

In operations such as those upon which he was now engaged all his skill as an amphibious commander was called forth. The enemy's strong-points were fixed, and could be destroyed by lightning raids. His own ship served as a floating battery, appearing now off one point and now off another, firing a few broadsides whenever a target offered, and then moving out of range of coastal fire. For long-range weapons he used mortars, which he also used mounted in the bows of a cutter. He also made use of a new invention, which had only once previously been used, and then with scant success, off Boulogne in 1806—Congreve's incendiary rockets.

A good example of his use of the *Imperieuse* as a floating battery occurred near Port Vendres, where he was cruising in company with the *Spartan*. After a landing had been made it was discovered that a large force of cavalry and infantry was approaching the coast. Cochrane withdrew his marines and packed them into ship's boats with all the supernumeraries he could muster clothed in the scarlet jackets of the Corps, and despatched the boats towards a point some miles away to make a feint at a landing. Away galloped the enemy's cavalry in that direction to head them off. The *Spartan* and *Imperieuse* were then warped close inshore, covering a place by which the enemy was bound to return. When they did so the cavalry was mown down by grape-shot fired from the guns of the frigates.

The climax of these operations was the defence of Rosas in November 1808. This town guarded the main road to Barcelona. The enemy having been pushed out of it, every effort had to be made to hold out until the junta of Gerona could raise sufficient troops to garrison it. Captain West of the *Excellent* had been there several weeks before Cochrane appeared, but he had come to the conclusion that its fall was inevitable in view of the 6,000 troops marching against it, and had withdrawn his marines.

Cochrane came ashore in the gig to reconnoitre the position and make contact with the eighty-odd Spaniards who remained under arms. The strong-points were the citadel in the town and Trinidad Castle outside the walls. The latter was a rambling edifice, built on the edge of a cliff, consisting of three towers, each standing above the next on account of the steep slope of the ground—"the whole presenting the appearance of a large church with a tower a hundred and ten feet high, a nave ninety feet high, and a chancel fifty feet." In view of the thickness of the walls, and the possibility of maintaining contact with the ship by means of rope ladders down the cliff, he decided that the position could be held, in spite of the fact that the French had already established entrenchments outside the town walls, and a 3-gun battery had been placed on a hill overlooking the highest tower of the castle. There were also plenty of Swiss sharpshooters at points of vantage.

On the morning of November 24 nearly a hundred men were landed, under the command of two lieutenants and Cochrane himself, to reinforce the handful of Spaniards already there. Boatloads of supplies followed them in, the *Imperieuse* providing covering fire by silencing the battery on the hill at a range of over 600 yards. By the time the party arrived a breach in the upper half of the highest tower was inevitable, so Cochrane decided to isolate the rest of the castle by breaking down the connecting dome and converting the interior into a vast mantrap. A sharply inclined plane of planks, well greased with cook's slush from the ship's galley to preclude finger holds, was constructed to lead down to a fifty-foot drop; the idea being that those forcing an entry by the breach high up in the wall would slide down the trap to destruction in the pit below. Barricades prevented access to the next tower, and these were festooned with a brilliant improvisation for barbed wire—lengths of chain barbed with fish-hooks.

Thus defended they waited for the French to make the first move. Unfortunately Cochrane, raising his head for an instant above the crenellated parapet, was struck in the face and had his nose broken by a splinter from a musket ball which hit the stonework beside him. It was excruciatingly painful, but Guthrie soon put things to rights.

An incident which occurred while they awaited an attack is related by Marryat in *Frank Mildmay*. It is highly characteristic of Cochrane's egotism, though it does not seem to have shocked his junior in the least:

> "While he himself walked leisurely along through a shower of musket balls from those cursed Swiss dogs, whom I most fervently wished at the devil, as an aide-de-camp, I felt bound in honour as well as duty to walk by the side of my captain, fully expecting every moment that a rifle ball would have hit me where I should have been ashamed to show the scar. I thought this funeral pace confounded nonsense; but my fire-eating captain never had run away from a Frenchman, and did not intend to begin then.
>
> "I was behind him, making these reflections, and as the shot began to fly very thick, I stepped up alongside of him and by degrees, brought him between me and the fire.
>
> " 'Sir,' said I, 'as I am only a midshipman, I don't care so much about honour as you do; and therefore, if it makes no difference to you, I'll take the liberty of getting under your lee.'
>
> "He laughed and said, 'I did not know you were here, for I meant you should have gone with the others; but, since you are out of your station, Mr. Mildmay, I will make that use of you which you so ingeniously proposed to make of me. My life may be of some importance here; but yours very little; and another midshipman can be had from the ship only for the asking; so just drop astern if you please, and do duty as breastwork for me!'
>
> "'Certainly, sir,' said I, 'by all means'; and I took up my station accordingly."

The position down in the town itself was perilous. The enemy's artillery opened a barrage with such precision of aim that the wall of the citadel was neatly undercut, so that the whole building collapsed about the defenders. At midnight on the 26th those on the castle walls heard the trumpet sound for the final assault that carried the town. Two thousand armed Spaniards turned up next day exactly six hours too late. Having kept their appointment in true Spanish fashion, they disappeared into the hills again.

The enemy was now able to transfer four more batteries on to the hill overlooking the castle. An assault might be expected at any hour. At dawn on the 30th Marryat was keeping watch from the wall overlooking the misty valley below, up which the attack was expected. "The captain came out and asked me what I was looking at. I told him I hardly knew; but there did appear something unusual in the valley, immediately below the breach. He listened for a moment, looked attentively with his nightglass, and exclaimed in his firm voice, but in an undertoned manner, 'To arms!—they are coming!' In three minutes every man was at his post; and though all were quick there was no time to spare, for by this time the black column of the enemy was distinctly visible, curling along the valley like a great centipede; and, with the daring enterprise so common among the troops of Napoleon, had begun in silence to mount the breach."

Cochrane's version of the incident is more melodramatic, but more unlikely. According to him, he awoke with an intuition of an attack. He joined the guard on the wall and, simply to pass the time, fired a mortar which happened to be pointing in the direction of the path along which their assailants must come. "Before the echo had died away, a volley of musketry from the advancing column of the enemy showed that the shell had fallen amongst them just as they were on the point of storming."

The assault was successfully repelled; but a few days later they heard that over a thousand men were preparing a second attack. Cochrane decided to evacuate a position which, after a month's siege, was no longer tenable. Trains of gunpowder were laid to blow up the remains of the castle, along with its invaders; booby-traps and delayed-action grenades were set about the place. At eleven o'clock on the morning of December 5 the ship's boats, along with those of the *Fame* and *Magnificent* which had returned to join her, grated on the beach at the bottom of the cliff to take off the defenders as they climbed down the rope ladders from the castle. The whole operation was successfully carried out under cover of a bombardment from the ships' guns.

Unfortunately the enemy was far too wary, after what they had experienced at Cochrane's hands, and delayed their entry until one of the powder trains had blown up part of the remaining walls. The other fire failed to explode. As the ship got under way Cochrane could see a pall of smoke arising from the debris, and the French flag floating over the ruins of what had once been Trinidad Castle.

For the whole period of the siege the losses sustained by the ship's company only amounted to three killed and as many seriously wounded. In view of the hundred-odd they had counted for dead among the enemy, and the delay imposed on all troop movements in that area, the episode was a signal success. Collingwood, in forwarding Cochrane's laconic despatch, admitted as much. "The heroic spirit and ability which have been evinced by Lord Cochrane in defending this castle, although so shattered in its works by the repeated attacks of the enemy, is an admirable instance of his lordship's zeal." Previously he had paid generous tribute to Cochrane's services: "Nothing can exceed the zeal and activity with which his lordship pursues the enemy. The success which attends his enterprises clearly indicates with what skill and ability they are conducted, besides keeping the coast in constant alarm—causing a general suspension of trade, and harassing a body of troops employed in opposing him." And again: "The zeal and energy with which he has maintained that fortress excites the highest admiration. His resources for every exigency have no end."

The contrast between this well merited praise and the lack of official commendation roused Cochrane's ire. But in that war of naval miracles the secretary of the Admiralty could not constantly be conveying their lordships' congratulations to every deserving officer. However, he had more legitimate cause for resentment at the conclusion of the cruise, when the only sign of official recognition of his services was a reproach that he had used more than his quota of sails, stores, gunpowder and shot!

Just before Christmas he renewed his attacks by rounding up a convoy of seventeen ships in Cadaques harbour, a few miles north of Rosas, and compelling the two armed escorts to scuttle themselves. They were later salvaged because, as Marryat remarks, "they were very beautiful vessels, and of a character much wanted in the peculiar warfare in which we were engaged." Nevertheless Cochrane was permitted to buy one, the *Julie*, as a private yacht after she had been condemned as a prize. Since the Spaniards in the port began to pilfer the captured merchantmen, he took the law into his own hands by selling the cargoes and distributing the proceeds at the capstan head, so that every man "got his whack" of silver dollars on the spot instead of waiting years for the receipt of prize money of a doubtful amount from official sources.

At the end of January 1809 he took the frigate back to Minorca and applied for leave. He and his men had certainly earned it, but two personal motives in particular urged him to return to England. He had seen enough of the proceedings of the Prize Courts in the Mediterranean to warrant an attack on them in Parliament. Moreover, he wished to suggest a better strategy to the authorities at home. In his view a small force based on Minorca could cut the Barcelona road completely; and if at the same time the islands off the west coast of France—Aix, Rhé, Oleron, etc.—were occupied it would be possible "so to harass the French coast as to find full employment for their troops at home, and thus to render any operations in Western Spain, or even in foreign countries, next to impossible."

We may not agree with him that the eight years of the Peninsular War was an expensive mistake, but we can appreciate his strategic insight in returning to the commando raids (badly executed as they were) of the Seven Years' War. His principle was the thoroughly sound one, indeed the classical strategy of a maritime nation, of an amphibious force utilising the mobility rendered possible by supremacy at sea, to harass a land power in possession of an extensive coastline. In such circumstances the point of attack is left to that power which has command of the sea (a phrase to be interpreted in terms of the weapons employed at any given date); and by the threat of impending landings at vulnerable points over a wide area, a very large force of the enemy can be immobilised, even when it is not actually engaged. But at that date there was no one in the government of sufficient intelligence to appreciate these ideas, though Cochrane suggested them in public and in private for years to come. When an expeditionary force was eventually decided upon—the Walcheren expedition—it was so badly organised and led that the result was a catastrophe.

However, when the *Imperieuse* anchored in Plymouth Sound on 19 March 1809, Cochrane's big chance had come.

CHAPTER VI

The Battle in the Aix Roads

A S SOON as Cochrane stepped ashore at Plymouth he was handed a letter from the second lord of the Admiralty:

"There is an undertaking of great moment in agitation against Rochefort, and the Board think that your local knowledge and services on the occasion might be of the utmost consequence, and, I believe, it is intended to send you there with all expedition; I have ventured to say, that if you are in health, you will readily give your aid on this business."

A few hours later a signal arrived by telegraph requiring his immediate attendance at Whitehall. Having posted up to London, he found Lord Mulgrave, the first lord, in an unusually cordial mood. This was not the manner in which junior captains were normally received: Cochrane's vanity was flattered, and he was curious to know exactly what was expected of him.

Mulgrave outlined the situation, which was indeed sufficiently serious to warrant this unusual procedure. An enemy force of eight line-of-battle ships, taking advantage of the bad weather which had driven Lord Gambier's Channel Fleet off their blockading station the previous month, had escaped from Brest, picked up more ships at L'Orient, and effected a junction with the Rochefort squadron in the Aix Roads. There was every evidence that Admiral Allemand proposed to break out in an attack on the West Indies, just as Villeneuve had succeeded in doing four years previously. As a matter of fact he had already lost his chance by failing to brush aside Stopford's small squadron in the Basque Roads outside his anchorage; by the end of March Gambier had reinforced Stopford, so that the British fleet now totalled eleven ships of the line, seven frigates and sixteen smaller armed ships.

Allemand's eleven big ships were anchored in a defensive, though extremely strong position, which invited attack by fireships. Unfortunately, Mulgrave explained, as he handed a letter from the commander-in-chief across the table, it was evident that Lord Gambier had no desire to make such an attack. A timid man, with strict Evangelical principles, he regarded the use of fireships as "a horrible mode of warfare, and the attempt hazardous if not desperate." Mulgrave had heard that Cochrane, when in command of the *Pallas*, had suggested some such form of attack. Would he now lead the fireships against the French?

Cochrane hesitated. In an unconvincing manner he at first declined the invitation. He was, he pointed out, an extremely junior officer compared with those in Gambier's fleet. If he accepted this appointment, all manner of ill feeling would be aroused in the fleet on the part of those who felt that they had been passed over. "The present is not a time for professional etiquette," Mulgrave assured him. But Cochrane insisted (though he did not say as much) in discerning ulterior motives in the offer. The Tory government had chosen him in order to break him, while they themselves would reap the benefit if he succeeded. Gambier, he imagined, was trying to shift the responsibility of such a desperate enterprise on to some one else's shoulders. But in justice to the latter it must be stressed that his letters show that he was perfectly willing to carry out any order sent to him, though at the same time he openly expressed his disapproval at this particular form of attack.

Cochrane also recalled the failure of the last fireship attack made by Popham off Boulogne. In his view a type of vessel that would explode with the force of a bomb was essential, in addition to the ordinary type of fireship, which was, as experience had shown, not such a terrible weapon as romantic stories of the Spanish Armada led the public to believe. An unusual combination of circumstances—an enemy force in an enclosed area, wind, tide and darkness in favour of the attacker—was essential to launching them; and even then their approach could be easily warded off by an enemy on the alert and armed with means of repelling them.

In the end he begged to be excused on the grounds of ill health, due to the exertions of his recent cruise. But Mulgrave, like a sensible man, was not so easily put off. The next day he insisted on Cochrane's acceptance of the offer. "My lord, you must go. The Board cannot listen to further refusal or delay. Rejoin your frigate at once. I will make all right with Lord Gambier."

Cochrane returned to his ship with mixed feelings, but exhilarated with the knowledge that of all the captains in England he had been chosen for such a task. Meanwhile Gambier was told to expect the arrival of a dozen transports to be converted into fireships, some mortar bomb vessels (five were promised, but only the *Etna* arrived) and the inventor Congreve himself with "a large assortment of rockets."

The *Imperieuse* joined the fleet in the Basque Roads on April 3. Just as Cochrane had foreseen, his arrival aroused indignation in the fleet as soon as the news went round that he was to lead the long-expected attack. The spirit of this fleet was very far from that of Nelson's "band of brothers." Many officers disliked Gambier's psalm-singing habits, the religious services he insisted upon, his distribution of pious tracts in every ship. Among the fire-eaters there was a genuine grievance that they had not been given the chance to lead such an attack. "Why could we have not done this as well as Lord Cochrane? Why did not Lord Gambier permit us to do this before?" were the embarrassing questions Cochrane heard on all hands. One hardy veteran, Admiral Sir Eliab Harvey, who commanded the *Téméraire* at Trafalgar, so far forgot himself that he insulted the commander-in-chief on his own quarter-deck, struck his flag in disgust and was court martialled for grossly insubordinate behaviour. Red with fury, he came on board the flagship shouting "he did not care; if he were passed by, and Lord Cochrane or any other junior officer was appointed in preference, he would immediately strike his flag, and resign his commission . . . he never saw a man so unfit for the command of a fleet as Lord Gambier." Shaking hands with Cochrane in the cabin of the captain of the fleet, he explained that he meant nothing personal, but he must say he regarded the appointment "as an insult to the fleet." He was shown over the side muttering imprecations against Gambier—"Well, this is not the first time I have been lightly treated . . . because I am no canting methodist, no hypocrite, no psalm-singer, and do not cheat old women out of their estates by hypocrisy and canting!"

Gambier himself received Cochrane well, and courteously explained the situation to him, though the arrival of this stormy petrel must have been far from welcome. There were plenty of reasons to make a timid man apprehensive of the success of an attack. The enemy fleet lay at anchor in the Aix Roads at the mouth of the river Charente.* To the north lay the island of Aix, fortified with a citadel of unknown strength. Almost joined to the island at low tide, the Fouras peninsula forms the north bank of the river. On the opposite side lies the Isle Madame, forming the southern bank. Its seaward extension is the Palles mudflat, only visible at low water; thence, with a narrow intervening channel, the mudbank shelves out in the long Boyart shoal, lying directly opposite Aix, and separated from it by a sea passage, called the Aix Roads, of something over a mile in width. Since little can be seen of the Boyart even at low water, and since Gambier had not risked taking soundings at its inner end, there was considerable argument about the exact width of this channel. The *Neptune Français* chart made it nearly two miles broad; the Master of the Fleet estimated it at little over a mile, and therefore covered by the guns of the Aix batteries. On the inner tip of the Boyart, nearest the Palles, there is to-day a fort built on a rocky excrescence of the shoal. In 1809 the French tried to establish a battery there, but the emplacement works were destroyed by a British frigate a short time before the battle. Had they succeeded, an attack could never have been launched, for it was just by these rocks that Cochrane found sufficient depth of water for his plan.

Between Aix and the Palles Flat the fleet lay at anchor in two indented lines, six ships of the line composing the outer line and five the inner, the whole guarded by three frigates on the seaward side, whose task it was to watch the mile-long boom which protected the fleet. On the chart of Fairfax, Master of the Fleet, which was accepted as the official chart at the subsequent court martial, this boom is not so much as marked, and its existence appears to have been unknown to

* See Plan of the Battle in the Aix Roads, page 61.

Gambier until Cochrane reconnoitred it shortly after his arrival. Since it was a formidable affair of spars, yards, beams and tubs weighted with stones and securely moored by $5^1/_4$-ton anchors and $31^1/_2$-inch cables (larger than anything in use in the British Navy), its construction must have been noticed if any attempt had been made to take soundings near the position. That, if anything, proves the truth of Cochrane's contention that Gambier grossly exaggerated the risk of taking the fleet in to attack the French. If, thought Cochrane as he used the lead along the northern edge of the Boyart, if sufficient depth of water can be found, not entirely out of range of the Aix batteries, but sufficiently so to enable big ships to pass in to attack the enemy after the explosion vessels had blown up the boom and the fireships have broken their formation, the destruction of their fleet is certain.

Apart from underestimating the width of the channel, Gambier overestimated the strength of the Aix fortifications. He kept on talking about the danger of red-hot shot from the citadel, which, he claimed, prevented any access to the Roads within. Napoleon shared his view: "You may quiet your apprehensions that the enemy will attempt something against the Isle d'Aix; nothing could be more insane than the idea of attacking a squadron at Isle d'Aix. I am annoyed to see you with such notions." Whenever Napoleon said anything about naval matters he was almost invariably wrong. Allemand and his officers on the spot were indeed justly apprehensive of a landing there. The island was only garrisoned by 2,000 raw conscripts; most of the guns pointed north, not south. As the event proved, it was perfectly possible to enter the Roads without serious damage, provided one kept close to the Boyart. Three seventy-fours succeeded in doing so, and where three had gone the rest could follow. It was just a question of daring to take a risk. Cochrane, who was not in command of the fleet, was prepared to risk the loss of three or four ships; Gambier, who was, dared not lose a single one.

Besides expecting an attack on Aix, Allemand was fully prepared for an attack by fireships, a factor which made Cochrane's problem all the more difficult. The French admiral had noted the arrival of numerous craft obviously intended for fireships, where Gambier lay about six miles west of the island. So he ordered his ships to anchor 170 yards apart with canvas unbent to afford as little inflammable material as possible. Frigates were posted in advance of the main lines, and relays of boats (seventy-three of them) patrolled the boom night and day (a precaution Cochrane circumvented by choosing a pitch-dark night, when it was blowing so hard that very few of them were on guard). Having thus secured what was naturally a strong position, Allemand awaited the outcome with composure. As a gesture of defiance, a British ensign was hung out from the "heads" of the *Calcutta* (a 50-gun East Indiaman captured in 1805 and now serving as the magazine and storeship for the proposed expedition)—an insult which those in the British fleet could see and appreciate.

The one thing he could not have foreseen was Cochrane's own explosion vessels. There were three of these (for some reason he only speaks of two in his autobiography)—one under Cochrane himself, assisted by his brother Basil and Lieutenant Bissell; one under Lieutenant Urry Johnson and Midshipman Marryat; and one in reserve moored to the stern of the *Imperieuse*. He describes in detail how they were constructed:

> "The floor of the vessel was rendered as firm as possible, by means of logs placed in close contact, into every crevice of which other substances were firmly wedged, so as to afford the greatest amount of resistance to the explosion. On this foundation were placed a large number of spirit and water casks, into which 1,500 barrels of powder were emptied. These casks were set on end, and the whole bound round with hempen cables, so as to resemble a gigantic mortar, this causing the explosion to take an upward course. In addition to the powder casks were placed several hundred shells, and over these again nearly three thousand hand grenades; the whole, by means of wedges and sand, being compressed as nearly as possible into a solid mass."

Many of the fireships—there were twenty-one of them all told, led by the 800-ton *Mediator*—were constructed with equally devilish ingenuity. Gunner Richardson describes how one of the victuallers, the *Thomas* of 350 tons, was constructed:

> "We made troughs and laid them fore and aft on the 'tween decks, and then others to cross them, and on these were laid trains of quick match; in the square openings of these troughs we put barrels full of combustible matter, tarred canvas hung over them fastened to the beams, and tarred shavings made out of brooms, and we cut out four portholes in each side for the fire to blaze out and a rope of twisted oakum well tarred

led up from each of these ports to the stanching rigging and up to the mast heads. We had captured lately several *chasse-marées* laden with resin and turpentine, which answered our purpose well. We placed Congreve's rockets at the yard arms, but this was an unwise proceeding, as they were as likely to fly into our boats when escaping, after being set on fire, as into the enemy's."

All was ready by the night of April 11. The combination of circumstances was so favourable that even Gambier could not delay matters any longer; a dark, windy night with a strong tide flowing towards the French fleet. While the main British fleet remained at its anchorage in the Basque Roads—over six miles from Aix, but not as much as fourteen, as Cochrane states—the advanced ships took up their stations as follows: the *Imperieuse* with three frigates astern of her (including Cochrane's old *Pallas*) was anchored off the inner edge of the Boyart. Slightly ahead of her, on both sides of the channel to mark its limits, the *Redpole* and *Lyra* sloops were anchored as lightships. As a diversion the *Etna* bomb vessel used her 13-inch mortars against the works on the island. In the evening Cochrane and the officers of the leading fireships foregathered on board the *Caledonia* to discuss the last details. Then he boarded his explosion vessel and raced down the rough water in the darkness towards the boom.

As he approached it he lit the fuse and jumped into the dinghy towing astern. He and his companions began to pull for the frigate as hard as they could against the strong tide. But the fuse, instead of burning fifteen minutes, lasted only half that time, and the vessel exploded with an appalling detonation while they were still close to it—so close that the burning fragments went flying over their heads. The second vessel, under Johnson, blew up a moment later, exactly where and when no one could say in that night of wind and darkness. The spot was probably about half a mile from the nearest French ship. According to the log of the *Imperieuse* the explosion occurred at 8 P.M.; according to the captain of a French frigate it was 8:30; at the court martial the time given was 9:30.

As they pulled back—and Cochrane's physical strength never stood him in better stead than at this moment—they passed the *Mediator* and a few of the leading fireships heading for the wreckage of the boom, which had been torn from its moorings by the force of the explosions. There still remained the third vessel; but when they reached

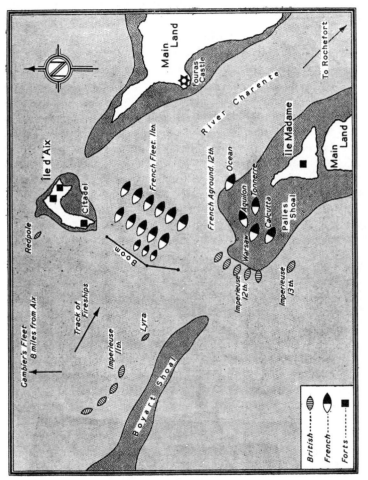

PLAN OF THE BATTLE IN THE AIX ROADS

the side of the frigate Cochrane found that it had been cut adrift in view of the dangerous proximity of a fireship off her course. As the leading fireships began to catch alight, and the incendiary rockets spurted into the air in all directions, the enemy fleet was illuminated and Cochrane could see something of the effect of his plan. So could those on board Gambier's ships: "All hands were up on board to behold this spectacle, and the blazing light all around gave us a good view of the enemy, and we really thought we saw some of their ships on fire." Cochrane, however, affected to be much displeased at the conduct of the fireships. Most of them had been prematurely ignited and abandoned long before entering the channel, with the consequence that only four out of twenty-one ever reached the enemy. Though Cochrane gives them no credit whatsoever, we know from French sources that their effect was just as he had intended. The mere threat of destruction was enough to throw the whole fleet into confusion. Here is Captain Proteau of *L'Indienne* frigate nearest the boom: "I was in a position $3^1/2$ cables length from my squadron when I saw at 9:30 under our starboard cat-head something floating at the boom. Suddenly there was an explosion; a quantity of rockets, grenades and shells exploded in the air without doing us the least harm, although we were within half a cable's length." This must have been the *Mediator* breaking through the wreckage of the boom. The effect was to drive the frigate aground on the Palles Flat.

Much the same thing happened to the flagship, *L'Océan:*

"At 10.0 we grounded, and immediately after a fireship in the height of her combustion grappled us athwart our stern; for ten minutes she remained in this situation while we employed every means in our power to prevent the fire from catching the ship; our fire engines and pumps played upon the poop enough to prevent it from catching fire; with spars we hove off the fireship, with axes we cut the chains of the grapplings lashed to her yards, but a *chevaux de frise* on her sides held her firmly to us. In this deplorable situation we thought we must have been burned, as the flames of the fireship covered all our poop. Two of our line-of-battle ships, the *Tonnerre* and *Patriote,* at this time fell on board of us; the first broke our bowsprit and destroyed our main chains. Providence afforded us assistance on this occasion. At the moment the fireship was athwart our stern, and began to draw forward along the starboard side, the

Tonnerre separated herself from us, and unless this had happened the fireship would have fallen into the angle formed by two ships and would infallibly have burnt them. The fireship having got so far forward as to be under our bowsprit, we left it there some time to afford the two ships above mentioned time to get far enough away to avoid being boarded by this fireship. While this fireship was on board of us we let the cocks run in order to wet the powder, but they were so feeble that we could not do that; we lost fifty men by this circumstance, who fell into the sea and were lost; our boats saved a great number."

As daylight dawned on April 12 Cochrane had the satisfaction of seeing that his part of the operation had succeeded to perfection. As the tide began to ebb he could see that every one of the big French ships was aground, save two which managed to anchor higher up the estuary, only to drag their anchors later in the day and run aground under the guns of Fouras Castle. The flagship was aground in shallow water off the northern tip of the Palles Flat; the *Calcutta* lay stranded on the southern side; the seventy-fours *Varsovie, Tonnerre, Aquilon, Regulus* and *Jemappes* lay to the landward of her on mud or rocks. It was April 12, the anniversary of Rodney's great victory of The Saints, and Cochrane confidently expected Gambier to lead in the main fleet to complete the work of destruction he had so admirably begun.

As soon as it was light enough to see the flags, he hoisted signals to apprise the commander-in-chief of the situation, since the latter was by now almost ten miles from the scene of action. I give the signals as logged by the *Caledonia*, for Cochrane, in his autobiography, muddles the order and is inaccurate as to the wording:

5:48 A.M.   *Half the fleet can destroy the enemy. Seven on shore.*
6:40 A.M.   *Eleven on shore.*
7:40 A.M.   *Only two afloat.*
9:30 A.M.   *Enemy preparing to heave off.*

That despairing sequence tells the story by itself. Cochrane could not believe his eyes when no answering move came from the *Caledonia*. The tide was beginning to flow again, and the enemy were preparing to float off on it. It is very probable that the blame for this disastrous immobility is due to the master of the fleet, who returned from the *Lyra* to the flagship at eight o'clock. By virtue of his position he was responsible for the safety of the ships, and he knew the tide was upon the last quarter of the ebb when Cochrane's first signal was made. It is probable that he advised the admiral against taking the big ships in until the tide had turned.

Thus it was not till about eleven o'clock that the fleet weighed. Half an hour later Cochrane had another shock when he saw it anchor again about three miles off Aix, and consequently about six miles from the nearest enemy ship. When asked at the court martial what induced him to do this, Gambier replied: "as the enemy was on shore, he did not think it necessary to run any unnecessary risk of the fleet, when the object of their destruction seemed to be already obtained." That, before a single French ship had struck her colours! It was the sort of "we have done very well" reply that infuriated Nelson. Only the *Etna* bomb and a few brigs appeared to assist Cochrane, who saw the *Océan* in process of heaving herself off as the tide rose.

But there were still several other ships securely aground, so at one o'clock he performed what has been called the bravest act of his career. He let the frigate drift down stern foremost to attack the remaining big ships on his own account. At the same time he tried to force Gambier's hand by signalling for assistance.

1:40 P.M. *Enemy superior to chasing ship, but inferior to fleet.*
1:45 P.M. *In want of assistance.*

At two o'clock he anchored in five fathoms and began to engage the 50-gun *Calcutta*. His position cannot have been that marked on the chart illustrating his own account of the battle, for, if so, he would have engaged the *Océan*, the nearest ship marked, and for a 38-gun frigate to have begun a duel with the 120-gun flagship exceeds even the bounds of Cochrane's temerity.

No sooner did the shot of the *Imperieuse* strike the *Calcutta* than the latter's captain led the way to abandoning the ship (after all, she was the magazine vessel) by climbing out of the stern windows. He was later shot for cowardice. Half an hour later the *Valiant* and *Revenge* line-of-battle ships, under Captain John Bligh, made a belated appearance, together with six frigates. As they took station on either side of the *Imperieuse* a cheer went up from her ship's company. "One of our ships of the line (actually the 44-gun *Indefatigable*) came into action in such gallant trim, that it was glorious to behold," writes Marryat. "She was a beautiful ship, in what we call 'high kelter'; she seemed a living body, conscious of her own superior power over her opponents, whose shot she despised as they fell thick and fast about her, while she deliberately took up an admirable position for battle. And having furled her sails, and squared her yards, as if she had been at Spithead, her men came down from aloft, went to their guns, and opened such a fire on the enemy's ships as would have delighted the great Nelson himself."

At 5:00 P.M. two more big ships, *Theseus* and *Caesar* (Rear-Admiral Stopford) moved in towards the scene of action, but the latter ran aground on the Boyart and remained out of range. From a gunner on board of her we have direct evidence that the fire of the Aix batteries was nothing like as fearsome as Gambier pretended: "We thought so little of [it] that we did not return their fire, although they fired pretty smartly at us with shot and shells, which made the water splash against the ship's sides; yet (thank God) they never hit."

As evening fell the supporting ships reaped the reward of Cochrane's initiative. At 5:30 the *Aquilon* and *Varsovie* struck. At 6:00 the *Tonnerre* was set on fire by her own crew and blew up; so did *L'Indienne* frigate. After darkness had fallen the day's work culminated in the accidental explosion of the *Calcutta*, which had previously surrendered to Cochrane's men. A "most dreadful explosion," Gunner Richardson calls it; "fortunately none of her fiery timbers fell on board our ship (the *Caesar)*; everything went upwards, with such a flash of red colour as illuminated the whole elements."

Before dawn the next morning Stopford sent three more fireships down upon the distressed vessels, but the only effect they had was to force Cochrane to shift his anchorage into the passage south of the Palles to avoid their errant course. At 4:00 A.M. the *Caesar* hoisted recall lights, and Cochrane's consorts left him one by one. As the *Indefatigable* passed him on her way out, Cochrane shouted an invitation to join him in attacking the *Océan;* but her captain could not hear what he said, and replied "I am going out to join the fleet." Cochrane answered that, in that case, the *Impérieuse* would shift to her berth to engage the enemy more closely.

Only the *Pallas*, now under the command of his friend Seymour, remained to assist him, together with four brigs and the *Etna* bomb, whose 13-inch mortars had now burst through constant firing.

A few minutes' sleep had apparently been snatched somehow during the past forty-eight hours, during which the losses sustained by the *Imperieuse* had been astonishingly light—three seamen killed, Gilbert and Marsden and a few seamen wounded. When the prospect of renewed action was announced at daylight on the 13th, the men tumbled up from below, cut away the wreckage, caulked the worst holes made by enemy shot, fished the damaged foremast. The brigs had already opened a gallant attack on the *Océan* when Cochrane saw the recall signal hoisted on board the *Caledonia*. He replied: *"If permitted to remain can destroy the enemy."* But shortly afterwards a boat brought the following letter from Gambier:

"MY DEAR LORD.—You have done your part so admirably that I will not suffer you to tarnish it by attempting impossibilities, which I think, as well as those captains who have come from you, any further effort to destroy those ships would be. You must, therefore, join as soon as you can, with the bombs, etc., as I wish for some information, which you allude to, before I close my despatches.

"Yours, my dear Lord, most sincerely,
"GAMBIER.

"PS.—I have ordered three brigs and two rocket vessels to join you, with which, and the bomb, you may make an attempt on the ship that is aground on the Palles, or towards Ile Madame, but I do not think you will succeed; and I am anxious that you should come to me, as I wish to send you to England as soon as possible. You must, therefore, come as soon as the tide turns."

It is an extraordinary message, because the postscript contradicts the recall order in the first part. Of course Cochrane only took notice of the promise of assistance and replied:

"MY LORD.—I have just had the honour to receive your Lordship's letter. We *can* destroy the ships that are on shore, which I hope your Lordship will approve of.

"I have the honour, etc.,
"COCHRANE."

By this time, however, the French were out of reach. Those which had run aground further up the river were throwing their guns overboard preparatory to heaving off as the tide rose. Fishing-boats were loading stores from the derelicts. There was nothing left for Cochrane to do. When, on the morning of the 14th, a more peremptory note arrived from Gambier, he had no alternative but to obey.

"My Dear Lord.—It is necessary I should have some communication with you before I close my despatches to the Admiralty. I have, therefore, ordered Captain Wolfe to relieve you in the services you are engaged in. I wish you to join me as soon as possible that you may convey Sir Harry Neale to England. . . ."

The scene on the quarter-deck of the *Caledonia* can be imagined. In the most pressing terms Cochrane urged the completion of the work of destruction before it was too late. At least Stopford's force might be sent in, if not the whole fleet. He explained that he spoke candidly as a friend, because if no more was done "a noise would be made in England." Much displeased, the admiral did not reply at first. Then he exclaimed: "If you throw blame upon what has been done it will appear like arrogantly claiming all the merit yourself." How little he understood Cochrane's character!

On April 15 the *Imperieuse* sailed for home. Clarendon's words in praise of Blake kept running in her captain's head: "He despised those rules which had been long in practice, to keep his ship and men out of danger, which had been held in former times a point of great ability and circumspection; as if the principal art requisite of a ship had been to be sure to come home safe again."

Many years later he and his friend Brougham visited Paris. In a letter Brougham recalls "the impression made upon all present when I took you to the Tuileries, when the name so well known to them was no sooner heard than there was a general start and shudder. I remember saying, as we drove away, that it ought to satisfy you as to your disappointment at Basque Roads, and you answered that you would rather have had the ships."

~

CHAPTER VII

The Court Martial

S IR, the Almighty's favour to His Majesty and the nation has been strongly marked in the success He has been pleased to give to the operations of His Majesty's fleet under my command. . . . I cannot speak in sufficient terms of admiration and applause of the vigorous and gallant attack made by Lord Cochrane upon the French line-of-battle ships which were on shore, as well as of judicious manner of approaching them, and placing his ship in a position most advantageous to annoy the enemy and preserve his own ship, which could not be exceeded by any feat of valour hitherto achieved by the British Navy."

The publication of Gambier's despatch was received with tremendous enthusiasm. The news of the victory came at a time when Napoleon was master of the Continent, and it heartened a war-weary nation which had been starved of the news of victory for the four years since Trafalgar. Bonfires were lit up and down the country; medals were struck; prints, which look like advertisements for a gala firework display, were published by highly imaginative artists; and Cochrane found himself the hero of the hour. On April 26 the King conferred on him the Knighthood of the Order of the Bath, the highest honour he could receive, and balladmongers sang his praises in the streets:

> *We poured in our shot and our rockets like hail*
> *Till at length that their courage began for to fail,*
> *Some were taken and destroyed, and some got on shore,*
> *The rest ran up harbour and would fight no more.*

> CHORUS:
> *So success to our sailors that sail on the sea,*
> *Who with COCHRANE undaunted, whenever they're wanted,*
> *They'll fight till they die, or gain the victory.*

> *So now, Master Bonyparte, cease for to brag*
> *Till you build some more ships for to hoist your white flag*
> *Which so often had been beat by the lords of the main;*
> *And if they dare face them, they'll serve them so again.*

> *So success, etc.*

Broadsheets are the best thermometers of public opinion: it is significant that in the ballad of the Battle in the Aix Roads Gambier's name is not so much as mentioned. Cochrane basked in nation-wide popularity for the proudest moment of his life. But he was under no illusion about the extent of the damage inflicted on the enemy, and he was not surprised when doubts as to Gambier's claims of a great victory began to percolate from the Channel Fleet. "I well remember," writes a junior officer, "the indignation which pervaded the whole fleet in witnessing the total want of enterprise, and even of common sense of duty, which permitted so many of the enemy's ships to escape when they were entirely at our mercy." Criticism of what the French called *"la mollesse de Lord Gambier"* began to find its way into the press within a few weeks of the battle, and talk about mismanagement and unenterprising conduct on the part of the commander-in-chief became general in London.

Imagine, therefore, Cochrane's feelings when it was announced that the Government was preparing a vote of thanks to Lord Gambier on what it variously described as his "brilliant," "glorious" and "unexampled" success. He immediately informed Lord Mulgrave that if the matter was raised in the House he felt it would be his duty as a Member of Parliament to oppose such a vote. Mulgrave earnestly begged him to desist, pointing out that such a course would be interpreted as an act of insubordination. With a somewhat insincere show of patriotism, Cochrane replied that it might not be his duty as a naval officer to criticise his commander-in-chief, but that as a representative of the nation as a Member of Parliament he refused to be a party to deceiving the public on a matter of such importance.

A few days later Mulgrave summoned him again. "Now, my lord, I will make you a proposal. I will put under your orders three frigates, with *carte blanche* to do whatever you please on the enemy's coast in the Mediterranean. I will further get you permission to go to Sicily, and embark on board your squadron my own regiment which is stationed there."

Cochrane dismissed the bribe without hesitation. It merely increased his conviction that he was acting in the public interest. His motives were certainly not entirely altruistic, but it is unfair to call his rejection of Mulgrave's bribe "unpatriotic." He preferred, says the great historian who makes this charge, to exploit a personal grievance instead of doing his country a service. But in those days wars did not provoke the bestial mass hatreds with which we are familiar to-day. Cochrane fought Napoleon because it was his duty as a naval officer. As far as patriotism was concerned he felt, as did the Whig Opposition, that it was just as important to attack corruption at home and to force a supine government to prosecute the war more vigorously, which was exactly what Gambier had failed to do. It was the Gambier affair which made him a crusader, because the injustice he suffered convinced him that until Gambier and the powerful clique which supported him was destroyed there could be no justice, nor even efficiency, at home in Britain. For him, patriotism began at home. It was a tragedy from the point of view of the success of his career in the Navy that he refused Mulgrave's offer; but a man of his character could not be expected to act otherwise.

The bait having failed, the Admiralty wrote demanding the charges which he proposed to bring against his commander-in-chief. Cochrane replied by referring them to the logs of the ships engaged. Thereupon Gambier demanded a court martial before the matter was raised in Parliament. That was in May; the court martial did not actually sit until July 26. According to Cochrane the delay was deliberate, in order to give Gambier time to prepare his defence, to obtain the services of the Admiralty solicitor, and to get notoriously hostile witnesses, such as Captain Maitland of the *Emerald*, sent out of the way on a distant station. Meanwhile the Admiralty could pick a suitable court, giving as their reason for the delay the preparations for the Walcheren expedition.

While his opponents carefully chose their ground, Cochrane showed all that ignorance of tactics which mark him as a failure as a politician. He congratulated himself on evading the Admiralty's attempt to make him appear as Gambier's prosecutor. He could not have made a greater mistake, for when the trial opened Mr. Bicknell, the official prosecutor, collaborating with a hostile court, was able to treat him merely as one of many witnesses. He was thus prevented from cross-examining Gambier or anybody else; he could not ask leading questions; as soon as he broached a point the defence might have difficulty in answering, he was interrupted with another question which led him away from the point at issue. He reaped the fruits of his impetuosity in raising the question, and by refusing professional advice he put himself in a false position before the trial opened.

The court martial was held at Portsmouth on July 26 on board the *Gladiator*, a hulk used for such proceedings. The President of the Court was Sir Roger Curtis, an honest man but a personal friend of Gambier and one who allowed himself to be influenced by knaves like Sir William Young, the senior admiral on the board. Young was the Plymouth port admiral with whom Cochrane had quarrelled in 1807, and whose inefficiency in fitting out ships he had publicly described in Parliament. Sir William's opportunity for revenge had come.

The official charge brought against Gambier was cleverly framed, for it was so vague that any lawyer could evade it: "It appears to us that the said Admiral Lord Gambier, on the 12th day of the said month of April, the enemy's ships being then on shore, and the signal having been made that they could be destroyed, did for a considerable time neglect or delay taking effectual measures for destroying them."

The resolution of a junior captain, however self-confident, who had the effrontery to bring his commander-in-chief to trial, must have faltered at the sight of the captains and admirals of the Channel Fleet resplendent in their dress uniforms crowding the decks as witnesses, the file of red-coated marines guarding the door of the main cabin, the board of admirals sitting behind the green baize table on which lay Gambier's sword. It was not the usual hole-in-the-corner court martial about some petty matter of discipline. It was an affair of national importance.

The first witnesses called were Mr. Stokes, master of the *Caledonia*, and Mr. Spurling, master of the *Imperieuse*. The latter was at once asked some awkward questions about the suspicious additions made in the margin of his log after the action. By whose orders were those additions made? Why were they not made at the time of the action? Spurling replied that he had added to the log after the action on his own initiative, because it was impossible to keep it up to date during the battle. True or not, the judge advocate had already prejudiced the Court against Cochrane by the suggestion that the logs had been tampered with to prove a case.

Then Cochrane was called. At first he tried to speak from notes he had prepared; when this was pronounced out of order, cleverly framed questions were put to him which prevented him from approaching the real point at issue—could Gambier have sent in help on the morning after the fireship attack? He described the disposition of the ships before the battle and was forced to admit that they were "judiciously placed," though he was not given the opportunity of pointing out that they had been so placed on his own advice. Only at the end of his evidence could he come to grips with the real question by stating that there was "anchorage out of range of shot and shell for at least six sail of the line," perhaps "a dozen or twenty sail." He was then asked if he closed to the attack at midday on the 13th with or without orders from the commander-in-chief?

"The doing of it was my own act."

In that case what did he mean by hoisting the signal of distress when he was in no distress?

He meant that he "wanted assistance" to attack the French, but there was no separate signal to express his meaning accurately.

"Was not assistance sent to you?"

"Yes, of a sort, but not early in the morning when it was signalled for." Warming to his subject, he allowed his feelings to carry him far beyond a direct answer:

> "I consoled myself with the supposition that his lordship
> intended a grand blow on the island and on the ships at
> once, although I thought this highly unnecessary and im-

prudent. I could not in any other way account for a proceeding which thus enabled the helpless French ships to
endeavour to escape undisturbed in to the river Charente.
Twelve o'clock arrived, no signal was made to weigh. Half
past twelve, still no signal——

"ADMIRAL YOUNG.—This is very improper. This is no answer to
the question. It is only calculated to make an unfavourable
impression against the prisoner.

"LORD COCHRANE.—I am bound to tell the truth, the whole
truth and nothing but the truth, and with submission to the
Court, if I am not permitted to state the circumstances
upon which my opinion is grounded, it is impossible I can
give a full answer to the question and until the Court hears
the whole of my answer, it is not possible that they can
form any correct judgment upon it, and must remain in ignorance of the fact.

"ADMIRAL YOUNG.—Lord Cochrane, you are bound to give a
direct answer to the question, and not to state that which
the Court are decidedly of the opinion is wholly irrelevant.

"THE PRESIDENT.—I really think since Lord Cochrane has gone
so far, the Court should hear the whole of his answer; we
can then judge if part of it should stand, or be expunged."

Upon this the Court was cleared. On the readmission of the press
Cochrane was permitted to continue, after a reprimand for applying
the word "ignorance" to the person who had proposed the question.
Why, he was asked, if you admit you received the signal for recall did
you not obey it? In reply Cochrane read Gambier's message of recall,
without, however, underlining the contradiction contained in it by
pointing out that the commander-in-chief promised to send ships to
support him at the same time as ordering his recall.

His lengthy cross-examination concluded with a series of questions about the charts used during the action. How did he know that
there was anchorage for six sail of the line? By the French chart taken
from the *Varsovie*. This showed the distance between Aix and the Boyart to be nearly two miles; it showed a depth of thirty-five feet at
low water off the Boyart, and between twenty and thirty feet off the
Palles Flat. As it was of French origin this chart was declared to be no
evidence and was flung under the table. Instead, the chart made by
Mr. Stokes of the *Caledonia* on information supplied by Mr. Fairfax,

the master of the fleet, was adopted in order, as the judge advocate ingenuously remarked, "to save a great deal of trouble." It certainly saved Gambier a lot of trouble, because the Aix–Boyart passage was marked as only a mile wide, and twelve feet of water was marked where Cochrane's chart showed twenty-five feet, apart from errors in the positions of ships. It was not till fifty years later that he had an opportunity of comparing the charts, and it was then that he discovered why Gambier was acquitted so easily.

Stokes's chart was adopted to prove Gambier's first line of defence—that there was not safe and sufficient anchorage for big ships, had they been sent in. Cochrane's idea of sending in half the fleet was, said Gambier, "preposterous and impracticable." If that was the case why, then, did he send in three seventy-fours under Captain Bligh, followed by two of the biggest ships under Stopford? What business had such ships as the *Revenge* and the *Caesar* in Aix Roads while so many ships of shallower draught remained at anchor several miles away? That was the sort of question Cochrane might have asked if he had been permitted to cross-examine the prisoner.

The commander-in-chief's second line of defence was that the passage was not wide enough to allow ships to lie out of range of shot from Aix citadel. About the efficacy of these batteries there was much disagreement. Cochrane's view was that "the distance was such that I might lie there for a week and not have been hit twice." Captain Broughton reported that "the fortifications were not as strong as we supposed." We have seen what Gunner Richardson has to say about the matter in his diary from his experiences in the *Caesar*. An officer in the French flagship himself admitted that "the batteries afforded us no protection at all, when the enemy forced the passage up the Road with the greatest ease."

At this point the Court adjourned for the week-end. When it reassembled on Monday, after additional time had been given to Gambier to prepare his defence, all the witnesses were ordered out of court. Cochrane immediately protested against this breach of custom.

"THE PRESIDENT.—Lord Cochrane, it is the wish of the Court, in the present instance, that the witnesses should be excluded.

"LORD COCHRANE.—The trial of Admiral Harvey is a case in point, where the witnesses were allowed to remain.

"THE PRESIDENT.—My Lord, the Court has discussed the measure in the present instance, and it is its wish that you should withdraw.

"Lord Cochrane bowed and withdrew."

While Gambier's defence, drawn up and read for him by his lawyer, Mr. Lavie (whom we shall meet again), was continuing in the great cabin, we can imagine Cochrane's feelings as he paced the half-deck. A few witnesses were later readmitted, but none of them favourable to the prosecution. Cochrane therefore wrote a note to the President, pointing out the injustice of these proceedings. By so doing he succeeded in getting Captain Seymour of the *Pallas* called. Seymour testified that to the best of his knowledge there was ample anchorage, to which Gambier replied "that he did not consider the evidence of the least consequence." Gambier's own defence turned the tables on Cochrane by converting the trial into a prosecution of his accuser rather than a defence of his own inactivity. He pointed out how inimical it was to naval discipline that a commander-in-chief should have to defend himself "against the loose, indirect accusations of an officer so much his inferior in rank." He stated, quite unwarrantably, that Cochrane had been general in his complaints of all the other officers, adding, as he pointed to the imaginary spot on the chart where the explosion vessels were supposed to have blown up, that Cochrane himself had failed in his objective. In all the subsequent part of the action he denied him any merit at all. It is hardly possible to believe that the man who referred to Cochrane in this way was the same man who had spoken so generously of his services in the despatch of April 14. After stressing the suspicious contradictions shown in the logs kept on board the *Imperieuse*, he concluded by stating that if he had acted on Cochrane's view "I am firmly persuaded that the success attending this achievement would have proved more dearly bought than any yet recorded in our naval annals."

The trial ended on the ninth day, after further cross-examination of witnesses favourable to the defence. At the last moment Cochrane sent another note begging the President to recall him to the witness-box. The Court did not think it proper to accede to his wish, but agreed that the letter should be entered on the minutes. The judge advocate then read the sentence of the court. The charge against the accused was found not to have been proved; the court was of the opinion that Lord Gambier's "conduct on that occasion, as well as his general conduct and proceedings as commander-in-chief of the Channel Fleet employed in the Basque Roads, between the 17th day of March and the 29th day of April 1809, was marked by zeal, judgment, and ability, and an anxious attention to the welfare of His Majesty's service; and doth adjudge him to be most honourably acquitted."

"Admiral Lord Gambier," the President added, picking up the sword in front of him by the blade, "I have peculiar pleasure in receiving the command of the court to return you your sword."

The Vote of Thanks was accordingly proposed at the next session of Parliament in January 1810. Mulgrave's motion in the Lords (in which Cochrane's name was not so much as mentioned) was supported by a former first lord with the statement that "he thought it extremely wrong that the Admiralty should have appointed Lord Cochrane at all." In the Commons there was a long and futile battle in which Cochrane tried vainly to have the whole case retried by moving for the minutes of the court martial. He compared Gambier's behaviour to that of Parker at Copenhagen, to whose recall signal Nelson had turned his blind eye. He was supported by many of the Whigs, Tierney, Whitbread and Burdett, who remarked sarcastically: "Lord Gambier's plan seemed a desire to preserve the fleet—Cochrane's plan, to destroy the enemy's fleet. He had never heard that the Articles of War held out an instruction to preserve the fleet. What if Nelson, at the Nile or Trafalgar, had acted on this principle?" Largely on account of a speech by Wilberforce, Gambier's co-religionist and friend, and some vicious attacks on Cochrane's personal character, his motion was lost by 161 votes to 39. When the Vote of Thanks was read he received the crowning humiliation of finding that the only thanks he received for his part in the action was for superintending "the brilliant and unexampled success of the difficult and perilous mode of attack by fireships"—an attack which he himself was the first to call a failure, and of which even Gambier had said that "they failed in the principal effect they were intended to produce."

Cochrane was defeated all along the line. More than that, every effort was made to rob him of the honour of effecting even a partial destruction of the enemy fleet. The Admirals were jubilant. "It will be a lesson to restless and inexperienced young officers," wrote one, "not to hazard a mischievous opinion tending to weaken the respect and confidence due to able and tried officers." Gambier's acquittal was regarded as a political victory over the Radicals. "What a tem-

pestuous world do we live in!" wrote the insufferable Hannah More
to Barham, lately first lord and a cousin of Gambier; "Yet terrible as
Buonaparte is in every point of view, I do not fear him so much as
those domestic mischiefs—Burdett, Cochrane, Wardle and Cobbett. I
hope, however, that the mortification Cochrane, etc., have lately experienced in their base and impotent endeavours to pull down repu-
tations which they found unassailable, will keep them down a little."

Nevertheless, the Battle in the Aix Roads was an important victory. Gambier might have made it as annihilating as the Battle of the
Nile, but Cochrane at least succeeded in paralysing the Rochefort
squadron for the rest of the war. Three line-of-battle ships had been
destroyed and three others rendered unfit for further service. Allemand was superseded and his successor promptly dismantled the
ships to defend the estuary against another such attack. And that it
was a strategic as well as a tactical victory is proved by the fact that
Guadeloupe and Martinique, the two richest islands in the French
West Indies, fell into our hands without a struggle shortly afterwards. The West India merchants could sleep quietly in their beds
once more, secure in the knowledge that another colonial expedition
on Napoleon's part was now impossible. More important still, the
blow to the enemy's morale was decisive: "It is first necessary to inspire our sailors with the spirit with which they were animated previous to this unfortunate affair. As it is, the greater part are completely
disheartened: every day I hear them lamenting their situation, and
speaking in praise of our enemy's. This, in my opinion, is the greatest
injury the English have done to us." So wrote one of the men who had
experienced Cochrane's methods of warfare. Napoleon's view is
worth quoting too, because it is such a contrast to the attitude taken
up towards Cochrane by his own countrymen. At St. Helena,
O'Meara mentioned that he had heard it said that "if Cochrane had
been properly supported, he would have destroyed the whole of the
French ships. 'He could not only have destroyed them,' replied the
emperor, 'but he might and would have taken them out, had your
admiral supported him as he ought to have done.... The French
admiral was a fool, but yours was just as bad.'"

THE COURT MARTIAL prevented Cochrane from joining the disastrous expedition to Walcheren, a flagrant example of the timid and
incompetent administration of the day. His frigate sailed under the
temporary command of the Hon. Captain Duncan, son of the famous

admiral, and some of the methods Cochrane had taught his men were used with good effect. Of course the elaborate plans he drew up for destroying the French fleet in the Scheldt were summarily rejected by the Admiralty.

This was the first public sign of the ill favour in which he was now held, though he himself does not seem to have realised how seriously he had prejudiced all chances for a successful career in the Navy. He had attempted to attack the dominant faction in politics; he was well known for his Radical views; since his election to Parliament he had taken every opportunity to rake the Government fore and aft for their corruption, their inactivity and their inefficiency; he was the personal friend of dangerous reformers like Cobbett and Burdett, and he was often the central figure at "seditious" meetings held in London and elsewhere. Now he had given the authorities a chance for revenge, for his attack on Gambier had turned out as nothing less than an official condemnation of himself.

The problem for the Admiralty was how to get him out of the Navy without putting themselves in the wrong. Such an attitude can be excused on the grounds that they had to consider the harmony of the whole fleet, in which a man of Cochrane's temper could easily breed trouble. But their real motive was political. A famous naval officer with a grievance who was also a Member of Parliament could make things exceedingly uncomfortable for the Government. They had no difficulty in rejecting his plans for coastal landings and commando raids by pointing out their lack of success in the days of the elder Pitt. The next step was to force him either to relinquish the command of his ship, or silence him by sending him abroad. The latter course had been successful in 1807. If he refused to go he would not be employed again and they would thus be saved the trouble of taking the dangerous step of dismissing him.

He was therefore abruptly informed that he had unjustifiably absented himself from his ship and that he must join her forthwith as she was destined for the Mediterranean. That meant a subordinate position in the blockading fleet off Toulon, no chance of honour, excitement or prize money. It would have been an intolerable situation for a man of his spirit and his gifts. On 11 June 1810, he replied in a long and confused letter which shows his embarrassment at the position in which he found himself. Since his plans had been rejected by the naval authorities, he declared he had "no alternative than to submit them to the wisdom of the House. . . . In conclusion I beg permission to say that I have got some objects of moment to bring forward in Parliament, and that as there is no enterprise given to the *Imperieuse*, I have no wish that she should be detained for me one moment."

That did not satisfy the Admiralty. The next day he received a letter from the Secretary requesting "to be distinctly informed whether or not it is your Lordship's intention to join your ship as soon as Parliament shall be prorogued. I shall be much pleased to receive an answer in the affirmative because I should then entertain hopes that your activity and gallantry might be made available for the public service."

Very handsomely put, for their lordships knew that whichever way he might turn he could not escape resigning either his command or his seat in Parliament. Cochrane expostulates too much in his account of the matter in his autobiography: "a more unjust order was never issued. . . . There is nothing worse in the records of the Admiralty even at that period." In his final letter he did exactly what they intended him to do: As the *Imperieuse* "is to proceed immediately on foreign service, I fear it is impossible for me to be in readiness to join her within the time specified." The next month she sailed without her old captain. Cochrane was not again employed in the Royal Navy for thirty-nine years.

The career of the sea wolf was ended. Yet by the age of thirty-five he had managed to write his name indelibly in the annals of naval history. No other captain of his age had done so much for his country in so short a time. As a frigate captain he had been a phenomenal success, for he showed time and again that he possessed every attribute such an officer should have—courage, energy, imagination, ingenuity, the ability to strike enthusiasm into his own men and terror into his enemies. He had made his fortune with prize money and won undying renown by the brilliance of his tactics. But his sin of pride proved his undoing. He thought too much of his own abilities to co-operate easily with others, and he loved a grievance almost as much as he loved the cause of justice and liberty. Politics attracted him now, because Westminster is the ideal place to vent a grievance. He felt that as long as his country was misgoverned in the way it had been for the past score years he could not throw himself wholeheartedly into the cause of her defence. The injustices he had suffered personally jaundiced his political outlook and lent fire to his attack on the Tory administration.

"The worst injury," said the *Annual Register,* "which the radical reformers have done to the country, has been by depriving it of Lord
Cochrane's services, and withdrawing him from that career which he
had so gloriously begun." But it was not the fault of his Radical
friends that he deserted the quarter-deck for the hustings. It was the
state of the country, the manifest iniquities of the borough-mongering faction, the gross scandals of naval administration, the injustices
daily inflicted by a reactionary legal system; these were the things
which made him a crusader in the cause of parliamentary reform.

PART II

Crusader in Parliament

CHAPTER I

⌇

The Cause of Reform

WRITING in 1859 as an old man of seventy-four Cochrane, by that date Earl of Dundonald, says: "It is strange that, after having suffered more for my political faith than any man now living, I should have survived to see former Radical yearnings become modern Tory doctrines. Stranger still they should now form stepping stones to place and power, instead of to the bar of the criminal court, where even the counsel defending those who were prosecuted for holding them became marked men." He lived long enough to share the fate of all reformers who outlive the struggle. When he entered Parliament in 1806 as a young naval captain he was, with Sir Francis Burdett, the only link between the House of Commons and the popular reform movement outside its walls. By the time the movement he had supported in its darkest hours had triumphed he had retired from the scene.

It is as a parliamentary reformer, not as an adventurous frigate captain, that he first appears in the role of a crusader. He seems to have regarded war as a profession, demanding of its participants the utmost skill and courage, and repaying their success with honour and prize money. It was something in the nature of a business, not a crusade inspired by the highest principles. There is no evidence in his writings that he ever appreciated the ideals at stake in the Napoleonic Wars; nor did many of his contemporaries. When honour and reward were not forthcoming in the measure he thought was his due, he had no hesitation in absenting himself from naval service to devote himself to attacking the enemy within the gates—the stranglehold of Tory corruption, which he detested so much more heartily than he disliked Napoleon. At first he tried to combine the professions of naval officer and Radical politician, but they soon proved incompatible, and when his naval career ran upon the rocks he devoted himself with the greatest energy, but with an almost complete lack of success, to a frontal assault on that jungle of corruption which his friend Cobbett used to call "the thing."

On his return from the successful cruise of the *Pallas* in the spring of 1806, he noticed an advertisement in Cobbett's *Political Register* of May 24, calling upon any public-spirited gentleman to come forward to contest the free borough of Honiton on "patriotic principles." He had long desired to get into Parliament, and the general election due to Pitt's death, together with the proximity of Honiton to Plymouth, gave him a chance to try his fortune. He was thirty years old, brimming over with self-confidence, his pockets full of prize money, and his mind restless with grievances about the conduct of the war at sea. His electioneering tactics were to prove quite as original, if not as successful, as those he employed at sea.

On June 8 a fanfare of trumpets announced his arrival from Plymouth, "accompanied by two lieutenants and one midshipman in full dress in one carriage, followed by another containing the boat's crew new rigged and prepared for action." To his surprise he found that Cobbett, together with that shady character, his uncle Cochrane Johnstone, who wished to see him on a business matter (probably to persuade him to invest his newly gotten gains in some City scheme of his own backing), had arrived from London the previous evening. Though it is doubtful if Cochrane knew anything about Honiton and its four hundred electors, Cobbett knew it well as one of the most notoriously corrupt boroughs in the country. It had been in the pocket of one family for most of the previous century, its last "owner" having represented it in no less than twenty-nine parliaments. "Who shall describe the gulph wherein have been swallowed the fortunes of so many ancient and respectable families?" writes Cobbett in the *Political Register*. "There was, the electors would tell you, no bribery. They took a certain sum of money each, according to their consequence; 'but this,' they said, 'came in the shape of a reward after the election, and, therefore, the oath might be safely taken.' "

In the present election a certain Mr. Cavendish Bradshaw was to be the rival candidate. Cobbett had apparently intended to oppose him, but he welcomed the appearance of such a promising candidate as Lord Cochrane. They were alike in many ways, these two reformers who became lifelong friends—energetic men, both of them, impetuous, irritable, inconsistent, and entirely independent in their views. Of the two, Cobbett, the farmer in homespun, the pattern John Bull, was the more honest; but Cochrane the aristocrat, the handsome young sailor, was obviously the more popular personality in an election. He was just the type to become the hero of the mob, and to allow the intoxicating fumes of popularity to influence him to rash decisions.

A brilliant amateur in politics, he regarded the Honiton election as a game. But Cobbett was in earnest. The recent attempt to impeach Melville, first lord of the Admiralty, on a charge of malversation of naval funds, had opened his eyes to the political situation. The Melville case transformed Cobbett from a scurrilous anti-Jacobin into an equally scurrilous Jacobin. It persuaded him that it was his duty, as an honest political journalist, to lead a crusade against "the THING," that mystical nexus of corruption centring around "the bloody tyrant, Wm. Pitt," his friends and his relations. Honiton gave him his chance to open the campaign, and Cochrane provided an energetic disciple. The two men saw eye to eye from the start. Cobbett too loved the sea; he had himself tried to join the Navy as a boy, but the captain on board whose ship he presented himself "thought I had eloped on account of a bastard" and sent him back to the plough. Later he tried to join the Marines, but found that he had enlisted in a regiment of the line by mistake. In the Army he experienced just the same abuses as Cochrane found in the Navy. When the two men shook hands on the principle that not a farthing was to be spent by way of a bribe during the course of the election, an alliance was founded which was to prove fruitful to the cause of reform.

The election opened on Monday with the summer sun blazing down on the hustings. Cavendish Bradshaw, secure in the knowledge that money counted more than words, did not waste time in speech-making, beyond warning his audience that Mr. Cobbett was a dangerous windbag. Cochrane followed with a polite speech pledging himself not to accept any sinecure or pension in the event of his election, a point which entirely failed to interest his hearers. Then Cobbett rose to turn the big guns of his invective on Bradshaw. The latter replied that, as Cobbett was well known as "a convicted libeller," no attention need be paid to his remarks. On this a riot broke out, Cochrane's naval boys being well to the fore. Above the hubbub the captain's quarter-deck voice could be heard calling for order, and it was only by sheer determination that Cobbett managed to make his voice heard at all. The meeting broke up in disorder.

Money, not principles, counted at Honiton. Cochrane had been considered a promising candidate by the inhabitants because they imagined his pockets were stuffed with prize money which, of course, he would spend sailor-fashion. This was made clear to him when canvassing began. "You need not ask me, my lord, who I votes for," leered one elector; "I always votes for Mister Most." The announcement that he intended to stand for "patriotic principles," which meant that he refused to bribe, naturally resulted in a sound defeat. Indeed, only his bodyguard of bludgeon-men saved him from physical violence at the polls.

Cobbett posted back to London to vent his wrath in the next number of the *Political Register,* convinced that his sole duty henceforward must be to attack with all the means in his power the system under which such dishonesty was encouraged.

Cochrane remained on the scene to spring one of those surprises which made his political career as exciting as his record at sea. With magnificent inconsistency he sent a bellman round the town to announce that "all who had voted for Lord Cochrane might repair to his agent, J. Townshend Esq., and receive ten pounds ten." The effect upon the electors of Honiton was electrical. Since Bradshaw's rate of payment was only five guineas a vote, all his supporters considered themselves cheated. Cochrane left the town secure in the knowledge that the next time he chose to contest the seat his success was certain.

His experience at the election had as profound an effect on him as it had on Cobbett. He began the election as a Whig, but he ended it as a Radical. Like Cobbett, he felt there was something seriously wrong with a political system which made a respectable country tradesman say, "I always votes for Mister Most." With the impetuosity which was so typical of him he plunged into the task of cleansing the Augean stables of political life, without considering into what dangerous waters such a crusade would lead him.

Fortunately another chance to try his fortunes at Honiton occurred that autumn before he was sent to sea again in the *Imperieuse*.*

With the ten-guinea bonus fresh in their memories the electors
flocked to the polls and Cochrane was triumphantly elected. It was
then hinted that another ten-guinea bonus was due to his supporters.

"Not one farthing!" was the reply.

"But, my lord, you gave ten guineas a head to the minority at the
last election, and the majority have been calculating on something
handsome on the present occasion."

"No doubt. The former gift was for their disinterested conduct in
not taking the bribe of five guineas from the agents of my opponent.
For me now to pay them would be a violation of my own previously
expressed principles."

"Will you not, then, at least give your constituents a public supper?"

"By all means. It will give me the greatest satisfaction to know
that so rational display of patriotism has superseded a system of
bribery."

But this time the biter was bit. The whole town, supporters, opponents, wives, children, friends, all turned up to the banquet. The
result was a bill for £1,200, which Cochrane refused to pay. For
eleven years he was dunned for the debt, until at last in 1817, when
he was a ruined man, his creditors closed on him by obtaining a warrant to put an execution into his house. For six weeks he managed to
keep the bailiffs from crossing his threshold. "I still hold out," he
writes to a friend, "though the castle has several times been threatened in great force. Explosion bags are set in the lower embrasures,
and all the garrison is under arms." At last the sheriff and twenty
constables, taking their lives in their hands, forced an entry through
a window and arrested him as he sat at breakfast. On examination
the contents of the bags proved to be merely charcoal dust.

When he returned from his first cruise in the *Imperieuse* early in
1807 he found that Parliament had again been dissolved on account
of the death of Fox. Once more he would have to undergo the rigours
of an election. According to his own account he was already so disgusted by the demands of the Honiton electors for places and pensions that he was determined not to seek re-election there. But we

---

* The date of his election given in his autobiography is incorrect. The actual date was October
1806; see the *Political Register* for that year.

may guess that the existence of an irate body of creditors and dissatisfied electors made the place somewhat inhospitable for him. Instead he determined to stand for the City of Westminster. It was the most momentous decision in his parliamentary career, for in the event of his election he would be thrown into the maelstrom of radical politics, this being the most notoriously Radical constituency in the country.

The Westminster elections of 1806 and 1807 are landmarks in political history, because they gave the Radicals their first representation in Parliament. At that date Britain was not ruled by the party system but by oligarchical groups of patricians, who had so far forgotten the traditions of party government that they were no longer known as the Whigs and the Tories, but as the Ins and the Outs. Neither group possessed unity or principles, for party government had deteriorated into a scramble for power and place. Hazlitt, indeed, compares the groups to two coaches which splashed each other with mud as they passed, but were both going to the same place by the same road. The best description of the political situation as it existed after the death of the opposing giants, Pitt and Fox, is to be found in a letter from Jeffery, the editor of the *Edinburgh Review*, to Francis Horner, the Whig M.P.

"Do you not see that the whole nation is now divided into two, and only two, parties—the timid, sordid, selfish worshippers of power and adherents of the Court, and the dangerous, discontented, half noble, half mischievous advocates for reform and innovation? Between these stand the Whigs; without popularity, power, or consequence of any sort, with great talents and virtues, but utterly inefficient, and incapable of ever becoming efficient, if they will still maintain themselves at an equal distance from both the prevailing parties. It is your duty then to join with that to which you approximate most nearly; or rather with whose aid alone can you snatch the country from imminent destruction. Is this a time to stand upon scruples and dignities? Join the popular party, which is every day growing stronger and more formidable, patronise a reform in Parliament."

At the outset of his political career Cochrane found himself in this dilemma. At first he called himself a Whig. But the party was leaderless and unprincipled, and his Honiton experiences showed him that more was at stake than the so-called Whig reformers dreamt of. On most occasions he found that he could vote with the fifty-odd members nicknamed "the Mountain," who rallied behind the fiery Whitbread, a rich brewer despised by the aristocrats of his party because he was a tradesman. When Whitbread attacked prevalent abuses Cochrane was with him, but when he began to demand that troops should be withdrawn from Spain he could only walk out of the House. Nor was "the Mountain" as Jacobinical as its name implied. Though Grey and other aristocratic Whigs had supported some measure of reform in the far-off days before the war, even "the Mountain" cold-shouldered extremists like Cochrane and Burdett in their demand for an extension of the suffrage. As a result of this parody of party government, the battleground of political principles shifted from the benches of the House of Commons to the hustings of the City of Westminster. Ever since the historic contests of Fox's early days, when the Duchess of Devonshire kissed the butcher's baby, this seat had been the centre of political interest because it was the largest and most democratic constituency in the country. It was a scot and lot borough in which every ratepayer was entitled to vote. Bounded roughly by Oxford Street on the north, Temple Bar on the east and Kensington Palace on the west, much of its area was composed of slums of the vilest description. It was reported to have 17,000 voters at a time when Grampound and Old Sarum had one or two, and the electioneering methods employed on the very steps of the Mother of Parliaments should have made every thinking man a reformer. Francis Place, the Charing Cross tailor, thus describes the election the year before Cochrane presented himself:

"My indignation was greatly increased when I saw the servants of the Duke of Northumberland, in their showy dress liveries, throwing lumps of bread and cheese among the dense crowd of vagabonds they had collected together. To see these vagabonds catching the lumps, shouting, swearing, fighting, and blackguarding in every possible way, women as well as men, all the vile wretches from the courts and alleys in St. Giles and Westminster, the Porridge Islands, and other miserable places; to see these people representing, as it was said, the electors of Westminster, was certainly the lowest possible step of degradation."

It needed a brave man to forsake the quarter-deck of a frigate to harangue that rabble. For some years the seat had been a quiet one on account of a bargain struck between Fox and his Tory opponent, but in 1806 Cobbett and Place began to educate the electorate and the floodgates to demagogy were opened. James Paull, a retired Indian merchant with a grievance and a hot temper, was the Radical candidate that year, but he was easily defeated by Sheridan the Whig and Admiral Sir Samuel Hood the Tory.

At a meeting of the new Radical organisation in the parlour behind Place's shop it was decided to run Sir Francis Burdett and Paull for the 1807 election. The former, who had spent £94,000 in two Middlesex elections, refused to spend a penny more but agreed to stand if elected. However, he and Paull quarrelled before the contest opened and both men were wounded in a duel. Place thereupon refused to put his services at Paull's disposal, and Paull refused to retire from the contest, with the result that he came bottom of the poll. Of Elliot, the Tory candidate who replaced Hood, there is nothing to be said except that he also retired before the end of the contest. On the other hand, Sheridan, the official Whig, was a name on everyone's lips since the golden days in which he had won fame as an orator and a dramatist; but in 1807 he was too often drunk and too often in debt to be a serious opponent.*

Into this crowded arena leapt Cochrane, fresh from the sea. Nobody knew anything about him except that he was a junior naval officer who had been returned for Honiton in the Whig interest the previous year. In the eyes of the mob he was considered to be Sheridan's opponent, but he proclaimed himself an independent without any party connections. Unlike Burdett he did not have the backing of Place's efficient organisation, the details of which have been preserved in the latter's guard books in the British Museum—ballads, slogans, inspired newspaper articles, posters proclaiming SIR FRANCIS A PLUMPER! NO TUMULTS! NO TREATING! etc. All that Cochrane had to

---

* In the Gillray caricature reproduced as frontispiece the results of the election are shown. The sub-title reads: "Election Candidates, or the Republican Goose (Burdett) at the top of the Pole (poll), the Devil helping him behind (Horne Tooke); also an exact representation of Sawney Mc. Cockran flourishing the Cudgel of Naval Reform lent him by Cobbett (in his pocket is a paper marked 'Charges against St. Vincent'), and mounting Triumphantly over a small Beer Barrel (Elliot)—together with an Old Drury Lane Harlequin (Sheridan) trying in vain to make a spring to the top of the Pole, his Broad Bottom always bringing him down again—and lastly, poor little Paul the Taylor done over, wounded by a Goose and not a leg to stand on (referring to the Paull–Burdett duel)."

rely on was his own compelling personality and a long purse, which enabled him to hire Richardson's Coffee House in Covent Garden for his committee rooms and Willis's Rooms in St. James's for the dinners he gave. He printed circulars begging for the electors' "interest and favour." He even hired a hack to write a broadside for him, entitled VICTORY! COCHRANE! AND REFORM! to be sung to the tune of *The Mulberry Tree*:

> *All hail to the hero—of ENGLAND the boast,*
> *The honour—the glory—the pride of our coast;*
> *Let the bells peal his name, and the cannon's loud roar*
> *Sound the plaudits of COCHRANE, the friend of her shore.*
>
> *From boyhood devoted to ENGLAND and FAME*
> *Each sea knows his prowess, each climate his name. . . .*
> *While he hurls round the thunder, and rides in the storm*
> *He is more than all this!—He's the FRIEND OF REFORM!*

On nomination day he opened the election in his own style. Leaping from the hustings platform, he balanced himself on the narrow bar which separated the constables from the mob with the acrobatic skill of one long used to manning a yard at sea. From this precarious position he harangued the mob, reports a newspaper, "at considerable length and with much animation. He observed that if the electors should not like him when they had heard him, they might reject him at once. He stood upon the footing of perfect independence unconnected with any person whatsoever." The roars of laughter which greeted this sally from a man so precariously placed showed that he had won the hearts of the mob. Sheridan tried to embarrass him by pointing out that the place of a naval officer in time of war was at sea, not on the benches of the House of Commons. Cochrane replied by asking "how were abuses in the navy to be pointed out without the presence of men to point them out, giving accurate information, and suggest remedies? . . . Naval officers might—and often did—effect more for their country in a few days than half those gentlemen who continued for seven years sitting on the cushions in the House of Commons, without speaking a word for the public good—nay, very often voting against it. (Laughter and applause). I am not a mere professed reformer, but the zealous friend of reform, earnestly desiring to see it thoroughly carried out as regards the many abuses which have crept into our constitution. A man representing a rotten borough (like Honiton) could not feel himself of equal consequence in the House with one representing a constituency such as the City of Westminster. Therefore I have taken the liberty of soliciting the suffrages of the electors of Westminster."

It was a clever address mingling all the arts of the demagogue, humility to his audience, threats to his enemies, promise of tangible reform, and above all an effective advertisement of his own colourful personality. At the end of the first day's poll the figures were: Cochrane, 112; Elliot, 99; Burdett, 78. Alarmed at his success the Tories attacked him venomously, and Place hired bugle boys "to animate the people and distribute handbills" on behalf of Burdett. On the third day he was still leading, but by the close of the poll on the fifteenth day Place's efficiency had displaced him. The final figures were: Burdett, 5,134; Cochrane, 3,708; Sheridan, 2,645; Elliot, 2,137; and Paull, 269. Poor Sherry found himself so far behind on the last day that "he begged hard to be permitted to make as respectable a show of numbers as he could, so Lord Cochrane took his inspectors away and Sheridan polled whom he pleased, and the same man over and over again as many times as he pleased."

For years afterwards the reform movement celebrated the triumph of the 1807 election with dinners all over the country. Yet it is significant that among the innumerable toasts drunk at the Crown and Anchor dinner which was the first of the series Cochrane's name was not mentioned. Burdett, as 'Orator' Hunt remarks with disgust (for he lived to see the insincerity of Burdett's opinions), "was now become the great political Idol, the political God; Lord Cochrane had not been kicked yet into a thorough patriot by the Government."

The reformers did not have to wait long for proof of Cochrane's "patriotism". He was the last person to become a back-bencher yesman. The mandate from his constituency, as well as personal inclination, urged him to a crusade against abuses. On July 7 he brought forward his first motion; "That a committee be appointed to enquire into an account of all offices, posts, places, sinecures, pensions, situations, fees, perquisites, and emoluments of every description . . . held or enjoyed by any member of this House, his wife, or any of his descendants." In his speech he detailed the charges, assessing, among other things, that there were eighteen placemen in the House whose emoluments totalled £178,994 of public money. It was a reckless motion and bad tactics, for the chancellor of the Exchequer had no difficulty in dismissing it as "much too general." An angry debate followed, in which Cochrane was supported by Whitbread and Sheridan, who had by now secured election elsewhere. Ultimately a compromise was reached by which the House agreed to have a list published of all places and pensions excluding those in the services. When this report did appear two years later it was found that seventy-six Members held places worth £150,000 and twenty-eight received pensions worth £42,000.

The Government now knew what to expect from this stormy petrel who had gained an entry into the House. After a bitter attack on Lord St. Vincent to which we shall return, care was taken to get Cochrane out of the way by sending him to sea again. The *Imperieuse* was refitted with surprising alacrity and her captain received orders to join the Mediterranean Fleet. By dint of keeping him at sea for two years he was excluded from the House until the summer of 1809.

He returned fortified with the laurels he had gained in the Battle of the Aix Roads. His shabby treatment in the Gambier court martial, and the redress he vainly sought afterwards in the House, combined to deepen his sympathy with the Radical cause. The campaign against corruption was prospering. Apart from the Finance Report already mentioned, Colonel Wardle tried that year to get the House to investigate his charges against the Duke of York's mistress for the sale of commissions in the Army; and in May, Cochrane supported Madock's attack on the Prime Minister and the Foreign Secretary on specific cases of selling seats in Parliament. The ministers were absolved by the borough-mongering majority on the excuse of "the extreme notoriety of the practice." "Good God!" exclaimed Canning, "was this the time to suppose that the character of the House of Commons was lost, and that the most hazardous experiments should be made to restore it?"

The ground for just such experiments was being prepared at the meetings of the reformers in the large hall they hired as their headquarters at the Crown and Anchor tavern in the Strand. The young naval officer who dared to mix with Cobbett, Place, and 'Orator' Hunt, "the man in the white hat," soon won an unenviable notoriety. But Cochrane loved the combined roles of crusader and martyr forced upon him after the Gambier affair. He cheered old Major Cartwright, the veteran reformer, when he moved: "That so long as the people were not fairly represented corruption must increase, our debts and taxes accumulate, our resources be dissipated, the native energy of the people be depressed, and the country be deprived of its best defences. The remedy is only to be found in the principles handed down to us by our forefathers, in a full and fair representation of the people in Parliament."

Cochrane followed this with what in that heady atmosphere must be regarded as a moderate speech attacking the inactivity of the Government, on which Burdett commented: "My dear Lord Cochrane, you don't know ministers. If you wish to get anything from them, you must go for a great deal more than you want." "Oh!" replied the sailor, "if those are your tactics, go on, I'll follow!"

The cause of parliamentary reform had been at a low ebb ever since Pitt's savage repression of the Corresponding Societies twenty years earlier. It was to the eternal honour of that eccentric old bore, Major Cartwright, now over seventy and as bald as a pebble, that he kept the banner of reform flying throughout the subsequent depressing epoch. Place tells how he used to come up to London to dine with him, "eating some raisins he brought in his pocket and drinking weak gin and water, he was cheerful, agreeable and full of curious anecdote. He was however in political matters exceedingly troublesome and sometimes exceedingly absurd." Cochrane was no more able than other people to share his curious notion that Parliament must be reformed in accordance with the Anglo-Saxon constitution.

Of course the bulk of the Whigs would have nothing to do with such extremists, but a few of them agreed to join the Reform Union founded by the major in 1811 to make "representation co-extensive with direct taxation." However it was too respectable a body to get anything done, even though Cochrane was a steward and Cobbett a member. The Hampden Club of 1812 was no better: a club which included Lord Byron, the duke of Norfolk, the earl of Oxford, as well as Lord Cochrane and Sir Francis Burdett, which limited its membership to those possessing property over the value of £300,000, was not going to do much for the working classes. The club would have died a rapid death—indeed Cartwright admitted that he was often the only member to attend its dinners—had not the undaunted old man founded less exclusive clubs in the provinces. Even then Cobbett opposed the scheme on the grounds that such organisations only invited suppression on the part of a reactionary government.

He was right. The Government had already begun to revive Pitt's methods of repression, particularly in their attacks on the freedom of the press. In February 1810 a poor, crazed individual known as Citizen Gale Jones, once a member of the London Corresponding Society abolished by Pitt, and now the organiser of a harmless debating society in Covent Garden, dared to protest against the exclusion of strangers from the debates on the failure of the Walcheren expedition. He was haled before the House and packed off to Newgate. Burdett lodged a protest against this example of official bullying, which he published in Cobbett's *Political Register*. The House judged this to be a breach of privilege and ordered that he too should be sent to prison. Burdett, however, chose to regard the Speaker's warrant as illegal and barricaded himself inside his large house in Piccadilly.

Here Cochrane joined his ally and the two hotheads prepared for a siege against the armed forces of the Crown. They had the mob with them, for anyone who passed the house without taking off his hat was plastered with mud. As there was no organised police force in those days, the rioters spread havoc through the West End, smashing windows, looting shops, bombarding passers-by with mud and abuse. The Ministers of the Crown, fearing to leave their houses, ordered out the military. On three successive nights the Horse Guards tried to clear the streets by riding down the pavements and beating the rioters with their flat swords; nevertheless skilfully placed ladders prevented the soldiers from approaching Burdett's house. The Foot Guards were also on duty, together with the Fifteenth Light Dragoons; a battery of artillery was posted in Berkeley Square, another in St. James's Park, a six-pounder in Soho Square and guns mounted at the gates of the Tower. The temper of the City was rising and everything pointed to a repetition of the Wilkes or the Gordon Riots.

Cochrane was in his element. The situation reminded him of the siege of Rosas, and without troubling about the niceties of the law he threw himself into the defence of Burdett's mansion as heartily as if the French were at the gates. One evening he drove up in a hackney coach with a barrel of gun-powder. He trundled it in at a side door and, without so much as by-your-leave to Burdett, began to knock away part of the front wall to prepare a mantrap for anyone who tried to force an entry. Place, hurriedly summoned from his shop, arrived to view these foolhardy preparations with horror. "It will be easy enough to clear the hall of constables and soldiers, but are you prepared to take the next step and go on?" Burdett decided that he was not. With difficulty he persuaded Cochrane that it was time for him to go away. "The gallant tar," writes Hunt, "then retired, apparently much disconcerted, and he was particularly requested to take away with him the cask of gunpowder."

Place, the tailor, superseded Cochrane in the post of commander-in-chief, and with his usual egotism imagined that it was by his efforts that the riot was suppressed. But before his futile scheme of raising volunteers in the City was ready Burdett allowed himself to be arrested by an enterprising constable, who climbed through a basement window to surprise the baronet at breakfast translating Magna Carta to his little son.

For the rest of the session the House debated whether Burdett should lose his seat or not. Cochrane, who frequently appeared at the doors of the House on the shoulders of an enthusiastic mob, staunchly defended his friend by presenting petitions in what Members called "indecent and impudent" language. The Government was genuinely frightened. The ministers had no wish to revive Wilkes in the person of Sir Francis Burdett, so it was decided that he should remain in custody in the Tower until the House rose in June.

The sequel shows that Burdett, as Cochrane guessed, did not have the stuff in him to become a political martyr. Place, a genius at advertising the popular cause, had organised a triumphal procession to escort him back to his home when he was set at liberty. But at the last moment Burdett lost his nerve and sneaked across the river in a rowing-boat. Place was forced to provide a substitute, and the large crowd which lined the route was regaled with the ridiculous spectacle of Citizen Gale Jones speechifying from the top of a hackney coach.

As a responsible Member of Parliament Cochrane does not come well out of this episode. His harebrained scheme of levying civil war in Piccadilly only served to make the Government's revenge more savage. From now on, he and his friends were marked men. It only needed the slightest mistake on their part for them to receive cruel punishment. That autumn Lord Ellenborough sent Cobbett to Newgate for two years with a fine of £1,000 for publishing a pamphlet on flogging. Cochrane had not long to wait before he too fell into the hands of the same judge. Meanwhile every attempt was made in Parliament and the ministerial press to get him to go to sea again. It needed a lot of determination to face the Tory sneers that he was neglecting his duty by remaining in Parliament, though as a matter of fact of the twenty-four naval Members only four were on active service; but he remained convinced that his duty lay at home, that true patriotism demanded that he should make use of his unique position to attack the enemy within the gates.

Outside the political arena he was altogether a different person. There was nothing of the flaming Radical about the man Miss Mitford met at Cobbett's house at Botley, "in the very height of his warlike fame, and as unlike the common notion of a warrior as could be. A gentle, quiet, mild young man, was this burner of French fleets, as one should see in a summer day. He lay about under the trees reading Selden on the Dominion of the Seas and letting the children (and children always know with whom they may take liberties) play all sorts of tricks with him at their pleasure."

CHAPTER II

Prize Courts and Secret Plans

OCHRANE entered Parliament primarily as a naval reformer. Naval administration had lately been the subject of debate, because the famous Tenth Report of the Naval Commission of Enquiry, originally set up by St. Vincent, but not published until the year of Trafalgar, had revealed a staggering degree of dishonesty and profiteering in the dockyards at home. It was the revelations in this report which forced Melville to resign. Why, then, if there was such an abundance of grievances to remedy, did Cochrane fail to achieve a single concrete improvement after ten years' campaigning?

In his *Naval Sketch Book*, Captain Glascock has some good advice for naval officers in Parliament: "On nautical topics observe a passive and dignified silence. The discussion of naval affairs and maritime matters to be left solely to landsmen." In his innocence Cochrane thought that he knew better than the landsman; but the latter was the more skilled politician: he knew far more about the vested interests at stake, since, if he was not a contractor himself, he was the friend or agent of contractors. Habitually underrating his enemies on land, Cochrane's protests proved ineffective against this wall of prejudice. At sea he took every possible precaution before attacking his objective; on land he went bald-headed at the most complicated problems.

Instead of catching his enemy unawares, he loaded the wrong person with abuse and then wondered why he never achieved his aims. In that jungle of corruption he was like a blind man fighting in the dark. He was a fluent but not an impressive speaker; he did not always verify his facts; nor had his mind ever received the training necessary for an effective presentation of a mass of detail. He preferred abuse and the theatrical gesture to a sober, forceful statement of a case. Meeting Shelley's father-in-law about this date, the latter, indeed, thought him the greatest fool possessing the faculty of speech he had ever encountered.

Nor had he any chance of achieving his aim as long as he was connected with the Radical interest. Supporters of the Government voted solidly against him, because they rightly regarded his efforts as attempts to make political capital out of naval abuses. And even those likely to prove sympathetic to his attempts to improve conditions in the Navy were alienated when it became obvious that he was exploiting personal grievances as much as attacking injustice for its own sake. As a crusader in naval matters he was never disinterested enough to be an effective advocate.

His defects as a parliamentary tactician are illustrated in the first speech he made on the subject in July 1807. This petulant outburst queered his pitch and made it difficult for him to be taken seriously later on. He had just returned from his first cruise in the *Imperieuse*, and he had seen with his own eyes the crazy, ill-found state of the ships sent to sea by the Plymouth command. His own ship had run the gravest risk of being wrecked on account of the unseaworthy state in which she was ordered out of harbour. Worse still, he had gone over the *Atalante* which, after four months of blockade, had sunk with all hands off the coast of Brittany simply because she ought never to have been sent to sea at all in her leaky state.

Having given an account of these things, he turned to the state of the naval hospitals. It is noteworthy that in what purports to be a verbatim account of this speech in his autobiography he entirely omits the passage which gave so much offence:

"Mistaken economy has even reduced the quantity of lint for the purpose of dressing wounds. To the ships there is not half enough allowed. This lint has been cut off by a person unworthily employed in the late administration as Commander-in-Chief. He did not know whether it was regular to mention

his name in the House (a cry from several parts of the House—
Name! Name!) His Lordship said that he had no hesitation in
naming Lord St. Vincent. Unworthy savings had been unworthily made, endangering the lives of officers and seamen.
Indeed, the grievances of the Navy are so severe, through
rigour and mistaken economy, that I can see nothing more
meritorious than the patience with which those grievances
have been endured."

To the angry replies which this attack evoked from Admiral
Hood, Admiral Harvey, Mr. Wyndham, and Mr. Sheridan, Cochrane
did indeed give definite instances in which the shortage of lint resulted in the death of men wounded in the service of their country.
Nevertheless most of the House agreed with Admiral Markham
when, purple with rage at the effrontery shown by this young man,
he demanded "In what condition was the Navy to be placed if an inferior officer could bring his commander-in-chief to the bar of the
House?" St. Vincent, who had suffered such attacks before, begged
the Whig leader to "bring in a Bill into Parliament to disqualify any
officer under the rank of rear-admiral to sit in the House of Commons; while a little, drunken, worthless jackanapes is permitted to
hold seditious language in the presence of flag officers of rank, you
will require a man of greater health and vigour than I possess to command your fleets."

Cochrane was promptly sent to sea again; but when he returned
to the charge three years later his behaviour continued to lay him
open to similar aspersions of insubordinate conduct on the part of
Admiralty officials. It was presumption, said the Secretary on one occasion, for a young man just turned thirty to set up in judgment
against men who had been captains before he was born. To which
Cobbett replied: "What has age to do with it? Lord Cochrane has had
more practical experience than half the admirals mouldering on the
back benches of the House. Was not your own Mr. Pitt Prime Minister at twenty-four?" As time went on and Cochrane became increasingly obstreporous, official replies became more and more libellous
in their implications. What right had he to sit in Parliament when a
frigate captain like himself was so much needed on the coasts of
North America? A squib in one of the Government papers was
widely quoted:

You fight so well and speak so ill,
Your case is somewhat odd,
Fighting abroad you're quite at home,
Speaking at home—abroad:

Therefore your friends, than hear yourself,
Would rather of you hear;
And that your name in the Gazette
Than Journals *should appear.*

His consistent enmity against Lord St. Vincent was particularly unfortunate because, had he been in a position to know, the latter was the one man who realised the extent of the scandals he deplored, and the one man who had actually tried to eradicate them. The series of Reports which resulted from the first lord's visitation of the dockyards, hospitals, timber yards and such like places in 1802 are in themselves sufficient justification for the violence of Cochrane's language. The examples adduced by a Radical Member of Parliament are nothing to the scandals unveiled in the official Reports: how of the 289 trees received at Deptford 144 were defective; how children of nine or ten, and men of seventy and over, received wages of between £14 and £17 a quarter; how cables were found to be anything from five to fifteen fathoms short on delivery. Admiral Markham himself estimated that one-third of the expenses of the Navy could be saved if the recommendations of the Reports were adopted. Fox begged the first lord not "to be intimidated by an insurrection of jobbers who were ever ready to set up the hue and cry against those who would bring their malpractices to light." It was in vain. St. Vincent was driven from office by a combination of vested interests, who camouflaged their aim by a pretence that they were insisting on the efficiency of the Navy. And where a first lord, backed by men like Fox and Grey, had failed, a young Radical captain could not hope to succeed.

The chief object of Cochrane's criticisms after 1810 was the administration of the Prize Courts, particularly in the Mediterranean. Here again was a crying scandal in which the landsman defeated the sailor every time, and here again Lord St. Vincent led the way to reform with his motion "that the officers of His Majesty's Navy should be allowed a larger proportion of the seizure in order that they might have an inducement to be more alert in the execution of their duty."

It was an important question because, according to Cochrane, "prize money ever formed the principal motive of seamen to encounter the perils of war." The two aspects of the complicated problem which he specifically attacked were the new regulations governing the distribution of prize money issued in 1808, and the dishonesty prevalent at the Courts where prizes were condemned. Though by the first the share of the individual seaman was increased, the captain's share was so substantially decreased that, in Cochrane's view, prize money ceased to be the incentive it had been. "It was the diminution of the prize money by recent regulations which principally induced me to leave the profession," he stated in the course of one of the debates. An unpatriotic view perhaps; but ideas have changed, and we have to remember that he entered the service penniless and without prospects, and that he had succeeded under the old regulations in making a fortune entirely by his own efforts—a fortune which would have been doubled had it not been for the peculations he was now about to attack.

What, indeed, was the point of risking life and reputation merely to enrich Admiralty officials and Maltese Jews? Whenever possible it was Cochrane's habit to avoid the courts by selling the cargo locally and distributing the prize proceeds at the capstan head, though this was strictly speaking an illegal procedure. When it was a matter of ships which had to be condemned as fair prize there was no alternative but to send them under a prize crew to Gibraltar or Malta. There the case was usually tried when the captor was absent on duty. His interests were looked after by an attorney or proctor, whom he could seldom nominate himself, and whose dishonesty was a byword in the service. If the prize turned out to be a neutral, the captor was liable for damages, though he had only acted in the service of his country. No wonder that in 1804 a commission stated that "gross and abominable frauds were practised upon sailors with respect to their prize money." The net result of all this, argued Cochrane, was that the enemy's coasting trade continued to thrive in spite of the blockade, largely because captains of patrolling warships had no incentive to destroy it.

A couple of instances will suffice to illustrate the injustice inflicted by the Prize Court at Malta on energetic officers. When he first reached the Mediterranean in command of the *Imperieuse* he had the misfortune to capture a pirate masquerading under the name of the *King George*, for which £500 reward had been offered. When he sent the prize back to Malta it appeared that some Prize Court officials had an interest in her, with the result that so far from receiving the reward the captors had to pay costs amounting to 500 double sequins. During one of his speeches in the House he unrolled this bill to impress his audience: it stretched from one end of the chamber to the other. An equally startling case was that of his friend Brenton who, for a prize valued at £1,025, received £285 when the costs of litigation had been deducted.

Finding himself at liberty early in 1811, Cochrane decided on a personal inspection of the Prize Court at Malta. He had suffered much at the hands of the officials there, and he wanted to know exactly how they arrived at the fantastic totals presented to their bills. Five per cent was the legal fee for condemning a prize. How did that five become seventy-five?

He set sail in his yacht *Julie,* one of the gunboats captured in Cadaques harbour which he had subsequently bought from the Gibraltar Court. However, he left her at Gibraltar for fear she might be mistaken for a warship in the Mediterranean. On his arrival at Malta his first discovery was that the marshal of the court was the same person as the proctor; similarly the deputy marshal held the office of deputy proctor; he was also the deputy auctioneer, the chief auctioneer living comfortably at home on two-thirds of the fees charged. The result of this extraordinary concentration of powers was a farcical table of bills:

For attending as Proctor	£2	0	0
For attending as Marshal	2	0	0
Fees paid by the Proctor to the Marshal	1	0	0
Fees paid by the Marshal to the Proctor	1	0	0

It was laid down in the regulations that the official list of fees must be conspicuously posted in the Court Room. Cochrane demanded to see the list, but nothing appeared to be known about it. Roaming through the building he discovered it stuck to the back of the door of the judge's lavatory. He tore it down and returned in triumph to the Court Room. Thereupon a warrant was issued for his arrest on the charge of contempt of court. After some argument he allowed himself to be arrested. The matter was purely formal, he was told, so he could stay at his inn, provided he gave bail. "Not at all," was his reply, "I will be no party to an illegal imprisonment of myself. I refuse to give bail, and if you want me to go to gaol, you must carry me by force, for assuredly I will not walk."

With the aid of a squad of Maltese soldiers he was carried off to a pleasant, airy room on the top floor of the town gaol. The turnkey, delighted at the prospect of so rich a prisoner, begged to know what his lordship would like for supper. "Nothing," was the answer; "I have been placed here on an illegal warrant, and I will not pay for so much as a crust. If I starve to death the Admiralty Court will have to answer for it."

Scratching his head, the poor man went off to ask the Court officials what was to be done with so obstinate a prisoner. All they could think of was to allow him *carte blanche* for anything he chose to order from the inn next door, hoping that that would keep him quiet. Cochrane was delighted with the news. He invited all his friends to give him the pleasure of their company at dinner. Night after night parties of hilarious naval officers dined sumptuously at his table. "From the character of our entertainments the bill when presented must have been almost as extensive as the court's fees."

The farce of his imprisonment delighted everyone save the embarrassed officials. After a few weeks one of the senior officers came to visit him. "Lord Cochrane, you must not remain here; the seamen are getting savage, and if you are not out soon they will pull the gaol down, which will get the naval force into a scrape. Have you any objection to making your escape?"

"Not in the least," replied the prisoner, "and it may be done; but I will neither be bailed, nor will I be set at liberty without proper trial."

A file was smuggled into his cell and after several days' work the centre bar across the window was sawn through. After a particularly uproarious banquet at the Court's expense, he made the gaoler drunk (not a difficult task) and let himself down with the aid of a rope into the street below.

He had many accomplices in the port, so that when he reached the harbour he found the *Eagle*'s gig lying ready to take him to a ship which sailed before dawn for Gibraltar. As she was carrying mails she was home long before the news of his escape reached the Admiralty, thus enabling him to tell his fantastic story to the House before the officials had time to prepare a defence. It was a good story and it made the Court extremely ridiculous, so much so that even the Admiralty promised to look into the matter. The only man who did not enjoy the joke was Lord Chancellor Eldon, the embodiment of the spirit against which Cochrane was fighting and the brother of a Prize Court judge; he declared Cochrane's speech "to be a species of mummery never before witnessed within these walls, and altogether unbecoming the gravity of that branch of the legislature."

It would be tedious to particularise Cochrane's attacks on other abuses—the injustice of the pensions, the waste of public money on civilian placemen, even the comical speech in which he estimated that the great Wellesley family received from the public purse an amount equal to 426 pairs of lieutenants' legs at the current rate of compensation. His facts were not always strictly correct, with the result that Croker, the new Secretary to the Admiralty and a formidable debater, could sometimes triumph over him and accuse him of vilifying the Service. But letters to the *Naval Chronicle* prove that many in the Service were grateful to their advocate, though some thought that his zeal outran his discretion. Even so, he was absolutely right when he argued that the misfortunes experienced in the American War were mainly due to war weariness and bad administration which made the Service unnecessarily unpopular with the seamen. His constructive proposals on this point were eminently sensible: "That a limitation of the duration of service should be adopted, accompanied with the certainty of a suitable reward; and that measures should be taken to cause the comfortable situations in the dockyards, the places of porters, etc., to be bestowed on meritorious decayed petty officers and seamen, instead of being the wages of corruption in borough elections."

During these years he was not only a critic of administration. He made plenty of suggestions as to the more effective prosecution of the war by reviving Chatham's strategy of combined coastal operations. A government busy with the Peninsular War, with the catastrophic failure of the Walcheren expedition fresh in their minds, had no time for such suggestions. Nevertheless arising out of them he evolved what for long was the most intriguing mystery of his career—his famous Secret Plans.

So famous and so secret have these plans become that in the early months of the late war it was possible for a leading daily newspaper to publish an article suggesting that these mysterious plans, lying ready in the pigeonholes of the Admiralty, provided a final answer to Hitler's threats of a secret weapon. The secret was indeed well kept for nearly a century, but since the publication of the Panmure Papers

in 1908 the mystery has been unveiled. Even then the publication
was so obscure that Cochrane's own grandson was unaware that the
matter was no longer a secret when he drew the attention of Kitchener, Churchill and others to the plans in 1914. The most valuable account of them has, indeed, not hitherto been published, because the
document containing it was only deposited at the Public Record Office a few years ago. A study of the evidence reveals Cochrane as the
inventor of chemical warfare, if we discount such primitive but effective methods as the catapulting of decomposing corpses into the
city of Jerusalem during the siege of A.D. 70.

On the inside of one of the versions of the plans occurs this challenge: "To the Imperial mind one sentence will suffice: All fortifications, especially marine fortifications, can under cover of dense
smoke be irresistibly subdued by fumes of sulphur kindled in
masses to windward of their ramparts." The idea of chemical warfare occurred to him on a visit to the sulphur mines in Sicily in the
year 1811. On 2 March 1812 he wrote a letter to the Prince Regent
submitting a plan of attack on Toulon, Flushing, and any other port
where Napoleon's fleets were blockaded. Besides using explosion
vessels along the lines of the "bomb" vessels used in the action of
the Basque Roads, he proposed "a measure of neutralising Marine
Batteries and Lines of Defence by Sulphur Vessels placed during the
night on the windward side of the Fortifications." These sulphur
vessels were to contain layers of sulphur and charcoal laid on a bed
of clay on the deck, so arranged as to admit a draught of air beneath.
The Spaniards, he pointed out, might have used such methods
against Gibraltar if they had had more imagination, "for the volumes of noxious effluvia, evolved from Masses of Sulphur and
Charcoal, burning close to the Lines, and driven by the wind into
the Interior of the place, would have destroyed every animal func-
tion, until the walls would have been in ruins."

Of course he pronounced the scheme to be infallible. "A hundred
millions employed in war could not complete the ruin of our maritime opponents so effectually as could be done by the simple
method indicated in my plans." But he found that expert opinion
was divided on the matter. The committee which met under the pres-
idency of the Duke of York in May 1812 pronounced against the
scheme, not so much on the grounds of the barbarity of this type of
warfare (as was the case when torpedoes were discussed at the time
of the Walcheren expedition), as because some of the members—

notably Cochrane's old enemy, Admiral Young—thought it was just another of his crazy schemes. To the inventor of the incendiary rocket, Major-General Congreve, the scheme seemed feasible, weather permitting. And Lord Keith was sufficiently impressed to invite him to submit a scheme for an attack on Toulon, which Lord Exmouth, then in command of the Mediterranean Fleet, turned down. For this particular attack Cochrane relied on the use of explosion vessels carrying 10,000 rockets, 2,000 barrels of powder, 5,000 carcasses (iron shells used for incendiary purposes), 5,000 shells and "as many grenades as can be spared." But the more carefully the original plans were studied, the more startling appeared to be the nature of the new weapon. In the end the Committee compromised by admitting that the plans were "so perfectly new to us that we cannot venture an opinion. . . . At the same time we cannot conceal our apprehension of the very doubtful success of an experiment from the various circumstances of Winds and Weather, Tides and Currents."

In the years after the war he served abroad in the role of liberator of Chili, Peru, Brazil and Greece, and for the time being no more was heard of his plans. But he was a singularly pertinacious character; and when he retired to private life after the conclusion of the Greek War of Independence and inherited the title of earl of Dundonald he did not lose sight of his plans. Periodic French war scares gave him the opportunity of refurbishing them and drawing the attention of the Government to them. "Two can play at that game," remarked the Duke of Wellington, and he refused to encourage the inventor.

The most important of these occasions was in 1846, when, to judge from the chart attached to his correspondence, Dundonald had Cherbourg in mind. The 1846 Commission rejected the plans on totally different grounds to those of earlier committees. Dundonald now made a smoke screen the preliminary of his attack with sulphur vessels. The commission, which reported at the beginning of 1847, was favourably impressed with this part of the plan; but, the report continues,

> "we have resolved that it is not desirable that any experiments should be made. We assume it to be possible that the plan contains power for producing the sweeping destruction the inventor ascribes to it; but it is clear this power could not be retained exclusively by this country, because its first employment would develop its principle and application. We

considered, in the next place, how far the adoption of the proposed secret plans would accord with the feelings and principles of civilised warfare. We are of unanimous opinion that Plans Nos. 2 and 3 [the sulphur attack] would not do so. We therefore recommend that, as hitherto, plans Nos. 2 and 3 should remain concealed. We feel that great credit is due to Lord Dundonald for the right feeling that prompted him not to disclose his secret plans when serving in war as naval commander-in-chief of the forces of other nations under very trying circumstances, in the conviction that these plans might eventually be of the highest importance to his country."

Dundonald's reaction to this and other rejections of his plans illustrates once more the persecution mania which mars so many pages of his thrilling record of his own career. "What can have been the cause of such neglect and contumely as I have suffered, under the full knowledge that such a secret weapon was in my power? There can only have been two causes—unmerited and personal aversion without reason, or want of political courage to put my plans into execution."

The Crimean War gave the indomitable old man (he was now seventy-nine) a final opportunity to have his plans adopted. The development of naval armaments, particularly in the matter of explosives, had made such strides since his plans were first evolved that he considered opinion would be more favourably inclined; nor did he feel himself too old to superintend their execution in person. "My dear Sir James Graham," he wrote to his friend the first lord in 1854, "were it necessary—which it is not—that I should place myself in an armchair on the poop, with each leg on a cushion, I will undertake to subdue every insular fortification at Cronstadt within four hours from the commencement of the attack."

He started his campaign of persuasion with a letter dated July 22 submitting "a simple yet effective plan of operations showing that the maritime defences of Cronstadt (however strong against ordinary measures) may be captured, and their red hot and incendiary missiles, prepared for the destruction of our ships, turned on those they protect." He offered his services to superintend the attack, "the success of which cannot fail in its consequences to free and ensure (perhaps for ever) all minor states from Russian domination."

Such ambitious political aims were rather breathtaking. However, the first lord asked him if he was willing to submit his plans to a naval committee consisting of Sir Byam Martin, Sir William Parker, one of the lords of the Admiralty, and the inspector-general of fortifications. He agreed under conditions of the strictest secrecy and appeared before the committee shortly afterwards.

He was asked how many vessels were required. "Twenty-four old iron colliers or iron lighters." How many officers and men? "About 144 for the smoke vessels and half the number for the sulphuric vessels—210 men." Protected by a small force of steamers, he proposed to ignite the sulphur about a mile to windward of the island forts which formed his objective. As for the cost, "the twenty-four vessels taken at £3,000 each—and coals for each £300—sulphur 200 tons £200—I should say £200,000 will do it all." Asked who should be responsible for fitting them out, "Lord Dundonald with some warmth declared he would have no hand in any contract; he would not subject himself to the ungenerous and unjust comments of malignant men." The memory of what he had suffered earlier in his career was evidently fresh in his mind! "The chance of success is so great that I can see no cause of failure." The Committee were not, however, impressed by the fact that he could offer no proof of their practicability beyond his observations in Sicily.

He then presented a memorandum summarising the project:

"Red hot shell and carcasses being now generally used in Maritime Fortifications it is manifest that attacking ships are infinitely more endangered than formerly when cold shot were the only missiles—especially during their approach, when deliberate aim can safely be taken from casemates and embrasures, before the guns of the ships can bear.

"To avoid this peril, it is proposed that Iron Vessels containing large masses of combustible materials (bitumenous coal and other matter) shall be kindled at a proper distance to windward of the Fortifications or Batteries to be attacked—so that dense vapours, more obscure than the darkest night, shall conceal the ships from the Batteries until they arrive at a proper position to batter in breach.

"If the assailing force, as there is great reason to believe, is still endangered by incendiary missiles, Sulphur Vessels may be conducted to appropriate positions the fumes from which will expel artillerymen from the strongest casemates, and drive them from their guns, wherever situated, within a mile of the burning Sulphur carried down the breeze.

"The works at Cronstadt are particularly exposed to this mode of attack, being partly insulated, and partly situated on a long sea wall running in the usual course of the prevailing wind, whereby one or two smoke and sulphur vessels would clear the whole range."

This plan was submitted to the Ordnance Office and Faraday was called in to give an expert opinion. On August 9 the Committee reported to the first lord. They described Dundonald's scheme as "hazardous, unpromising of success, and by probable failure likely to bring discredit on the service, and to give the enemy cause of boastful advantage calculated to improve his ebbing strength in the great struggle in which we are engaged." They thought it extremely doubtful that the smoke screen would be dense enough to cover the approach of the sulphur vessels, and they pointed out that the attacking force would not be able to occupy the forts on account of "the pernicious influence of the sulphur cloud. The whole scheme is beset with difficulties, and we think it cannot be regarded otherwise than as a rash enterprise, with every chance against its success."

Faraday's report was included to support this opinion:

"The proposition is correct in theory—namely dense smoke will hide objects, and burning sulphur will yield fumes that are intolerable, and able to render men involved in them incapable of action, or even to kill them.

"But whether the proposition is *practicable* on the scale proposed and required is a point so little illustrated by any experience, or by any facts that can be made to bear upon it, that for my own part I am not able to form a judgment."

After recounting his own experiences on Vesuvius, Faraday continues:

"If a ship charged with sulphur were burning in current of air a continuous stream of sulphuric acid fumes mixed with air would pass off from it. This stream being heavier than air would descend and move along the surface of the water, and, I expect, would sink perpendicularly, and expand laterally so as to form a low broad stream. Its noxious heights would soon be less than 15 or perhaps even 10 feet (but I cannot pretend to more than a guess) and its width by degrees more and more. The water over which it would have to move would tend continually to take part of the noxious vapour out of it. Now 400 tons of Sulphur would require 400 tons of oxygen, and that it would find in about 1,740 tons of air. Supposing this product were mixed with ten times its bulk of unaltered air it would make near upon 20,000 tons of a very bad mixture, and one, which, if a man were immersed in it for a short time, would cause death. . . . All I need add is that if the project were known or anticipated, it would not be difficult for the attacked party to provide Respirators which would enable the men in a very great degree, or even altogether to resist a temporary invasion of any atmosphere such as that described."

On receipt of this report Graham told the inventor that the Committee judged the adoption of the plans "inexpedient" at the moment, and he quoted certain passages to soothe his feelings; but he did not include Faraday's report. Hence Dundonald remained convinced that his plans were practicable, and so when the Aberdeen Government fell from power (largely on account of the inefficient and uninspired way in which the war was being conducted) he felt it his duty to approach Palmerston, the new prime minister, on the question in a letter dated 13 February 1855. The latter got into touch with Graham to find out what had been done, and when he was informed of the Committee's report he let the matter rest. Not so the indefatigable inventor. In March he aired his feelings in a vague and optimistic letter to *The Times*, and in April questions were asked on his behalf in Parliament which Palmerston found it difficult to answer without giving away the nature of the secret. Ultimately the first lord (now Sir Charles Wood) stated definitely that the plans had been rejected.

A final memorandum presents the plans in their latest stage, although he appears to have contemplated as well the ignition of naphtha by means of balls of potassium floating on the water:

"Materials required for the expulsion of the Russians from Sebastopol—

"Experimental trials have shown that about five parts of coke effectually vaporise one part of sulphur.

"Mixtures for land surface, where weight is of importance, may, however, probably be suggested by Professor Faraday, as to operations on shore I have paid little attention.

"Four or five hundred tons of sulphur and two thousand tons of coke would be sufficient.

"Besides these materials, it would be necessary to have, say, as much bitumenous coal, and a couple of thousand barrels of gas or other tar, for the purpose of masking fortifications to be attacked, or others that flank the assailing positions.

"A quantity of dry firewood, chips, shavings, etc., would also be requisite quickly to kindle the fires, which ought to be kept in readiness for the first favourable steady breeze.
"7 AUGUST 1855.   DUNDONALD.

"*Note.*—The objects to be accomplished being specially stated, the responsibility of their accomplishment ought to rest on those who direct their execution. There is no doubt but that the fumes will envelop all the defences from the Malakoff to the Barracks, and even to the line-of-battle ship *The Twelve Apostles* at anchor in the harbour.

"The two outer batteries, on each side of the Port, ought to be smoked, sulphured, and blown down by explosion vessels, and their destruction completed by a few ships of war anchored under cover of the smoke."

Forwarding this memorandum to Panmure (Secretary of State for War in the new Government) Palmerston writes: "I agree with you that if Dundonald will go out himself to superintend the execution of his scheme, we ought to accept his offer and try his plan. If it succeeds, it will, as you say, save a great number of English and French lives; if it fails *in his hands* we shall be exempt from blame, and if we come in for a small share of the ridicule, we can bear it and the greater part will fall on him. You had best, therefore, make arrangement with him without delay, and with as much secrecy as the nature of things will admit of." But before anything could be done Sebastopol had fallen and with it Dundonald's last chance of success.

The secret plans must not, however, be accounted a failure, for their story does not end with the conclusion of the Crimean War. On Dundonald's death they were bequeathed to his friend Professor

Lord Playfair, who later returned them to the Dundonald family on the understanding that they should only be divulged "in case of national emergency."

In the autumn of 1914, therefore, the inventor's grandson, the twelfth earl, tried to interest those responsible for the direction of the war in the plans, unaware of the fact that one version of them had been published in a somewhat obscure fashion six years previously. As he was an Army man he first approached Kitchener, who showed his customary blindness to novel methods in warfare. Since the plans were the invention of an admiral, Kitchener considered the Admiralty was the proper authority, although the earl made it clear that the prevalent winds on the Flanders Plain would favour the adoption of the plans in that theatre of war. It was equally characteristic that Winston Churchill at the Admiralty immediately realised the potential value of the smoke screen project; as for the gas attack he made it clear that he did not intend to depart from the rules of war as laid down by international convention since the death of the inventor. He authorised experiments to be put in hand, and an Admiralty Committee on Smoke Screens, of which the earl of Dundonald was appointed chairman, was set up in March 1915. However, unfettered by humanitarian scruples, the enemy struck first. On the morning of April 22 the first German gas attack took the Allied troops in the Ypres salient completely by surprise.

So much for the warnings Cochrane's Secret Plans contained for his own countrymen. However, his invention of the smoke screen, developed by the energy of his grandson, can be said to have saved many more lives than his intended sulphur attack would have destroyed. His grandson reaped the reward, for, as Lord Hankey told him, "there is no doubt that you gave the impetus which led to the adoption of smoke screens with the happiest results." Accounts of the activities of the small craft in such attacks as that on Zeebrugge echo strangely Dundonald's own intentions against Cronstadt: "The small craft would be sent first along shore and there anchored, to screen by their smoke operations about to take place."

At that date the inventor had replied to the objection that his plans were inhuman in these terms: "No conduct that brought to a speedy termination a war which might otherwise last for years, and be attended by terrible bloodshed in numerous battles, could be called inhuman, and that the most powerful means of averting all future war would be the introduction of a method of fighting which, rendering all vigorous defence impossible, would frighten every nation from running the risk of warfare at all."

This is not the place to enter into the usual debate on the force of the inventor's argument. In the age of the atomic bomb that excuse for the terrible discovery upon which he had stumbled has a very familiar ring.

CHAPTER III

~~~

The Stock Exchange Trial

BOUT MIDNIGHT on Sunday, 20 February 1814, a tall young man in a grey military overcoat with a white cockade in his hat knocked at the door of the Ship Inn, Dover, and demanded to see the landlord. He explained that he was the bearer of important news and that he must have pen and ink at once to write a note to the port admiral. Asked what the news was he replied brusquely: "Don't pester me with questions; you will know of it tomorrow." As he sat down to write he threw open his coat, disclosing a scarlet uniform with a large star on his chest.

> "To the Hon. J. Foley, Port Admiral, Deal, Dover.
> "21 February 1814. One o'clock A.M.

"Sir,
"I have the honour to acquaint you that the *L'Aigle* from Calais, Pierre Duquin, Master, has this moment landed me near Dover to proceed to the Capital with despatches of the happiest nature. My anxiety will not allow me to say more for your gratification than that the Allies obtained a final victory; that Bonaparte was overtaken by a party of Sachen's Cossacks,

who immediately slaid [sic] him, and divided his body between them. General Platoff saved Paris from being reduced to ashes. The Allied Sovereigns are there, and the white cockade is universal; an immediate peace is certain. In the utmost haste, I entreat your consideration and have the honour to be, Sir,

"Your most obedient humble Servant,

"R. Du Bourg,
"Lt.-Colonel and Aide-de-Camp to Lord Cathcart."

Despatching a post-boy with the note, Du Bourg, as he called himself, summoned a coach and set off to London in the greatest haste.

The fog that morning made it impossible for the admiral to telegraph the news by the visual means of communication then in use. However, Du Bourg lost no time in spreading his tidings wherever he changed horses. As befitted the bearer of such news, he tipped lavishly in gold napoleons. By nine o'clock he was at Lambeth, where he paid off his postchaise and hired a hackney coach driven by a drunken sot called Crane. "Number 13 Green Street," he cried as he slammed the door, and the coach went rattling off over the cobbles towards Lord Cochrane's house.

Arrived at his destination he asked to see his lordship immediately. Lord Cochrane, said the footman, was not at home; he was at Mr. King's, the lamp manufacturer in Cock Lane. "Ask him to return at once," said Du Bourg, as he sat down to scribble a note for the man to take. The servant found his master discussing with Mr. King the details of a convoy lamp which he hoped to patent in the near future. He was annoyed at the interruption, for he had only just arrived at the lamp works, having breakfasted late with his uncle, Cochrane Johnstone, and Mr. Butt, his agent on the Stock Exchange. They had driven up to the City together, Cochrane leaving his friends to go on to the Stock Exchange while he got out to visit the lamp works. He was expecting news of his brother who had been wounded in Spain, so he did not trouble to decipher the signature scribbled at the bottom of the note handed to him. He took it for granted that this request for his immediate return was from some brother officer with news of his brother's health.

He returned to find, not the officer he was expecting, but a comparative stranger of his acquaintance who had been introduced to him under the name of De Berenger. They had met once or twice at dinner at his uncle's house, where De Berenger (such indeed was his real name) had been introduced to him as a talented sharpshooter who had had the misfortune to run into debt. Hearing that Cochrane had been appointed flag captain to his uncle, Sir Alexander Cochrane, the new commander-in-chief on the North American station, and that he was fitting out the *Tonnant* frigate preparatory to sailing, he begged a passage in her to escape his creditors. Cochrane was sorry for him, but he declared that he could not take him on board without the Admiralty's permission. Apart from this he knew nothing whatever about the man.*

De Berenger appeared to be in a highly excited state. He apologised profusely for the freedom with which he had summoned Cochrane back to the house, but he explained that his affairs had reached a crisis. His creditors demanded £8,000 and he had no hopes of satisfying them. Could not his lordship reconsider his decision and take him to America? When Cochrane again refused the other appeared greatly hurt. At least, he begged, you will not refuse me the loan of a change of clothes. He confessed that he was a prisoner within the Rules of the King's Bench (privileged debtors were allowed a certain amount of liberty outside the prison), and he explained that he could not return in the green sharpshooter's uniform he was then wearing without exciting the suspicion that he had broken bounds. It became a matter of the first importance later on that Cochrane swore De Berenger was wearing a green uniform, though at Dover he was certainly wearing scarlet regimentals.

Naturally Cochrane was willing to do the unfortunate man this small service. Clothes were lying about the room preparatory to being packed for America. Picking up a black coat and an old hat he pressed them on De Berenger and allowed him to change his uni-

---

* That Cochrane proposed to do himself well now that he was back on active service is proved by his wine bill: For the undermentioned wines shipped in the *Tonnant*.

54 doz. Old Red Port	....	£170	2	0
60 " Vidonia	....	189	0	0
10 " Claret	....	60	0	0
124 " bottles	....	31	0	0
2 Pipes fine Madeira, 218 gallons	....	294	6	0
4 Hogsheads Red Port, 240 gallons	....	240	0	0
19 Half Chests, etc.	....	23	0	0
		£1,007	8	0

form. Having done so, the young man rolled up his green uniform in a towel, picked up a portmanteau he had with him and drove off "in great apparent uneasiness of mind" in the very coach by which Cochrane had arrived.

Meanwhile tremendous excitement reigned in the City. The news of Bonaparte's defeat reached the Stock Exchange at ten o'clock. A party of French Royalists had been seen cheering *"Vive le Roi"* as they drove down Cheapside. A boom set in and Government stocks were rocketing. For the past few weeks Omnium and other gilt-edged stock had fluctuated wildly in response to rumours buzzing about the City during Napoleon's last campaign before the gates of Paris. On February 17, Omnium stood at 25, on the 19th at $26^3/_4$ and when the market opened on Monday the 21st at $27^1/_2$. The fresh news forced them up to $30^1/_4$ at noon and to 32 in the afternoon. Then, because there was no official confirmation of the news, they dropped to 28. On Tuesday they were back again at $26^1/_2$.

Suspicions of a deliberate hoax were soon aroused. Somebody must have made a fortune that Monday morning. An inquiry disclosed an enormous turnover on the part of one particular group. Cochrane Johnstone, Esq., had sold £141,000 Omnium and £100,000 Consols; his friend, Mr. Butt, £224,000 and £168,000; Butt's client, Lord Cochrane, had sold £139,000 Omnium, and half a dozen others had sold lesser amounts. On March 7, £250 reward was offered by the Committee of the Stock Exchange for the arrest of the man calling himself Du Bourg who had started the rumour.

What was Cochrane doing in these unsavoury financial circles? Prize money won years before had enabled him to invest in various stocks, among which was the Omnium holding bought in the winter of 1813 when prospects of an Allied victory appeared to be bright. Not being a financier, he had engaged Mr. Butt, once a clerk in Portsmouth dockyard and now a stockbroker, as his agent. Early on February 21 Butt acted on instructions given him when Cochrane first began to dabble in stocks and shares to sell out at one per cent rise. Had he waited a few hours he could have sold out at a far higher profit, a fact which goes far to refute Cochrane's supposed complicity in a financial conspiracy.

The reaction of the speculators involved was characteristic. Cochrane Johnstone, Member of Parliament for Grampound, the rottenest of rotten boroughs, and heavily in debt as a result of playing the market ever since he was cashiered from the Army some years before, flew into a rage and threatened to take proceedings against the officials who had conducted the inquiry. Cochrane Johnstone's previous history had been a peculiarly unsavoury one. If half the allegations made against him by his enemies were true he was a thoroughly nasty person, and, we suspect, an evil influence on his nephew. Apart from being cashiered from the Army on a charge of dishonesty, he had been a slaver, a smuggler and a corrupt administrator in the West Indies. He had made a profiteer's fortune out of the Peninsular War by selling Birmingham muskets, costing seventeen shillings apiece, to the Spanish patriots at a rate of three guineas each. It is not in the least surprising that such a man should have engineered another financial ramp, which involved the honour of his nephew. Of Mr. Butt we know little, except that he was a stockjobber and pretended to be equally incensed when the inquiry was set on foot.

Cochrane's conduct, on the other hand, was entirely above-board. When, on March 8, he heard the news that a reward had been offered to identify a man who had been traced to his house on February 21, he applied for leave of absence to come up to London to swear an affidavit detailing his movements on that day. Between those two dates he had been down at Chatham, fitting out in preparation for sailing to America. His affidavit appeared in the press three days later, and helped the authorities to identify the mysterious Du Bourg with Random de Berenger (what a name for an adventurer!). Actually the authorities seem to have had a suspicion that this was the case before Cochrane's testimony was received.

Having satisfied himself that Bow Street runners were on the track of the culprit, he returned to Chatham to complete his work there before sailing for America. A few days later a Thames waterman fished out of the river a scarlet uniform with a star, which was identified by Mr. Solomon the tailor as having been sold to De Berenger three days before his masquerade as Du Bourg. Finally, on April 8, De Berenger himself was arrested at Leith while trying to flee the country under another assumed name.

Cochrane's composure was rudely shattered when, on April 20, he read in the papers that a Grand Jury had returned a true bill of charges against De Berenger and those presumed to be his associates. Charles Random de Berenger, Sir Thomas Cochrane commonly called Lord Cochrane, Andrew Cochrane Johnstone, Richard

Gathorne Butt, Ralph Sandom, Alexander McRae, Peter Holloway and Henry Lyte were charged with unlawfully conspiring by false news to induce the subjects of our Lord the King to believe that Napoleon Bonaparte was dead, and thereby to occasion a rise in funds and to injure such of the king's subjects as should on the 21st of February 1814 purchase any share in the said funds.

The Stock Exchange, of course, prosecuted in the first place. But since a naval officer was involved they had to approach the first lord of the Admiralty, who directed them to the attorney-general. This was tantamount to a Government prosecution, and the Solicitor for the Admiralty represented the Stock Exchange at the trial. He was no other than Mr. Lavie, Cochrane's opponent at the Gambier court martial. Cochrane, indeed, always maintained (though there is no direct evidence that it was so) that Croker, the secretary to the Admiralty, was responsible for these curious arrangements. He and Croker were old enemies in Parliament and out of it, and it is possible that Croker made these arrangements for the conduct of the prosecution in order to put an end to a career which he felt was a mischievous influence in the service.

Even when he found himself accused of criminal conspiracy Cochrane failed to realise the seriousness of the situation. Convinced of his own innocence, he was wilfully careless over the preparation of his defence. In fact he behaved in exactly the contrary manner he used to adopt when preparing for a battle at sea; instead of scrutinising every detail to ensure success, he behaved as if the whole business was no affair of his. Yet he was now faced with an enemy far more dangerous than any he had encountered in his naval career. Berenger's visit to his house trapped him in a plot engineered by a gang of financial sharks; but he was so confident that the evidence would clear him of all suspicion that he did not take the trouble to realise the danger in which he was involved. True, he consulted his solicitors, who briefed Scarlett (later Lord Abinger) as counsel; but when the brief was drawn up only parts of it were read to him. As his friend Burdett admitted, his mind was so full of his lamp patent (he sent the specifications to the Admiralty four days after the hoax took place) that he paid no proper attention to his position. The result was that when the trial came on his own counsel never spoke at all, valuable witnesses for the defence were never called, and to his surprise Johnstone's counsel, Serjeant Best, chose to defend all the three accused together. This ill advised policy meant that he had to stand or fall with the two crooks who had involved him in the affair. Three Lord Chancellors and one Lord Chief Baron later put it on record that in their opinion he would have been acquitted if he had not been defended in this way.

On the day on which the rest of London was celebrating the arrival of the Emperor of Russia and the King of Prussia the trial opened quietly at the Guildhall before Lord Ellenborough, Lord Chief Justice of the Court of the King's Bench. Cochrane's luck was certainly out, for no judge in the country was more notoriously hostile to a man of his political principles. Ellenborough had sent Cobbett to Newgate with a fine of £1,000 for a pamphlet on a scandalous case of flogging in the Army, and his conduct at "Orator" Hunt's trial had been so prejudiced that it shocked the entire legal profession. A High Tory of the Eldon school, he was not the man to give unbiased attention to a case involving a Radical demagogue. His descendants have pursued Cochrane's memory with as much venom as Cochrane attacked Ellenborough's good name during his lifetime. Probably the conduct of the trial was no worse than many other trials during that reactionary epoch, but no one can read the shorthand report of the proceedings without feeling that the judge was definitely hostile to the defence from the very start.

Cochrane himself never attended the trial. "I was not in court because my lawyers, for reasons unknown to me, were solicitous that I should not appear." But the best lawyers of the day were there: Park, Scarlett, Best and Brougham (later Lord Chancellor) for the defence; Gurney for the prosecution. Gurney was a clever Quaker who had once been a personal friend of Cochrane and before whom the affidavit had been sworn, though not actually settled, as Cochrane would have us believe. We have already commented on the surprising appearance of Mr. Lavie, as solicitor for the prosecution. As for the jury, Cochrane declares that it was packed, but there is no evidence to suppose that this was so.

The trial opened on 8 June 1814. Gurney opened in his fiercest style, concentrating the attack on the absent Cochrane, for the evidence was quite sufficient to prove beyond dispute the guilt of the others. After a long speech he called a procession of witnesses (two at least of whom had been bribed) to support his description of De Berenger's movements. What with the Dover innkeeper, the postboys, Crane the coachman, the man who found the uniform and the Jew who sold it, the case for the prosecution was a lengthy business.

The evidence did not finish till ten o'clock in the evening, the jury being cooped in that stuffy courtroom for fifteen hours of a summer's day. When the last witness had been cross-examined everyone assumed that the Court would adjourn until next morning. Not a bit of it: Ellenborough appeared determined that the case for the defence should not receive the same careful attention of fresh minds.

> "I should wish to hear your opening (he told Best); there are several gentlemen attending as witnesses who, I find, cannot, without the greatest public inconvenience, attend tomorrow.
>
> "MR. PARK.—The difficulty we feel, I am sure your Lordship will feel as strong as we do, is the fatigue owing to the length of our attendance here.
>
> "*Lord Ellenborough* having repeated his objection to postponement.
>
> "MR. PARK REPLIED.—I have undergone very great fatigue, which I am able to bear; but I would submit to your Lordship the hardships upon parties who are charged with so very serious an offence as this if their case is heard at this late hour; and then a fresh day is given to my learned friend to reply.
>
> "LORD ELLENBOROUGH.—It will not be a fresh day when you will be here by nine o'clock, and the sun will be up almost before we adjourn; I will sit through it if you require it, rather than that."

In spite of the late sitting, which lasted till three in the morning, important witnesses like the first lord of the Admiralty had to appear just the same the next day, and the court reassembled at ten, not nine o'clock. So much for Lord Ellenborough's excuses.

In the flickering candlelight Serjeant Best rose wearily to his feet in that fetid courtroom. Addressing the haggard jury he begged them to overcome their fatigue and pay as close attention to the case for the defence as they had to the prosecution. For the charge was a grave one: "Upon the issue of this question depends whether the accused are to hold that situation in society which they have hitherto held, or whether they are to be completely degraded and ruined." Recalling the public character of Lord Cochrane, a man who had done so much for his country and who occupied such an important position in the public eye, he asked the jury whether a man so circumstanced was likely to commit so sordid a crime.

There are said to be two types of advocates: those who plead the strongest points in a defence, and those who concentrate on defending the weakest points, leaving the stronger to make their own impression. Best was a counsel of the former school. Neglecting the defence of the client who had actually briefed him, he concentrated on rebutting the attack made by the prosecution on Lord Cochrane. The three chief accused had to stand or fall together according to the misconceived strategy of the defence. As the case against Johnstone and Butt looked so black, Best considered he could secure an acquittal by proving Cochrane's innocence and thereby exculpating the others.

The first point he made was that but for his lordship's affidavit De Berenger would never have been identified with Du Bourg. (This, as we have seen, was not strictly true.) He went on to point out that a man who was privy to such a hoax was not likely to be guilty of the incredible folly of meeting the chief conspirator so openly at his own house. If Cochrane had known De Berenger's business he would have arranged to meet him anywhere rather than at No. 13 Green Street. Moreover the evidence had brought nothing to light which could connect him in any way with the crime, apart from the coincidence of De Berenger's visit and the sale of his stock on February 21. None of the banknotes found on De Berenger when he was arrested could be traced directly to him, though many were traced back to Johnstone and Butt; nor did any of De Berenger's papers refer to him in any way. As for his transactions at the Stock Exchange, Best showed that it was nothing unusual, that he had been selling stock as far back as November, and that such sale as there had been was made on Butt's initiative acting on general instructions issued by Cochrane a long time previously. Had Cochrane been a party to the conspiracy his gain would have been much greater, for he would have sold out later in the day when the price was higher, as the other two had done.

It was an able piece of pleading for which Cochrane was never sufficiently grateful. But it slurred over the weakest point which inevitably became the chief point at issue during the trial: the colour of the uniform De Berenger was wearing when he arrived at the house in Green Street. In his affidavit Cochrane swore that he was wearing a green sharpshooter's uniform underneath his military grey coat; all the evidence brought by the prosecution was to the effect that he was wearing the same scarlet uniform in which he was first seen at Dover.

This was the only point in the affidavit which was at variance with the evidence, and naturally the prosecution made the most of it. Gurney even exaggerated it into an argument that Cochrane was guilty of perjury in swearing to what he must have known to be the wrong colour; the discrepancy, he suggested, really invalidated the whole affidavit and proved Cochrane's complicity in the crime. Of course Ellenborough stressed the point in his summing up: "How," he asked, "could Lord Cochrane, had he been innocent, have failed to notice the scarlet uniform when De Berenger stripped off his coat to change into the clothes so opportunely provided for him?" Lord Cochrane, he told the jury, must have seen the accused "fully blazoned in the costume of that crime."

Unwisely, Best did not contest the discrepancy. He suggested that possibly Cochrane might have been mistaken about the colour; being accustomed to seeing De Berenger in green, he thought, when he swore the affidavit three weeks later, that green was the colour— "there being nothing to fix on his lordship's mind the colour of the uniform." But if only Cochrane could have been cross-examined he would have been able to clear up the difficulty before the prosecution could have had time to make the most of it. The explanation he gives in his *Letter to Lord Ellenborough* is perfectly credible. It was later proved at the trial of one of the witnesses for the prosecution on the charge of perjury that De Berenger had indeed arrived at Dover in a green uniform before he appeared at the inn in scarlet regimentals. He could therefore, Cochrane suggested, have changed back from the red to the green on one of two occasions—either when the postboy noticed that the blinds of the coach were drawn up on their approach to London, or, more probably, during the long wait while the footman was fetching his master from the lamp works.

Ellenborough adjourned the first day's sitting at three A.M., an hour when few of the jury can still have been awake. The court met again at ten o'clock on Thursday morning. The cross-examination of a score of witnesses was followed by another long speech from Gurney pressing home his attack on the point of colour. Then came the summing up, which took three hours to deliver. Cochrane's complaints about it are perfectly justified: "There does not occur in the whole course of your Lordship's charge even the shadow of a suggestion in my favour." The judge, indeed, not merely posed all the questions for the jury, but gave them the answers, in peculiarly forcible terms. His language throughout was suggestive of guilt, and no judge can be called impartial who talks about the accused having committed a crime before the jury has had the opportunity to decide whether a crime has been committed or not.

At 6:10 P.M. the jury retired. At 8:40 they returned with a verdict of guilty.

According to the curious procedure of trials in the old Court of the King's Bench there was an interval between the verdict and the judgment during which an appeal might be lodged for another trial. But as the judge presiding at the original trial was permitted to decide if a re-trial should be held the accused seldom got a second chance. Cochrane cannot have been in a hopeful frame of mind when, on June 14, he himself appeared for the first time before the stern figure of Lord Ellenborough. He begged to be permitted to present evidence overlooked at the first trial; but Ellenborough cut him short by saying that his plea was not in order since the chief conspirator had admitted his guilt by fleeing to the Continent. Cochrane tried to talk him down, but the judge's interruptions became so peremptory that he could not finish his speech. The entire proceedings did not take ten minutes.

On June 20 the accused were summoned to receive judgment at the hands of Mr. Justice Le Blanc. Serjeant Best moved in restraint of judgment. He began by fighting a long legal duel with Ellenborough, who was on the bench, though he did not pronounce judgment. Then, before sentence was delivered, Cochrane was allowed to speak for the first time. He aimed at securing a suspension of judgment, so he elaborated in more forcible language the points already made by his defence. By this time he knew that he was fighting a losing battle, and there is a note of apprehension in his speech unusual for so self-confident a man:

> "It has been my very great misfortune to be apparently implicated in the guilt of others with whom I never had any connexion, except in transactions, so far as I was apprised of them, entirely blameless. I had met Mr. De Berenger in public company, but was on no terms of intimacy with him. With Mr. Cochrane Johnstone I had the intercourse natural between such near relatives. Mr. Butt had voluntarily offered, without any reward, to carry on stock transactions in which thousands as well as myself were engaged in the face of day, without the smallest imputation of anything incorrect. The other four defendants were wholly unknown to me. . . . The pretended

Du Bourg, if I had chosen him for my instrument, instead of making me his convenience, should have terminated his expedition and found a change of dress elsewhere. He should not have come immediately and in open day to my house. I should not rashly have invited detection and its concomitant ruin. . . . Is it not next to impossible that a man conscious of guilt, should have been so careless of his most imminent danger? . . . I look forward to justice being rendered my character sooner or later; it will come most speedily, as well as gratefully, if I shall receive it at your Lordship's hands. I am not unused to injury; of late I have known persecution; the indignity of compassion I am not yet able to bear. To escape what is vulgarly called punishment would have been an easy thing; but I must have belied my feelings by acting as if I were conscious of dishonour. I cannot feel disgraced while I know that I am guiltless. Under the influence of this sentiment I persist in the defence of my character. I have often been in situations where I had an opportunity of showing it. This is the first time, thank God, that I was ever called upon to defend it!"

His appeal availed him nothing. The next day Mr. Justice Le Blanc pronounced sentence. "That you, Sir Thomas Cochrane, otherwise called Lord Cochrane, and you Richard Gathorne Butt, do severally pay the King a fine of one thousand pounds; . . . that all you the six defendants [Cochrane Johnstone and McRae had already fled the country] be severally imprisoned in the custody of the Marshal of the Marshalsea of our Lord the King for twelve calendar months; and that during that period you, Charles Random de Berenger, you, Sir Thomas Cochrane, you, Richard Gathorne Butt, be severally set in and upon the pillory opposite the Royal Exchange in the City of London for one hour between the hours of twelve at noon and two in the afternoon."

CHAPTER IV

In the Wilderness

WITH THE PUBLICATION of that savage penalty the whole structure of Cochrane's life crashed in ruins. The sentence would have broken a lesser man; but he was always a fighter and, in spite of the almost mortal blow, he remained buoyed up by the conviction of his innocence. Even if it meant taking the rest of his life to do it—as indeed it did—he was determined to fight the injustice of the verdict with all the means in his power. "As for pardon," wrote Creevey, "he will die sooner than ask it. I find many people take the field for him as to innocence, or at least have doubts." The mob had no doubts, as Lord Eldon discovered when he was hissed in his coach owing to his identity being mistaken for that of Lord Ellenborough.

Two of the principals had admitted their guilt by fleeing the country before sentence was delivered. Butt, in whose innocence Cochrane had a strange belief, followed them as soon as he heard the verdict. De Berenger had been in prison on another charge for some time, and the others confessed. Cochrane alone, as befitted the sole innocent man in that gang of crooks, remained to take his punishment. Since the trial involved a man of his political reputation it was generally regarded as a political event. In this ostensibly Stock Exchange matter men saw a trial of strength between the Government and the Radicals. "Although as yet he was generally believed to be guilty," wrote Lord Campbell, "the award of this degrading and infamous punishment [the pillory] upon a young nobleman, a Member of the House of Commons and a distinguished naval officer, raised universal sympathy in his favour." But Campbell is certainly wrong when he goes on to suggest that Ellenborough's death was hastened by an uneasy conscience. The matter never cost that tough old Tory a single night's sleep. The scanty group of faithful Radicals naturally saw Cochrane as the victim of a judge who openly expressed the views of the Government from the bench. Burdett, indeed, told his bankers that he considered himself fortunate that no stock of his was sold that day; if it had been, he would now be sharing Cochrane's fate. To many others it came as a shock to find that their Member had been gambling on the Stock Exchange. Place regarded it as "more than sufficiently disgraceful"; but Cobbett, much as he hated stockjobbers, stood by his friend. The trial and all the subsequent events were fully reported in the *Political Register,* which was always full of propaganda in Cochrane's favour. The public interest in the event was so great that the paper reached a record circulation of 7,000 copies.

Thus encouraged, Cochrane found a certain pleasure in regarding himself as a political martyr. The truth is that he was the victim of circumstantial evidence, that the conspirators had indeed made him "their convenience"; but the trial itself was by no means as unfairly conducted as he would have us believe in what he ingenuously calls "my unvarnished tale" in his autobiography. Writing that account at the end of his life fifty years later he still hints darkly "that a higher authority than the Stock Exchange was at the bottom of my prosecution"; he still professes to regard De Berenger as a Government agent employed to implicate him in a criminal conspiracy; he still detects collusion between his enemy Croker, secretary to the Admiralty, and the committee who prosecuted him.

Possibly; though there is no real evidence to support the allegation. None the less the sentence was surprisingly savage for so common an offence, and the naval authorities certainly acted with indecent haste in expunging his name from the Navy List within a week of the result. Then, on July 5, he was expelled from the House. But here at least he was given the opportunity of defending himself. Unfortunately, as the leader of the Opposition said when he spoke in his favour, Cochrane's speech ruined his case more effectually than his worst enemy could have done. Smarting from a sense of injustice, he launched into a violent personal attack on the character of Lord Ellenborough. The wild career of his invective could not be checked, though Castlereagh was able to warn reporters that they would be liable to prosecution for libel if they printed his speech in its entirety. The result is a string of asterisks (or "asterisms," as they were then called). Reading the speech in Hansard is therefore like reading a letter after it has been censored: "I would rather stand, in my own name, in the pillory every day of my life than I would sit upon the Bench in the name of *** If there is any meaning in the word 'packed' as applied to juries *** This *** judge *** In short, he was *** Never in the history of this country," he declared as he withdrew when the vote was taken, "was a case of such gross and cruel injustice recorded."

Burdett, Whitbread and Ponsonby spoke in his defence, but he was expelled from the House by 140 votes to 44. Cochrane Johnstone, on the other hand, was expelled without a single dissenting voice.

A few days later the young and chivalrous Lord Ebrington appealed for clemency, if not for justice, on Cochrane's behalf. He begged the House to annul that part of the sentence which condemned him to the pillory. His generous effort was rewarded with an ungrateful letter from the prisoner, who objected to being treated as an object of mercy; but Ebrington had the consolation of being congratulated on his speech by Napoleon in an interview at Elba six months later: "You were right," said the emperor; "such a man should not be made to suffer so degrading a punishment."

Cochrane never did stand in the pillory because Castlereagh intervened to say that the Government proposed to abolish its use except in cases of perjury. The reason for such an access of generosity was their fear of the consequences if Cochrane was forced to undergo such an ordeal. It would have been the signal for a riot, especially as Burdett announced his intention of standing in another pillory alongside his friend.

Meanwhile Burdett was making a good deal of political capital out of his friend's misfortunes. Soon after his expulsion from Parliament a mass meeting of five thousand electors was summoned to nominate their ex-member for the ensuing election. The mob cheered "Cochrane! Cochrane for ever!" while Burdett inveighed against Governmental injustice. After a scathing reference to the way Ellenborough had conducted the trial, Burdett said, to quote the report in *The Times* of July 12:

"It now remained for the electors of Westminster to vindicate
the character of an illustrious person who had rendered great
services to the country *(loud applause):* services which, even if he
had been guilty of the meanness imputed to him, should, as he
thought, have protected him from the degrading infamy which
it was now intended to have inflicted upon him. *(No! No! from
many persons, as expressing the hope that the sentence would not be
inflicted).* He should hope that the malice of his enemies would
not prevail; but even if he were to suffer that degrading punishment, he would confidently look for his acquittal to the un-
packed and uncorrupted verdict of his constituents and his
countrymen at large. He said, that if Lord Cochrane was to
stand in the pillory, he should feel it his duty to attend also *(loud
shouts of applause which lasted for many minutes)."*

At the same time what Cobbett called "the hellish craft" of corruption was at work to prejudice the electors against their favourite.
On the eve of the election a letter was published in *The Sun* describing a conversation in a tavern with the old earl of Dundonald. As
usual at this date, the old man was very drunk; but he was understood to say that just before the trial his son had kicked him down-
stairs because he tried to put him on his guard against his uncle.
Apart from this, he claimed that the Aix Roads affair was entirely his
own idea; that his son had robbed him of all share in the merit of its
success; and that he had left his father in penury for the past few
years. Cobbett fairly shrieked with rage when he heard of this trick
to discredit the popular candidate. For his part, as soon as he heard
of it, Cochrane wrote a dignified denial of the charge, pointing out
that he had given his father over £8,000 in the last ten years, and that
he could not be held responsible for "the unfortunate state" of his father's mind in extreme old age. In Scotland, indeed, the old man had
long been known as "daft Dundonald."

There were other candidates in the Westminster election that
July—Sheridan, Cartwright and even Cochrane's late counsel,
Brougham; but they all retired from the contest when they saw
that Cochrane still retained the support of the mob. "It is understood," Brougham told Grey, "that an arrangement has been made
to choose him this one time, and that he is not to come forward
again in case of expulsion. The great thing was to keep all together
and avoid splitting."

The generous support of his constituents and of political societies in other parts of the country warmed Cochrane's heart as he lay in prison. But his enemies were not yet done with him. A final attack on his good name was made by the Secretary of State when he ordered the Bath King-of-Arms to remove Lord Cochrane's banner from above his stall in Henry the Seventh's chapel. On August 11 his coat of arms was unscrewed, the helmet and sword taken down, and his banner kicked down the steps of the Abbey. This gratuitous insult of stripping him of the honours he had won in battle marks the nadir of his chequered fortunes. It is the measure of the hatred he had inspired in Governmental circles by his persistent campaign against places and pensions, against the inefficiency and the injustice of Old Corruption.

THE KING'S BENCH was a prison for gentlemen. Cochrane refused the privilege of the rules which enabled prisoners to go outside for short intervals, but he was able to receive friends and relations in his comfortable two-roomed quarters. His young wife, heavily veiled, was a frequent visitor. Of course, with his romantic temperament, it had been a runaway match undertaken in opposition to the wishes of his father and his uncle Basil, who promptly cut him out of his will. The lady's name was Katharine Corbett Barnes, and they were married secretly in Scotland in 1812, Cochrane returning to London two days after the event. It was a love match and the most enduring success he ever achieved. For fifty years they lived a devoted couple, chiefly because Lady Cochrane always showed an inexhaustible sympathy for the difficult but lovable man who was her husband.

There is a delightful picture of the two of them at home in the memoirs of Samuel Bamford, written shortly after Cochrane's release. The author was a humble Lancashire weaver who had come up to London for the first time to hand over to Cochrane one of the many working-class petitions he presented in Parliament.

"On arriving at his house in Palace Yard, we were shown into a room below stairs, whilst Lord Cochrane and Hunt conversed above; a slight and elegant young lady, dressed in white, and very interesting, served us with wine. She is, if I am not misinformed, now Lady Dundonald. At length his lordship came to see us. He was a tall young man, cordial and unaffected in his manner. He stooped a little, and had somewhat of a sailor's gait in walking; his face was rather oval; fair naturally, but now tanned and sunfreckled. His hair was sandy, his whiskers rather small, and of a deeper colour, and the expression of his countenance was calm and self-possessed. He took charge of our petitions, and being seated in an armchair, we lifted him up and bore him on our shoulders across Palace Yard to the doors of Westminster Hall; the old rafters of which rung with the shouts of the vast multitude outside."

Afterwards they visited Burdett's house.

"He was one of our idols. Still I could not help my thoughts from reverting to the simple and homely welcome we received at Lord Cochrane's, and contrasting it with the kind of dreary stateliness of this great mansion and its rich owner. At the former place we had a brief refection, bestowed with a grace which captivated our respect; and no health was ever drunk with more sincere good will than Lord Cochrane's: the little, dark haired and bright eyed lady seemed to know it, and to be delighted that it was so. But here scarcely a servant appeared, and nothing in the shape of refreshment was seen."

Cochrane was too active a man to sit and mope in prison. Throughout the winter he was busy with inventions, particularly an oil lamp for street lighting which was actually adopted by one parish in Westminster, until the invention of gas lighting (which owed much to the experiments of his father) ruined the success of his project. He also composed a lengthy, muddled *Letter to Lord Ellenborough* which he published at his own expense—a badly argued presentation of his case which had little of the effect intended. But his impatience soon got the better of him. He never had much respect for the law, so he listened sympathetically to Cobbett's silly proposal that he should escape as he had done in Malta. The excuse was that it was illegal to imprison a Member of Parliament on such a charge. That was a mere pretence. By the spring Cochrane was ready to do anything to break the monotony of prison life. On March 6 he made the attempt.

His rooms were on the top story, on a level with the prison wall and only a few feet from it. Somehow he obtained a short length of rope with which he made a slip knot. When the night watchman had passed on his rounds, Cochrane threw the rope across to catch one of the spikes on the wall. For a man of his agility it was an easy matter to swing himself across, balance on the wall, and then let himself down on the farther side. Unfortunately the rope snapped when he was twenty-five feet from the pavement. He fell heavily on his back, but managed to crawl to the house of his old nurse, where he lay concealed for a few days.

The hue and cry was raised immediately his absence was reported next morning. The news even overshadowed another rumour which reached London that same morning, that Napoleon had escaped from Elba. But the bills posted gave such a faulty description of his appearance, and the police system was so inefficient at that date, that he escaped capture, in spite of the three hundred guineas reward. Every day the newspapers were full of rumours as to his whereabouts: he had fled the country, he was hiding in an apothecary's shop in the City, he was at Hastings, in the Channel Islands, at Cobbett's house. Yet all the time he was living quietly at his own country house, Holly Hill in Hampshire.

He must have known that he could not long escape capture. Yet he appears to have been convinced of the legality of his flimsy excuse, for on March 20 he astonished the officials of the House of Commons by walking into the lobby "dressed in his ordinary usual costume, grey pantaloons, frogged great coat, etc." An undignified scene followed. While one official tried vainly to prevent him entering the chamber, another ran off to fetch the constables. Indignant members compelled him to retire, since he had not yet taken the oath and could not therefore occupy his seat.*

Then Bow Street runners, accompanied by a strong posse of tipstaves, appeared on the scene. Cochrane refused to budge. The police, he shouted, had no authority to issue a warrant inside the House. There was a struggle, in which he was over-powered and dragged struggling out of the building. When he was searched for arms all that could be discovered was a packet of snuff. "If I had only thought of that before!" cried the infuriated prisoner, "you should have had it in your eyes!" Once outside the precincts he agreed to go quietly. Accompanied by four constables, he was driven back to prison in a hackney coach.

It is typical of the attitude of the Government newspapers that

---

* Another account states that the chamber was empty, as it was still early in the day; having already taken the oath in the clerk's room, he sat down on the right of the speaker's chair.

one exaggerated the story about the snuff into a report that Cochrane had admitted that he brought it on purpose to blind his captors, "observing that he had found the use of a similar weapon when in the Bay of Rosas"; another paper called it vitriol.

After this mad escapade Cochrane was locked in the strong room of the prison, a narrow cell, ill ventilated and partly underground. The damp oozing through the walls from a nearby cesspool forced him to burn charcoal to fumigate the stagnant atmosphere, but he was overcome by the fumes. Within a few weeks he became so ill that his brother insisted on calling a doctor, who certified that "Lord Cochrane is affected with a severe pain of the breast. His pulse is low, his hands cold, and he has many symptoms of a person about to have typhus or putrid fever."

Under these circumstances his friends did all they could to persuade him to pay the fine when his term of imprisonment was up in June. At first he refused, but the conditions of prison life were beginning to tell even on his iron frame and at length, on July 3, he paid the £1,000 fine. He endorsed the banknote (which was for long preserved at the Bank of England) with a protest with which he concludes his autobiography:

> "My health having suffered by long and close confinement, and my oppressors being resolved to deprive me of property or life, I submit to robbery to protect myself from murder, in the hope that I shall live to bring the delinquents to justice.
> "COCHRANE.
> "King's Bench Prison, July 3rd 1815."

The world in which he found himself at liberty was a world intoxicated with the news of Waterloo. He himself had little inclination to exult over the triumph of a foe who always referred to him in generous terms, even though he had spent the happiest time of his life in fighting him. The ordeal through which he had just passed made him more self-centred than ever. His one feeling now was a determination to continue relentlessly his search for justice.

In the 1816 session of Parliament he opened his new campaign with a farcical attempt to impeach Lord Ellenborough. His speech on the thirteen charges he brought against his judge took over four hours to deliver; he was never at a loss for words where a personal grievance was concerned. But, as before, he made the mistake of overstating his case, and he only succeeded in exasperating a sparse audience which was by now thoroughly bored with the rights and wrongs of his case. After the motion had been defeated by eighty-nine votes to none, he announced in a final burst of anger: "So long as I have a seat in this House I will continue to bring these charges forward, year by year and time after time, until I am allowed the opportunity of establishing the truth of my allegations."

Outside the House he was more successful. He prosecuted one of the late witnesses for perjury and won his case, incidentally proving the truth of his argument that De Berenger must have changed his uniform before he met him. But he was not yet free of the meshes of the law. In August he was summoned at the Guildford Assizes on the charge of escaping from prison. He went down from London in a lighthearted frame of mind, accompanied by Burdett and other political friends. His defence was that he considered that he had been illegally imprisoned because he was a Member of Parliament. The verdict of the jury was magnanimous: "We are of the opinion that Lord Cochrane is guilty of escaping from prison, but we recommend him to mercy because we think his subsequent punishment fully adequate to the offence of which he was guilty." The words were greeted with loud applause, whereupon the judge ordered the court to be cleared and imposed a fine of £100.

Cochrane refused to pay. But his constituents responded nobly with a penny collection which, according to his own account, not merely paid this fine but the original £1,000 fine as well. This can ardly have been the case, since we find him in 1856 demanding £1,000 as part of the reinstatement money due to him; however, we know for certain that soon afterwards he paid over most of the Westminster subscription to Hone in order to pay his fine when condemned by Ellenborough for the publication of blasphemous parodies.

Of more importance than these sordid legal squabbles, in which he was invariably worsted, was the continuation of his crusade for parliamentary reform. Ever since he first sat for Westminster in 1807 he had pledged himself to this cause in successive election addresses. Now peace had come, the small Radical group—for the Whigs still held aloof—considered the time opportune to renew their demands. Ministers could no longer pretend that reform was impossible in face of the danger abroad. No longer could they blame Napoleon for all their sins of omission. Nevertheless peace brought no relaxation in the stringent rule of a reactionary government, rather the opposite. Discontent born of the high cost of living due to the new Corn Laws, unemployment consequent on demobilisation and a post-war slump, spread trouble through the land. The people cried for bread, while Luddites smashed machinery in the north and pauperised peasants burnt the hayricks in the south.

A stormy meeting held in the London Tavern in July 1816 shows the part Cochrane was playing in these troubled times. In inception it was a charity meeting of the Association for the Relief of the Manufacturing and Labouring Poor. The duke of York was in the chair, the dukes of Kent and Cambridge, the Archbishop of Canterbury and the Bishop of London were on the platform. Cochrane, accompanied by a group of working men who detested patronising charity of this description, determined to shake the complacency of the ruling classes by showing that the true cause of the national distress was political and not economic. After the duke of Kent had proposed a reasonable motion that distress was due to the transition from a war to a peace economy, Cochrane rose and "offered himself to the attention of the meeting, but was for some time unable to proceed, his voice being lost in the huzzas and hisses which his presence called forth." When the tumult subsided he was heard to say that the burden of parasitic placemen was a fundamental cause of the national distress. The duke begged him "not to urge any political principle," to which Cochrane agreed after some argument. He sat down to re-draft his motion, but the chairman took advantage of the lull in the proceedings to take a snap vote of thanks and close the meeting before he could proceed with his attack. Amid much confusion the duke bowed to the audience and "immediately withdrew amidst loud hissings and cries of Shame! Shame! A trick! A trick!" Chairs and benches were thrown about, men punched and fought each other, and the meeting broke up in disorder.

Cochrane acted more effectively in furthering the cause when, in December, he persuaded Cobbett to revise his *Political Register* with the aim of increasing the range of Radical propaganda among the working classes. He advised him to bring out a cheap weekly paper containing popular statements of the reformist aims. The result was a series of pamphlets at 2d. each or 12s. 6d. a hundred, which earned the name of "Tuppenny Trash." However, the Gagging Acts passed after the Spa Fields riots successfully silenced it after a short term of publication.

A man of his courage who found himself by now one of the most popular leaders in the country was not to be deterred by the increasingly reactionary spirit displayed by the Government. After what he had suffered he had nothing more to lose, and the heady wine of mob acclamation warmed his sore heart and encouraged him to assume the role of a demagogue. The age-old method of petitioning Parliament gave him ample opportunity to act the part with conviction. In January 1817 he presented monster petitions from every part of the kingdom. As has been seen, Bamford describes the enthusiasm with which the mob chaired him to the House as the representative of their demands. Stirred by the ovation he had received outside, he forced embarrassed Members to hear what the men of Bristol thought about placemen, and how the outspoken villagers of Yorkshire considered that taxation without representation was nothing better than slavery. Some of the politer petitions were accepted, with reluctance. But, as the Chartist agitation showed later, mass petitioning has no effect on a recalcitrant government which refuses to be hustled by mob violence.

The year 1817 was a bleak one for the popular cause. Fears of riots, and indeed of revolution, stiffened the Tories in their attitude to the Reform movement. A Secret Committee, of which Wilberforce was a member, was set up to examine "certain practices, meetings and combinations evidently calculated to endanger the public tranquility . . . and to bring into hatred and contempt the whole system of our laws and constitution." Wilberforce in his diary adds: "Remember to pray in earnest against sedition, privy conspiracy, and rebellion." The manufacture of evidence by spies and *agents provocateurs* went on apace. After the Gagging Acts came the suspension of Habeas Corpus. At no date in modern times have the liberties of the English people been so circumscribed; never has reaction ruled with such unabated rigour. Meetings were suspended, popular leaders persecuted whenever they dared to open their mouths. Many took refuge in exile: Cobbett fled to America; Byron, embittered and insulted, left to trail his bleeding heart across the Continent; Shelley in Rome castigated the rulers of Britain in the name of human liberty. Every month saw a thinning in the ranks of the reformers at home.

When, on May 20, Burdett proposed a motion for parliamentary reform, Cochrane was his sole supporter. "Reform we must have," he said, "whether we will or no. The state of the country is such that things cannot much longer be conducted as they are. There is a general call for reform. . . . I am satisfied that the present state of corruption is more detrimental to the country than a despotism."

A year later, on 2 June 1818, he made his last speech in support of the same motion, though he confessed that he did not entertain much hopes for it in the present temper of the House. "As it is probably the last time I shall ever have the honour of addressing the House on any subject, I am anxious to tell its members what I think of their conduct. It is now nearly eleven years since I have had the honour of a seat in this House, and since then there have been very few measures in which I could agree with the opinions of the majority." After a final fling at the burden of the placemen, he concluded, in sentences broken with emotion which aroused more sympathy than any of his invectives had done before: "The feelings of my heart are gratified by the manner in which my constituents have acted towards me. They have rescued me from a desperate and wicked conspiracy which has nearly involved me in total ruin. . . . I hope His Majesty's Ministers will take into their serious consideration what I now say. I do not utter it with any feelings of hostility—such feelings have now left me—but I trust they will take my warning, and save the country by abandoning the present system before it is too late."

A few months earlier the patriots of Chile had offered him the command of their navy in their fight for freedom. He accepted the post with enthusiasm. Here at last was a chance to return to his own profession, to win honour in battle, and at the same time to pursue his crusade for freedom in the active sort of life he loved and for which his talents eminently fitted him. He was tired of verbal quarrels, of endless arguments which never prevailed against the entrenched forces of Old Corruption. The Whigs were unresponsive to his cause; the Radicals were in exile or quarrelled amongst themselves. England had nothing left to offer except a vicious circle of discontent and repression. And all the time the dishonour he had suffered rankled in his mind: "The cursed recollection of the injustice that has been done to me is never out of my mind."

Even with his boundless self-esteem he must have felt that at home he was fighting a vain battle. He never had the temperament of a successful political leader. But with a sword again in his hand he could seek a world elsewhere.

PART III

Crusader at Large

CHAPTER I

~~~

The Liberation of Chile and Peru

I N FEBRUARY 1818 the Chilean envoy in London wrote to his government: "I have extreme satisfaction in informing you that Lord Cochrane, one of the most eminent and valiant seamen of Great Britain, has undertaken to proceed to Chile to direct our navy. He is a person highly commendable, not only on account of the liberal principles with which he has always upheld the cause of the English people in their Parliament, but also because he bears a character altogether superior to ambitious self-seeking."

Ever since Napoleon had invaded Spain, the Spanish and Portuguese colonies in South America had been in a state of revolt, and even before that there had been movements in emulation of the French and American revolutions. Parts of the continent, notably the north under Simon Bolivar the Liberator, had by now achieved their independence; but elsewhere the uneasy movement towards liberation from the mother countries was still in progress. On the Pacific coast the patriots, led by San Martin and O'Higgins, were in a desperate situation. Peru was firmly held by Spanish garrisons, which also occupied important strongholds in the south. Chile had indeed proclaimed her independence, but the resumption of a blockade was feared because a hostile fleet still ruled the seas and thus controlled the lines of communication and supply. Even though the Royalists received little or no support from Spain, the independence of the new republic was doomed unless that fleet was destroyed.

As soon as he accepted the invitation to command a navy which hardly existed Cochrane, with characteristic vision of the potentialities of modern inventions in warfare, decided on the necessity of a steamship. Under his direction an odd-looking sailing vessel with two auxiliary 45-h.p. engines, a retracting paddle, and two funnels placed abreast, was built at Maudeslay's yard at Rotherhithe, the pioneer firm in this sort of work. Apparently she was originally intended for the Arctic, for at first she was named the *North Pole* and a device depicting the North Star was painted on her stern. Retaining this crest, Cochrane renamed her the *Rising Star.* However, such was the urgency of the demand for help that he had to leave her to be completed by his brother. Ultimately she reached Chile, but not till 1820, by which time the fighting was over. Her claim to be the first vessel to use steam on the Atlantic crossing cannot be justified, for the American *Savannah* was actually the first to do so in 1817; nevertheless the *Rising Star* was the first steam-vessel to enter the Pacific, her passage thither being the longest on record. Even then it is said that her engines only worked for nineteen hours during the voyage.

In August 1818 Cochrane embarked with his wife and their five-year-old son, Tommy, in the 300-ton merchant ship *Rose.* On their arrival at Valparaiso, the port of the capital, Santiago, they received a tremendous welcome, the more so because the little Chilean squadron was celebrating its first lucky victory, the capture of a Spanish frigate now known by the patriotic, if unromantic, name of *O'Higgins.* General Bernardo O'Higgins, the illegitimate son of an Irish immigrant, was Supreme Director of the Republic more on account of the victories of General San Martin than his own prowess in the field. Cochrane always respected the man since, in spite of his laziness and weakness, he was about the only honest man on the Pacific coast at that date, and therefore the one man whose orders the new admiral always loyally obeyed. The trouble was that he was incapable of ruling by himself. As the Chileños said: "There is too much wax and too little steel in his composition; however, there are few better and many worse men than Don Bernardo." It was with the powers behind him, the corrupt, cold-blooded Zenteno, minister of marine, and the latter's enigmatic patron, General San Martin, that Cochrane inevitably quarrelled.

Having seen service in Spain, where he was brought up, San Martin had returned to South America to head the liberation movement some years previously. A brilliant march west over the Andes and two crushing victories at Chacabuco and Maypo had secured the independence of Chile. Everyone expected the successful general to install himself as director of the new state, for he was known to be an ambitious man. But for his own reasons he handed the post to O'Higgins, who, by the time Cochrane arrived, was little more than a well-meaning puppet in his hands. It seems that San Martin intended to fly higher, to become director of the richer, but as yet unconquered, province of Peru; his apparent generosity over the directorship of Chile merely allowed him to await the right moment for an attack on the stronger Spanish forces in the north. John Miers, an English copper manufacturer who knew him well, describes him as a weak, uneducated man, though with great abilities as a soldier and "an unusual share of cunning." His bushy black whiskers hid a treacherous mouth. Miers used to tell him that a country like Chile was not yet ready for republican institutions, and that an enlightened despot would be far more suitable; "on these occasions the eyes of the general used to glisten, and he readily assented to the truth of these observations."

Crusades have always been notorious for their internecine quarrels. Mrs. Graham, a Valparaiso resident and a great admirer of Cochrane, thought that his arrival would pacify the conflicting parties which San Martin was playing one against the other. "The state of the Chilean navy required a man of prudence as well as courage, of temper as well as firmness, and in no one man did these qualities ever meet in so eminent a degree. . . . His singularly gentle and courteous manner, which veiled while it adorned the determination of his character, was admirably calculated to conciliate all parties."

Prudence was, of course, the very last virtue Cochrane possessed. He never in his life acted the part of peacemaker and conciliator. True, everything went well at first, owing to the patriotic disinterestedness of the Chilean admiral, Blanco Encelada, who agreed to serve under a foreigner; but it was not long before friction arose, and, as before, Cochrane left the scene of his victories full of anger and grievances.

The 'navy' which he was appointed to command consisted of two East Indiamen, now named the *Lautaro* and *San Martin*, of forty-four and sixty-four guns, four American and English brigs mounting eighteen or sixteen guns each, and the recently captured 48-gun frigate *O'Higgins,* the flagship of the squadron. Most of the officers were foreigners, and there were some two hundred seamen. Of the former Cochrane counted among his supporters Captain Wilkinson, who had just succeeded in selling the government the two East Indiamen; Captains Crosbie and Forster, who took it in turns to act as his flag captain; and Henry Cobbett, the young savage who had bullied Marryat in the midshipman's berth long ago on board the *Imperieuse.* The best officer of the lot, and a firm admirer of Cochrane, was a Peninsular veteran, Major Miller, now Commandant of Marines. Indeed the best account of the war is to be found in his *Memoirs,* a far more impartial account than Cochrane's own *Narrative of Services,* two dull volumes of grievances written to justify himself shortly before his death, though it was evidently the latter which inspired Henty's uncritical novel of his adventures on this coast—*Cochrane the Dauntless.*

The rival faction which took shape on the arrival of the new admiral was led by two ex-naval men, Captain Guise, a gentleman with no mind of his own, and Captain Spry, his parasite, whom Mrs. Graham calls "a low-minded man." Having bought an 18-gun brig out of the British Navy, they had hawked her round South America till they found a purchaser in the Chilean Government. Already they had the ear of Admiral Blanco and they viewed the appointment of a rival with jealous eyes. "Two Commodores and no Cochrane" was what they wanted; but Blanco's unselfish decision brought their dangerous plan of a divided command to nothing.

Such were the men Cochrane met in the round of entertainments with which he was greeted. Mrs. Graham describes him as he appeared in his forty-third year: "Though not handsome, he has an expression of countenance which induces you when you have looked to look again and again. It is variable as the feelings that pass within, but the most general look is that of great benevolence. His conversation, when he does break his ordinary silence, is rich and varied; on subjects connected with his profession or his pursuits, clear and animated; and if ever I met with genius, I should say it was pre-eminent in Lord Cochrane." His young wife won all hearts—"a flattering specimen of the beauty of England," says the gallant major. Indeed she enraptured the populace when she rode up to review the army on horseback: *"Que hermosa! que graciosa! qué ariosa! es un angel del cielo!"*

This favourable impression was heightened by a banquet on St.

Andrew's day, at which Cochrane appeared in the costume of a
Scottish chief, to the stupefaction of the Chileños. But after a series
of such entertainments Cochrane suggested that it was really time to
get on with the war against Spain, about which the people of Santiago did not seem to be particularly interested. The first move was to
reconnoitre Callao, the port of Lima, the Peruvian capital. When he
did at last set sail the squadron proved smaller than he had intended, for one of his three accompanying ships promptly mutinied.
Just as the flagship *O'Higgins* was leaving the harbour, the admiral
saw his five-year-old Tommy being carried down to the last boat on
the shoulders of some seamen, waving his cap in the air and shouting *"Viva la patria"* for all he was worth. As the ship was already under way he could not be set on shore again. There was nothing for
it but to take him with them and allow the sailors to cut out a little
midshipman's uniform for him and make a pet of him generally.
Some weeks later, when they went into action, a shot took off the
head of a marine standing beside him, spattering the child with
blood. Running up to his horrified father he cried, "They have killed
poor Jack, Papa, but indeed the shot did not touch me; indeed I am
not hurt." "Put your head in the hole the shot made and stay there,"
was the reply, "no shot will ever come through the same hole
again." Miller was standing by when this happened, and he was
amazed at the cool accuracy with which Cochrane calculated the
flight of shot—"There comes one straight for us; but don't move, for
it will strike below us."

Callao was strongly held by warships in the harbour and batteries on the shore. The first attack was abortive, partly because of the
fog, in which one of the Chilean ships managed to desert, and partly
because the date happened to be that of the annual inspection of
posts, which were for once fully manned. However, San Lorenzo, an
island three miles off the coast, was occupied and an explosives lab-
oratory set up there under Miller. Besides compelling the Spanish
fleet to keep in port, Cochrane succeeded in capturing two treasure
ships, the contents of which he distributed on a generous scale to
win over the support of the Peruvians and to gain information. Wild
rumours were started to appal the Spaniards (Cochrane always had
the lowest opinion of Spanish morale). "El Diablo" was here with
his fantastic explosives; Drake's drum was sounding on that coast
once more.

Cochrane spent the summer fitting out another expedition against

Callao. His mind had always run on pyrotechnical methods of warfare, so he decided that a plentiful supply of rockets were necessary, together with the inevitable explosion ship. Orders were given for a thousand rockets to be constructed under the superintendence of a Mr. Goldsack, one of Congreve's assistants, who had come out with Cochrane. But the second attack failed worse than the first. Rafts were built on the lines of monitors and Miller and his assistants were provided with air-tight metal cuirasses as life-belts. But the rafts went adrift, Miller's left hand was shattered by a premature explosion and the rockets refused to go off, owing to the poor quality of the metal used. It was later discovered that the work of constructing them had been left to Spanish prisoners, who had taken the opportunity to fill the shells with rags, sand and manure.

Chile expected great things of her new admiral. When he returned a second time without any spectacular success to his credit it became clear that he would have to do something quickly if confidence was to be restored. Without waiting at Valparaiso for the recriminations of his employers, he continued south in the *O'Higgins* alone to reconnoitre Valdivia, the strongly fortified southern harbour still held by the royalists. In January 1820 he arrived off the mile-wide fiord leading to the town. Knowing that the arrival of a Spanish frigate was expected, he sailed boldly in and demanded a pilot. The pilot came on board, accompanied by several officers who had come to welcome their compatriots; all were promptly seized and compelled to give valuable information as to the state of the defences on the southern shore. The town of Valdivia lay fifteen miles up the estuary, the narrow mouth of which was protected by batteries and forts on either side. The strongest of these was Coral Castle on the southern shore, but all the forts were well placed on the tops of cliffs, and only one place gave any hope for a landing.

"Well, Major," he said to Miller after they had seen how formidable the defences were, "Valdivia we must take. Sooner than put back it would be better that we all went to the bottom. Cool calculation would make it appear that the attempt to take the town is madness. There is the one reason why the Spaniards will hardly believe us in earnest, and you will see that a bold onset, and a little perseverance afterwards, will give a complete triumph; for operations unsuspected by the enemy are, when well executed, certain to succeed, whatever the odds."

Reinforcements were necessary, so he sailed north to borrow four hundred soldiers off the governor of the next province. With these men on board two small transports, the *Intrepido* and *Montezuma*, he might be able to repeat his old trick of a *coup de main* on an unsuspecting foe. On the other hand, the flagship was in a lamentable state with eight inches of water in the hold, and of the two naval officers on board, one was under arrest and the other incapable of carrying out his duties. Cochrane had therefore to act as commander-in-chief of the expedition, officer of the watch, and first lieutenant in his own ship. One night, when he was worn out with fatigue and the ship lay becalmed off the coast, he turned in to snatch a brief rest after telling the midshipman of the watch to call him if a breeze sprang up. Of course the boy fell asleep. In the middle of the night they were awakened by a rending crash as the ship ran on a rock, her rigging entangled in the branches of some trees, her false keel ripped off and floating astern in the darkness. Half-dressed, Cochrane ran up from below to find every one of the six hundred men on board preparing to abandon ship. He pointed out that no one could hope to reach the shore through that surf and proceeded to give an example of what a fine seaman he was, even at the age of forty-three. Stripping off his shirt, he climbed down into the bilge to stop the leak with his own hands. A stream anchor was got out and the ship hove off the reef, but not before the water had reached the powder magazine and soaked the ammunition. "Never mind," he told his men, "trust to the bayonet; that is the weapon the Spaniard likes least."

Thus, with a sinking ship and a flooded magazine, he sailed to attack one of the strongest points on the coast. Anchoring the flagship some way off shore, he prepared to make a landing, from the two smaller vessels, on the one practicable beach. Spanish colours were hoisted to forestall possible interference from the shore batteries, all the troops were hidden below and the boats kept out of sight by being lowered on the seaward side. Just as everything was ready, one of the boats drifted astern. A sentry on the point sighted it and a brisk fire opened from the most seaward of the defences. Miller was told to make a dash for it through the surf. He and his men effected a landing and the Spaniards were driven up the cliffs at the point of the bayonet.

It was now late in the evening. Miller waited till darkness fell. Then, following the admiral's orders, he climbed the rocky path towards the first big fort, while the gallant Ensign Vidal attacked with a larger force in the flank, scaling the fort by swinging over the palisade on the branch of a tree and then tearing down the palings to bridge the ditch. Surprised flank and front, the Spaniards abandoned the fort and fled towards their next defences at the Coral Castle. But the Chileños followed close on their heels and beat them from fort to fort. When dawn broke Cochrane, who had maintained contact from a gig rowed along the shore, saw his men surrounding the last of the fortifications on the southern side. The defenders of the northern forts abandoned their posts as soon as they saw the flag of liberation flying from the castle. Cochrane signalled the ships to move in, and soon town and garrison surrendered—not a moment too soon, for the *Intrepido* ran aground in the harbour, and the *O'Higgins* had to be careened before she could put to sea again. The "Gibraltar" of Chile had been captured by a single ship and half the number of the opposing force; the total loss suffered by the patriots was seven men killed.

The chief credit for this brilliant exploit goes to Cochrane for his skilful plans and to Miller for his gallant leadership, all the more remarkable because of his recent wound. The capture of Valdivia completed the freedom of Chile, and allowed the republicans to turn all their attention to Peru; furthermore it enabled them to float a loan on the London market. But Zenteno, the Minister of Marine, chose to be ill-pleased at the news. It was "an act of madness," he declared, and the admiral deserved hanging for acting without orders. Guise and Spry were equally incensed because they had been left out of it. Making common cause with them, Zenteno had the effrontery to appoint Spry flag captain to the admiral on his return. Cochrane was furious. He was determined Spry should never tread his quarter-deck as long as he remained in command. San Martin intervened to allow the admiral his point, but Cochrane made matters worse by arresting Guise on "several acts of direct disobedience and neglect of duty." A warm correspondence ensued, Cochrane demanding a court martial, Zenteno refusing it. Furthermore, no reward was forthcoming for the men of the *O'Higgins*. Refused satisfaction on this point, Cochrane played his trump card: he sent in his resignation. A petition from all the officers in the fleet (except Guise and Spry) begged him to withdraw it. Ultimately a compromise was patched up and the details of the next move in the war were discussed in an unfriendly atmosphere.

It was decided to send a large combined force of 4,200 men and seven ships against the capital of Peru and its port, Callao. The command of the army was given to San Martin. So far Cochrane had no cause to quarrel with him, but the General's subsequent actions justified the distrust he and others felt for him. On the other hand it must be admitted that in an enterprise of this kind no one could be more difficult to work with than Cochrane, his native egotism heightened by his recent brilliant successes.

Disagreement began as soon as they sailed. San Martin wished to land at a point south of Lima. Cochrane preferred a frontal attack. They compromised by landing a small force south of the port to take the capital in the rear, while the main force under San Martin disembarked at Ancon, fifty miles north of the capital. Having done this Cochrane withdrew most of the ships, ostensibly to blockade Callao. Secretly, however, he was determined on another surprise: an attack on the Spanish fleet in the harbour. From what he had seen of San Martin's methods of warfare, he fancied the General would be too timid to allow him to do this if the matter was broached at a formal council of war.

Callao, he knew, was heavily fortified. Under the guns of the castle lay the Spanish flagship, the 44-gun frigate *Esmeralda* in the middle of a semicircle of twenty-seven gunboats protected by a boom and guardships. This was the force he proposed to attack with three ships. Furthermore, to avoid international repercussions, he would have to avoid two neutral ships lying in the roadstead, one American, and one British. His enemies called him reckless, so it is worth studying the care with which he prepared this, the most brilliant example of a cutting-out expedition in naval history. His plans prove clearly enough what Captain Basil Hall (whose ship was at that moment lying off shore) calls his "matchless intrepidity and inexhaustible resources in war."

The first thing was to fool the Spaniards into the belief that he did not intend to attack. Two of his ships were sent out of the Roads, the *O'Higgins* remaining apparently as an inshore blockading ship. Then the date of a carnival was chosen, when most of the Spanish crews would be on shore. One hundred and sixty-eight volunteers were carefully picked and detailed orders circulated to the officers commanding them. Fortunately his secretary and interpreter, Stevenson, has preserved them for us:

"The boats will proceed, towing the launches in two lines parallel to each other, which lines are to be at the distance of three boats' lengths asunder.

"The second line will be under the charge of Captain Guise, the first under that of Captain Crosbie. Each boat will be under the charge of a commissioned officer, and the whole under the immediate command of the admiral.

"The officers and men are all to be dressed in white jackets, frocks, or shirts, and are to be armed with pistols, sabres, knives, tomahawks or pikes.

"Two boatkeepers are to be appointed to each boat who, under no pretence whatever, shall quit their respective boats, but are to remain with them therein and take care the boats do not get adrift.

"Each boat is to be provided with one or more axes, which are to be slung to the girdles of the boatkeepers. The frigate *Esmeralda* being the chief object of the expedition, the whole force is first to attack that ship which, when carried, is not to be cut adrift, but is to remain in possession of the patriot seamen to ensure the capture of the rest. On securing the frigate the Chilean seamen and marines are not to cheer as if Chileños; but in order to deceive the enemy, and give time for completing the work, they are to cheer *'Viva el Rey!'* The watchword and countersign, should the white dress not be sufficient in the dark, are *'Gloria'* to be answered by *'Victoria.'* "

Since he was dealing with a crew largely composed of Latin Americans these orders were followed up with an inspiring address, in which he reminded his men that "one hour of courage and resolution is all that is required of you to triumph." But he relied chiefly on the British volunteers, and as they climbed over the side into the boats he spoke to them in their own language: "Now, my lads, we shall give them such a Gunpowder Plot as they will not forget in a hurry."

It was the night of November 5. At ten o'clock, fourteen boats carrying 240 marines and seamen pushed off from the sides of the *O'Higgins* and pulled towards the enemy with muffled oars. As his launch led through the gap in the boom Cochrane had the misfortune to collide with a guardboat. The challenge was given, but a pistol held to the head of the sentry and a whispered threat was enough to ensure the man's silence. In a few minutes they were alongside the frigate, her spars looming above them in the darkness. As the boat grated against the side, Cochrane jumped out to lead the way up the

starboard gangway. Gaining the deck, he was knocked back into the
boat by a blow from the sentry's musket, a thole pin piercing his back
as he fell. However, he was on his legs again in a moment, only to receive a musket ball through the thigh. Had not Crosbie's party
swung over the port rail just in time, the admiral would have been a
dead man. In a moment the deck was a scrambling heap of men. The
boarders had entered by the waist, dividing the Spaniards on deck
into two parties, one driven to the fo'c'sle and the other to the quar-
terdeck, while the boarders guarded the hatches to keep down those
skulking below. A quarter of an hour's struggle was enough.

"Fore top there?" shouted Cochrane to the party he had detailed
to take possession of that part of the ship.

"Ay, ay, sir," came the welcome reply.

"Main top there?"

"Ay, ay, sir."

Those of the enemy who had not been cut down leaped overboard, or surrendered themselves with their comrades below. But the
patriots had scarcely gained possession of the ship when the guns of
the coastal batteries roared out. Their captain had taken precautions
for just such a contingency. Noting what coloured lights the neutrals
in the harbour were showing that night, he had brought with him
similar lights to be hoisted to confuse the enemy target. After some
erratic shooting, the guns ceased fire as suddenly as they had begun.
The Spanish flagship was securely in the hands of the patriots, together with her admiral and two hundred seamen.

Meanwhile Cochrane had bound up his leg with a handkerchief
and was directing operations from a hammock. Towards three o'clock
giddiness, due to loss of blood, compelled him to return to his own
ship to have his wounds properly dressed. Guise, as senior officer,
was left in command. He immediately made the mistake of cutting
the *Esmeralda* adrift, thereby making it impossible, as Cochrane had
intended, to use her guns against the adjacent warships. Before dawn
brightened the sky her topsails were set and she was steered triumphantly out of the harbour.

The capture of the enemy flagship was a brilliant exploit, boldly
conceived and bravely carried out with remarkably small loss, an
outstanding example of Cochrane's gift of combining foresight with
daring. Every move had been calculated to confuse the enemy and
yet maintain orderly action on the part of his own men. Every man
knew beforehand exactly what he had to do and every contingency

was provided for, even though Guise's folly spoilt the full effect. Even San Martin was generous in his praise. He wished to rename the frigate after her captor, but Cochrane refused, so she was called the *Valdivia* instead. It remained for a subsequent Chilean government to name a battleship after him.

But San Martin's behaviour during the next six months did nothing to improve their relations further. It is an elementary axiom in warfare that the effect of a success is doubled if it is exploited immediately. But just as Gambier's inertion had thrown away the fruits of Cochrane's skill in the Aix Roads, so San Martin failed to show any enterprise whatever after the cutting out of the *Esmeralda*. Throughout the whole of the winter and the spring he sat idly encamped, at one time even retreating further north instead of advancing on Lima. Moreover, just as he had tried to force Gambier's hand, Cochrane was now equally anxious that San Martin should advance. Intoxicated by his own success, he tactlessly suggested that if the general would give him a thousand men he would take Lima himself by a frontal assault on the capital. No one could accuse a man like San Martin of cowardice. His own excuse for his suspicious inactivity was that he was waiting for the people of Lima to show their sympathy for the cause of liberation. Indeed some difficulty was encountered in winning over the population: the native element had nothing to gain by a change of masters; the merchant classes were appalled by the prospect of the ravages of open war in their country; and the Spanish upper classes were naturally hostile. Cochrane's own explanation of San Martin's inactivity was that he was preserving his army to further his own ambitions later on. Eventually, on 6 July 1821, the Spanish Viceroy left the capital of his own accord. Even then the "liberating" general hesitated for a week before he entered the city, and marines from Captain Hall's ship, the *Conway*, had to be called in by the civic authorities to maintain order in the meantime. Further south, Cochrane and Miller had captured Arica on their own account during the interval, without letting the general know of their plans.

On July 28 Peru was declared an independent state at a mass meeting in the central square of the capital. Both Cochrane and San Martin were there to receive the thanks of the populace, the latter being somewhat piqued by the omission "brave," which was applied to his colleague and not to himself. However he redressed the balance by distributing a medal of his own design on which the inscription read: *"Lima secured its independence on the 28th of July 1821 under the protection of General San Martin and the liberating army."* Imagine Cochrane's feelings! A week later, without notifying his admiral, the liberator proclaimed himself Protector and dissolved the popular council. San Martin had at last achieved his ambition.

In ignorance of this decisive move Cochrane visited the palace to demand the payment which had been promised to himself and his men before they left Chile. San Martin replied abruptly: "I will never pay the Chilean squadron unless it is sold to Peru, and then the payment must be considered part of the purchase money."

Cochrane was taken aback. "But by such a transaction the squadron of Chile will be transferred to Peru by merely paying what is due to the officers and men for service done to that state."

The other turned angrily to order his two ministers, who were standing by, to leave the room. Realising the importance of witnesses at such a scene, Cochrane begged them to remain, explaining that, as he was not master of the language, he wished them to interpret for him in case he used an offensive expression by mistake.

"Are you aware, my lord, that I am Protector of Peru?"

"No, but I hope the friendship which has existed between San Martin and myself will continue to exist between the Protector of Peru and myself."

Rubbing his hands together San Martin laughed. "I have only to say that I am Protector of Peru!"

Stung by the man's insulting attitude, Cochrane replied: "Then it becomes me, as senior officer of Chile, to request the fulfilment of all the promises made to Chile and the squadron; but first—and principally—the squadron."

"Chile! Chile!" shouted the general, "I will never pay a single *real* to Chile. As to the squadron, you may take it where you please and go where you choose." He began to pace the room in a rage, then, halting before the admiral, he said in a different tone, "Forget, my lord, what is past."

"I will when I can," returned Cochrane, as he turned on his heel to leave the room. San Martin caught him up at the top of the stairs: "Will you accept the post of Admiral of Peru?" Without deigning a reply Cochrane ran down the stairs to return to his ship. It was clear, he told his secretary in his dramatic way, that after what had passed his life was not safe on shore.

That did not prevent him from sending the Protector a letter full of "sound advice" on the evils of dictatorship. The lecture only served to stiffen San Martin's attitude. He replied with a proclamation promising the seamen full pay if they would join the service of Peru. This cut the ground from under the admiral's feet, for his crews were destitute and desperate. Round-robins in the illiterate style of the lower deck kept coming in. Many of his officers could not be relied upon to maintain discipline. Spry, indeed, disobeyed orders so openly that he was superseded by Crosbie; whereupon the former took refuge on shore and was rewarded by being appointed San Martin's naval aide-de-camp. In vain Cochrane protested that the promises of payment had been signed jointly before the expedition left Valparaiso. Nothing was forthcoming, replied the Protector, unless the squadron was turned over to Peru, that is, to himself.

Meanwhile a force of 3,000 Spaniards was allowed to march past Lima to extricate a vast quantity of treasure and stores from Callao, without any effort being made to intercept them. Much against his personal inclination, Cochrane landed to beg the general to cut off their retreat with at least a part of his huge army of 12,000 men; but every proposal was coldly received. "My resolutions are taken. I alone am responsible for the liberties of Peru." What the general's conception of "liberty" meant, the inhabitants of Peru were soon to learn at their cost.

Payment for the mutinous squadron remained Cochrane's chief care. As San Martin refused to honour his word unless the admiral deserted from the Chilean service, the latter took matters into his own hands. Hearing that the general kept his own, as well as the public funds, on board his yacht at Ancon, Cochrane sailed up there and seized it with all possible form of legality. Meticulous accounts of the distribution of public moneys to the squadron were forwarded to the Chilean government and a voucher was collected from each seaman as a receipt of wages. San Martin's own treasure was left untouched, and Cochrane refused to take any payment for himself.

It was now the general's turn to be offended. Guise and Spry were persuaded to detach their ships from Cochrane's squadron, and other crews followed in response to renewed promises of an increase of pay if they deserted. The culminating affront was a letter from the so-called minister of the interior.

"MY LORD.—Your note, in which you explain the motives which induced you to decline in complying with the positive orders of the Protector temporarily to restore the money which you forcibly took at Ancon, has frustrated the hope which the Government entertained of a happy termination to this most disagreeable of all affairs. . . .

"You will immediately sail from this port to Chile, with the whole squadron under your command, and there deliver up the money which you have seized, and which you possess without any pretext to hold it. . . .

"I have to complain of the style of your Excellency's secretary, who, perhaps from his ignorance of the Spanish language cannot express himself with decency—his soul not having been formed to conceive correct ideas."

Instead of obeying the order, Cochrane determined to pursue the two remaining Spanish frigates on the coast, which were reported to be cruising to the northward. Only three loyal ships accompanied him, and the O'Higgins was in such a state that she nearly foundered in a gale off the Mexican coast. The cruise was a failure, and even the tough Major Miller admits that the privations they endured could seldom have been surpassed. They did not succeed in finding the Prueba frigate because San Martin's agents got in touch with her first and persuaded her to surrender to him. Furthermore, the Protector was doing his best to put Cochrane in the wrong with the British authorities as well as with the government of Chile by spreading the rumour that he was attacking neutral shipping on a piratical cruise of his own, and that his allegiance to Chile was purely nominal—all this from the very man who had tried to persuade him to desert to the Peruvian service.

What Cochrane was in fact doing, and had been doing for some months past, was attempting to crush the contraband trade being carried on by British merchants from Spanish ships. In his view the merchants were little more than smugglers, since they tried to evade the customs regulations set up by the new state. In the merchants' view (in which the so-called Protector now tried to confirm them) Cochrane was a pirate and a traitor. They invoked the protection of the British Pacific squadron under Commodore Hardy and Captain Basil Hall, who demanded an interview. At this Cochrane had no difficulty in justifying his actions, and henceforward British trade was carried on through more regular channels.

After several months Cochrane returned from his futile chase of the remaining Spanish men-of-war in the Pacific. He did, indeed, capture one frigate. However, when he looked into Callao on his way south, he found the *Prueba* already anchored under the guns of the castle ready to fire on him if he attacked. Even the Chilean schooner *Montezuma*, which he had himself captured some months previously, was now flying Peruvian colours. The *Prueba* might have surrendered to Peru, but he was not going to allow Chilean ships to desert in this way. A warning shot forced the *Montezuma*'s crew to haul down the offending flag, and a party was sent on board to run the officers on shore. Then a messenger arrived from the Protector, renewing his offer of the post of Admiral of Peru, together with his private Order of the Sun set in diamonds. Cochrane threatened to kick the man overboard if he did not leave the ship immediately.

Angered by the general's behaviour, and disgusted by the reign of terror which had by this time broken out all over Peru, Cochrane continued south for Chile. On the morning of 3 June 1822, the *O'Higgins* anchored in Valparaiso Bay. Mrs. Graham's maid came running in to her mistress: "Señora, he is come, he is come!" "Who is come, child?" "Our admiral, our great and good admiral. Come out on the veranda and see!"

His work in destroying the Spanish naval force in the Pacific achieved, Cochrane wished to retire to his private estate at Quintero, a beautiful landlocked bay a few miles north of the capital, which he hoped would become the naval base of the new state. He felt better after receiving the thanks of O'Higgins, particularly when a medal was issued, this time attributing all the credit for the liberation of Peru to the navy. "Thank God," he replied, "my hands are free from the stain of labouring in any such work [as the establishment of tyranny in Peru], and, having finished all you gave me to do, I may now rest till you command my further endeavours for the honour and security of my adopted land."

~

CHAPTER II

In the Service of Brazil

I N THE SUMMER of 1822 Cochrane regarded Chile as his adopted land. As soon as he went on leave he began to improve his Quintero estate and built himself a handsome house there in the local style. But the great earthquake which occurred in November that year destroyed everything, including valuable biographical records. At about the same time political developments in Chile forced him to change his mind about the future.

He had done as much as any other patriotic leader to secure the independence of the new Pacific states; but in South America independence was far from guaranteeing that liberty and justice for which he had really been fighting. The emancipated states had only succeeded in entering upon a century of military dictatorships and political adventurers. The revolution that autumn in Peru, which exiled San Martin to die of poverty many years later in France, was but the first of an interminable series. Whether the Protector's exile was a voluntary emulation of Washington's withdrawal from public life, or whether public opinion, backed by threats from Bolivar in Colombia, forced him to resign, is a debated point. Cochrane at any rate saw in it a just retribution for his treachery in usurping power. In a long letter to Francis Place, in which he catalogues the exactions and persecutions carried on under the general's regime, he writes with typical Radical optimism: "Would to God that all people on whom tyrants tread would act with the spirit of the gentle Limeños!"

As soon as the new government in the north was formed, he had the satisfaction of hearing that the following resolution had been passed:

> "The Sovereign Constituent Congress of Peru, contemplating what the liberty of Peru owes to the Hon. Lord Cochrane, by whose genius, fortitude, and valour, the Pacific is freed from deceitful enemies, and the standard of liberty planted on all the coasts of the South Sea, Resolve—
>
> That the Junta of the Executive Government in the name of the Nation, renders to Lord Cochrane, admiral of the Squadron of Chile the most sincere sentiments of gratitude for his efforts in favour of this people, heretofore tyrannised over by a powerful force, but now [i.e. after the fall of San Martin] arbiter of its own strength. . . .
>
> *"27 September 1822."*

A year later the Spaniards recaptured the town, and the war had to be fought all over again.

On his return to Chile Cochrane's first efforts had been directed towards payment of his squadron, together with a request for six months' leave for himself. He was successful in obtaining the latter only. For five months officers and men remained at Valparaiso without the payment of a dollar. When it looked as though the men would mutiny and sack the town, Cochrane intervened again on their behalf. By using forcible measures he gained his point, though the administration, at the last minute, attempted to seduce the loyalty of the men by only paying them and leaving their officers to shift for themselves. In the end Cochrane obtained part payment for his own services over the past two and a half years; of prize money, or reward in other forms, he received only the vaguest promises.

He had not been long in retirement before General Freyre, an insubordinate provincial governor in the South, decided that the time was ripe to oust the feeble O'Higgins. There was a suspicion that Cochrane would join him in his *coup d'état*, but though he sympathised with Freyre in getting rid of a corrupt administration, in the shape of men of the stamp of Zenteno who were trying to persuade

O'Higgins to dismiss all foreigners, he considered that it was not for a man in his position to meddle with internal politics. Besides, he was too loyal to his old friend O'Higgins to treat him as a despot of the San Martin pattern. To prove his neutrality he shifted his flag to the schooner *Montezuma,* which he took with him to Quintero.

In this uncertainty a timely invitation arrived from Brazil: *"Venez, milord, l'honneur vous invite—la gloire vous appelle. Venez—donner à nos armes navales cet ordre merveilleux et discipline incomparable de puissante Albion."* Cochrane's reply to this language was guarded, the more so since he must have heard something of the despicable character of Don Pedro, the young Portuguese regent who had just assumed the title of "Constitutional Emperor of Brazil"—whatever that meant. "I am, of course, free for the crusade of liberty in any quarter of the globe"; but, he added, he did not wish to commit himself until he had satisfied himself that the Brazilian Government did not "differ so widely in its nature from those I have been in the habit of supporting as to render the proposed situation repugnant to my principles."

However, by the beginning of next year the political situation in Chile left him little choice. It became clear that he would not be able to remain much longer undisturbed in his retirement on his estate. A final batch of proclamations in his best Latin-American style bade farewell to those for whom he had fought so well.

> "MY FELLOW COUNTRYMEN,— . . . It is now four years since the sacred cause of your independence called me to Chile. I assisted you to gain it. I have seen it accomplished. It only remains for you to preserve it. I leave you for a time, in order not to involve myself in matters foreign to my duty, and for reasons concerning which I now remain silent that I may not encourage party spirit. You know that independence is purchased at the point of the bayonet. Know also that liberty is founded on good faith and on the laws of honour, and that those who infringe upon these are your only enemies; amongst whom you will never find
>
> "COCHRANE."

On 18 January 1823 he struck his flag. Mrs. Graham, his guest at Quintero after the earthquake had destroyed her own house, and who had helped him to print the proclamations by the new lithographic process Cochrane had introduced, describes the scene. After

a cheerful camp meal of roast potatoes (for they all lived in tents after the earthquake), Crosbie was told to pull out to the ship and strike
the admiral's flag. As the pennant came fluttering down, a salute was
fired. "He received the flag without apparent emotion, but desired it
to be taken care of. Some of those around him appeared more
touched than he was."

Accompanied by the invaluable Crosbie and Grenfell he arrived
at Rio in March. Six other naval officers who attempted to join him
were struck off the Navy List at home in consequence of the Foreign
Enlistment Act, which made Cochrane himself for the time being an
outlaw. The rulers of the new South American republics of the last
century with whom Cochrane came in contact were not an estimable
set of men: San Martin was bad enough, but Don Pedro was worse.
Yet Cochrane remained on friendly terms with him to the end, chiefly
because he insisted on treating him as an English constitutional
monarch whose position was outside politics—a fiction which the
emperor strove to maintain, though the manner in which he tore up
the constitution and dissolved assembly after assembly was certainly
not in accordance with British practice. He was, says Cochrane, "induced to become" emperor; but from all accounts he did not need
much inducement.

As Cochrane had to quarrel with someone, he quarrelled with the
ministers instead. By the time the new admiral appeared, Rio and the
surrounding territory had secured independence; but the vast northern provinces of Maranham, Para and Bahia still refused to acknowl-
edge the new emperor. As there was no land communication
between the two areas, and no "patriotic" navy worth speaking of,
the Portuguese fleet secured the loyalty of these rich, though unde-
veloped areas. It was to destroy this fleet and reduce the north that
Cochrane was invited.

His experience of corruption and double-dealing on the Pacific
coast put him on his guard. He entered into negotiations about his
new contract with all the canniness of his Scottish nature. The Brazilian Government had the audacity to offer him the pay of a Portuguese admiral, notoriously the worst in the world. Cochrane
insisted on the same pay as he had received in Chile—$8,000 a year.
After some haggling about the rate of exchange this was agreed to.
Further, he extorted a promise that all prizes should become the
property of the captors. Needless to say this promise was not kept;
indeed the reverse occurred, for after the war the successful admiral

was involved in expensive litigation about the matter. But at least he gained his final point, that he should be appointed first admiral and not junior admiral, as the opposition demanded.

Where the other admirals would have come from it is difficult to say, for Cochrane found the so-called Brazilian navy in a parlous state. There was one line-of-battle ship in reasonable condition, the *Pedro Primiero*, rated as a seventy-four but only carrying sixty-four guns, together with half a dozen small and worthless ships. The flagship's crew consisted of 160 English and American sailors, 130 black marines (emancipated slaves, who considered it beneath their dignity to clean their quarters or their equipment without the assistance of batmen), and the usual riff-raff of the waterfront. The crews of the other ships consisted exclusively of the last class.

In his first action off Bahia this rabble showed what it was worth. Cochrane led to the attack, signalling to the rest of the squadron to follow him. No attention whatever was paid to his signal, and for the rest of the action "half the squadron was wanted to look after the other half." After it was over he sat down to write the most damning description of a fleet any commanding officer can have ever written. Everything, he told the government, was wrong: the ships leaky, the powder mouldy, the masts and sails rotten, the crews mutinous. The only sensible thing to do was to gather all the best men into two ships and send the dregs back to port. Having done this, he was able to defeat the Portuguese fleet with the two remaining ships and succeeded in freeing an area twice the size of Europe.

The enemy fleet, he learned when he put to sea a second time, consisted of thirteen ships, including one line-of-battle ship and five frigates. It lay at anchor nine miles up the river at Bahia, some five hundred miles north of Rio. Cochrane began with a remarkable piece of reconnaissance. He was known as a skilful navigator, but the way he took his big ship up the unknown river in the dark was one of the most notable feats in his career. As usual he was careful to choose a night when he knew that most of the enemy officers would be on shore. Thus when the presence of his ghostly flagship in the midst of the squadron was reported by a white-faced sailor to the Portuguese admiral at midnight, the latter was incredulous. "What? Lord Cochrane's line-of-battle ship in the midst of my fleet? Impossible! No large ship can have come up in the dark!" Actually it was not the dark that was worrying Cochrane, but the hazard of the wind, for, having prowled around the enemy squadron, the wind dropped, and his only method of escape was to drift out to sea stern foremost.

Enemy morale was fast ebbing. Rumours were spread about that Cochrane was preparing to send fireships up the river to burn the shipping at anchor. Knowing El Diablo's reputation, the Portuguese admiral was taking no risks. The whole fleet, together with all the merchantmen and transports in the river, was ordered to put to sea. Lying off the point with his two ships, Cochrane allowed this enormous convoy of thirteen warships and over sixty merchant vessels to get well clear of the estuary. Then, in the darkness, he slipped between them and the land and drove them out to sea, harrying them as a dog harries sheep. He had plenty of sea room; the enemy force would assuredly huddle together for protection; and he knew that the superior sailing qualities of his flagship would enable him to outmanœuvre any possible interference on the part of the warships in the van. But even with his courage and skill he could not capture the entire convoy, so orders were sent to the smaller ships which had joined him to cut off the topmasts and stave in the water-casks of as many ships as he could compel to surrender, thus forcing them to put back to the American coast without even a prize crew on board.

The amazing chase started in 13° S., and finished in 5° N., in the neighbourhood of the Canaries. Night after night the *Pedro Primiero* dashed in amongst the convoy, firing broadsides right and left, hulling and dismasting everything within range. Before the warships could tack to the assistance of the terror-stricken merchantmen, Cochrane had manœuvred his ship out of range, and was lost to sight in the surrounding darkness. Of the sixty vessels which set out from South America only thirteen reached Lisbon.

Shortage of ammunition compelled him to abandon this "feat without parallel in the history of war," as our greatest military historian calls it. He returned to occupy the coastline around Bahia without opposition. Maranham, an enormous province near the mouth of the Amazon, was next liberated. Here he made superb use of a *ruse de guerre;* arriving with the news of the surrender of Bahia, he pretended that his ship was but the van of a big force moving up from the south. "Sir," he peremptorily told the Portuguese commandant, "the naval and military forces under my command leave me no room to doubt the success of the enterprise in which I am about to engage, in order to free the province of Maranham from foreign domination. . . . I am anxious not to let loose the imperial troops of Bahia upon Maranham, exasperated as they are at the injuries and cruelties exercised towards themselves and their countrymen. It is for you to decide whether the inhabitants of these countries shall be further exasperated by resistance, which appears to me unavailing and alike prejudicial to the best interests of Portugal and Brazil."

An attempt was made to compromise, but the inflexible attitude of the admiral ultimately compelled the Portuguese officials, led by the local bishop, to come on board the flagship to tender their submission. Out of the clemency of his heart Cochrane promised free transport back to Lisbon for the Portuguese troops, provided they embarked immediately—it was important to get them out of the way before the ruse was discovered.

A single ship without a soldier on board had captured an enormous province. Encouraged by this second success, Cochrane instructed Grenfell, his second in command, to sail on to Para and repeat the trick there. The interior of this even vaster province was as yet unexplored: all that was necessary was to appear off the mouths of the Amazon and intimidate the towns thereabouts. Grenfell's threat was equally successful, the only blood to be lost being his own when an attempt was made to assassinate him.

Without appreciable casualties Cochrane had secured the independence of all the northern provinces of Brazil by a spectacular combination of enterprise and bluff. Admittedly the opposition was never in a fighting mood, but a single false step on his part, any failure to exploit the situation, any political or diplomatic mistake, might have resulted in prolonging hostilities for a year or more. Cochrane may have been a hot-head where domestic politics or his own career was concerned, but when he was making use of diplomacy as a weapon of war he was surprisingly sure-footed. If, for example, he had not sent Grenfell ahead to bluff Para into submission it would have been months before his main force could have appeared off the coast to enforce it, and meanwhile the southern provinces might have reverted to their Portuguese allegiance.

The fighting over, it was his duty to reduce the conquered territories to some semblance of order, a far more difficult task than the defeat of the Portuguese fleet. The comic opera of his constitution-manufacturing opens with the declaration of the independence of Maranham and an invitation to the inhabitants to elect a democratic assembly of which even old Major Cartwright would have approved. "Citizens! Let us proceed gravely and methodically, without tumult, haste or confusion, and let the act be accomplished in a manner worthy of the approbation of His Imperial Majesty." This to a population of half-castes and traders! Not to be outdone, they for their part, produced an extraordinary letter to the emperor:

> "What was our joy when unexpectedly we saw the *Pedro Primiero* summoning our port! Oh! 26th of July 1823! Thrice happy day; thou wilt be conspicuous in the annals of the province, as the sentiments of gratitude and respect inspired by the illustrious admiral sent to our aid by the best and most amiable of monarchs will be deeply engraven on our hearts and those of our posterity. Yes! August Sire! the wisdom, prudence, the gentle manners of Lord Cochrane contributed still more to the happy issue of our political difficulties than even the fear of his force."

The comedy ceased when Cochrane returned to Rio to claim his reward. The Portuguese faction were by now making their influence felt, and they resented his ill advised efforts to persuade the emperor to dispense with their services. His successes in the north merely rendered him, in their eyes, the more dangerous. To them his effort to secure a more genuinely democratic constitution was mere hypocrisy. It was either he or they who were to rule by influencing the emperor, and he was a foreigner. So instead of receiving any prize money for the one hundred and twenty vessels captured, the treasures of palaces, customs houses and government stores which had fallen into his hands, the tribunal offered to pay his men three months' wages. An attempt was then made to reduce the victorious liberator to the rank of port admiral, and Grenfell was put under arrest.

More than insults followed. Late one evening the wife of a French resident ran in to tell him that his house was surrounded, and that an attempt would be made at the naval review next day to search his ship for the treasure reputed to be hidden on board. Seeing suspicious-looking soldiers hanging about the entrance of his house, Cochrane slipped out by a side door, climbed the garden fence, and took horse to invoke the protection of the emperor.

The gentleman-in-waiting refused him entrance so late at night. Cochrane insisted. "The matter on which I come is fraught with grave consequences to His Majesty and the Empire."

"But His Majesty retired to bed long ago."

"No matter. In bed or not in bed I demand to see him by virtue of my privilege of access to him at all times. If you refuse to concede permission—look to the consequences!"

Hearing this altercation, the emperor appeared in his nightshirt. Cochrane explained the reason which forced him to disturb so august a personage at such an hour. He begged His Majesty's assurance that trusted persons should accompany him on board when the proposed search was made. "Depend upon it, they are not more my enemies than the enemies of your Majesty and the Empire, and an intrusion so unwarrantable the officers and crew are bound to resist."

"Well," the emperor replied cheerfully, "you seem to know everything; but the plot is not mine, being convinced that no money will be found more than we already know of from yourself."

Between them they decided that the best thing to do was to postpone the review. "I will be ill in the morning—so go home and think no more of the matter."

For once Don Pedro kept his word. At the levee which Cochrane attended next morning it was announced that His Majesty had been taken ill in the night; on which the emperor caught the eye of his admiral and they both burst out laughing, to the astonishment of the bystanders.

Early in 1824 news arrived that a rebellion had broken out in Pernambuco. Cochrane was asked to suppress it. Since he could not man his ship without money he refused, unless the emperor personally guaranteed the naval force a sum of $200,000. With this promise (which was never kept) he put to sea at the beginning of August. Arrived off the town he threatened a bombardment if the rebels did not submit. After an unavailing attempt to buy him off with an enormous bribe, their commander decided to surrender.

Having done his work Cochrane sailed back to Maranham to see how his constitution was getting on. Since he had been honoured with the title of Baron of Maranham, together with the promise of a vast estate (consisting chiefly of jungle) he considered that the inhabitants were in a special sense his protégés. Instead of the democrat's dream, he found anarchy and bloodshed. The president of the Junta was attempting to overawe the town with black troops, while the members of the Junta fought among themselves. Cochrane dismissed the president, dissolved the Junta, and ordered another general election. But he was getting tired of exhorting the inhabitants to loyalty to the central Government now he knew what that

Government was worth; and by now he must, in spite of all his optimism, have come to the conclusion that a democratic constitution such as even England did not possess at that date was hardly suitable for the inhabitants of an equatorial region. By the beginning of 1825 he confesses himself "heartily sick" of Brazil. Up in Maranham he was left entirely to his own devices, no instructions, no payment, no supplies being vouchsafed him from Rio. As the climate was ruining his health he sent in his resignation three times without any acknowledgment whatever. When no reply was forthcoming to his fourth resignation, he decided to cruise north in search of health and rest.

Such at least are the reasons he gives for his suspicious arrival off the Azores in the *Piranga* frigate. There he discovered (most opportunely) that a mast was sprung and that the provisions had turned bad in the hold. It was clearly impossible to return across the Atlantic without refitting; but to what port could he take his ship? Portugal was hostile; Spain equally so; France had not yet recognised the independence of Brazil; in England he was in danger of arrest under the Foreign Enlistment Act. At a council of officers it was decided, nevertheless, to risk a visit to Portsmouth. On June 25 the *Piranga* arrived at Spithead. Before anchoring Cochrane took care to inquire whether a salute on the part of the Brazilian ship would be answered by the same number of guns. To his immense relief the Port Admiral agreed, and for the first time the new Empire was saluted by a European power. It was Cochrane who called a new world into existence, years before Canning coined the phrase.

An angry correspondence with the Brazilian envoy in London ensued. There was the usual wrangle about payment and provisioning, and awkward questions were asked. Why had he appeared in England without orders? What treasure had he absconded with? Why should the Brazilian Government pay a crew whose loyalty was so suspect? The admiral was ordered to return forthwith to Rio. But the admiral was now on leave in Scotland and refused to rejoin his ship until she was provisioned. Obviously his status in the Brazilian navy was becoming increasingly obscure. At last the question whether he had resigned or not was settled by the outcome of the peace negotiations between Brazil and Portugal in November 1825.

Of course it would be ridiculous to claim, as Cochrane would have us suppose, that he originally sailed for South America with the exclusive aim of a crusader in the cause of democratic institutions. To establish liberty was, no doubt, his principal object. But it must be clear to those who have followed his career so far that he was by nature a fighting man with a sword for sale in any cause consonant with his libertarian principles. He enjoyed fighting, that was his career; but he never hesitated to demand full recompense for his services. Money runs Justice a very close second in his career, and with Money he was never as successful as with Justice. Politically, the causes for which he fought did triumph in the end, though not entirely on account of his own exertions; financially, he never received his just reward.

After so many quarrels it is not surprising that this was so. The impetuous sailor, though a Scotsman, was as wax in the hands of politicians of Portuguese extraction. Even if such men had wished to honour their country's word, they were never long enough in power to do so. With the distance of the ocean between debtor and creditor subsequent governments could afford to ignore his repeated requests for justice. Chile generously gave him a draft for $120,000 on Peru, which Peru refused to honour. Brazil, like Chile, sequestrated the estates which it had granted him. Neutrals involved him in scores of lawsuits over the capture of prizes. After years of haggling and recrimination Chile granted him £6,000 in 1845, and ten years later promised him admiral's pay for life. Since he claims that he was £25,000 out of pocket when he left that country, and since he was by that date eighty years of age, neither the grant nor the promise was exceptionally generous; nor was his brother ever paid the £12,000 due for the *Rising Star*. From Brazil he personally never received a penny, until just before his death an exceptionally honest government granted him half the interest on the sum originally promised; at a later date £40,000 of the £100,000 originally claimed was paid to his descendants.

Shortly after his return to Scotland he received an ovation from his own countrymen which must have compensated him in some measure for the shabby treatment his devotion to the cause of liberty had earned him on the coasts of South America. Sir Walter Scott describes the scene in verses more generous in conception than inspired in manner. Cochrane and his wife were attending the theatre at Edinburgh. A reference to South America having been introduced in their honour, the entire house rose to cheer the heroic pair. The applause was so spontaneous and so unexpected, considering the circumstances in which they had left their native land eight years previously, that Lady Cochrane broke down and wept.

CHAPTER III

~~

The Greek War of Independence

AFTER HIS EXPERIENCES in South America, Cochrane's behaviour in embarking on yet another crusade in the cause of liberty may seem somewhat inept. He had learned by his treatment at the hands of so-called patriots that the motives of those who fought in the sacred name of freedom were not necessarily as idealistic as his own; that however efficiently he discharged his duties he would meet with little gratitude at the hands of such men. But the Greek War of Liberation was a cause which roused enthusiasm in every liberal's heart. As the first post-war expression of that nationalistic sentiment which Napoleon's career had kindled in Europe, it carried a particularly irresistible appeal to a generation fed upon the wisdom of classical writers. Such enthusiasts made no distinction between the inhabitants of Athens in the age of Pericles and their descendants who began the revolt with a massacre of fifteen thousand Turks on Easter morning 1821. But whatever the character of its progenitors, the cause prospered in every sense save the military one. Funds and material were raised by Philhellene Committees, who successfully exploited the generosity of enthusiastic liberals in every capital. Byron sanctified the crusade by his death at Missolonghi in 1824; Shelley cast a glow of opalescent optimism over the whole sordid business; and the inevitable Sir Francis Burdett launched stirring appeals on behalf of the London Committee, a body which combined philanthropy with a keen eye for the financial chance in a typically English way.

In spite of his lack of a classical education, it was inevitable that Cochrane should be caught up in the movement. He had received an invitation to lead the Greek naval force soon after the outbreak of the revolt, but in view of his commitments in South America it was not until August 1825 that he was free to accept the post. By that date, writes Midshipman Keppel, who met him in South America, "he was, in the estimation of the Old World and the New, the greatest man afloat." The situation in Greece, however, was by now so depressing that even the best friends of the patriots were forced to admit that only a consummate genius in warfare could save them. The Sultan had invited his redoubtable vassal, Mehemet Ali, the almost independent Pasha of Egypt, to assist him in return for a promised reward of vast provinces in the Near East. Mehemet's son, the terrible Ibrahim, had, by the date of Cochrane's arrival, invaded southern Greece, and the end of the revolt looked near.

Burdett knew that Cochrane was just the man for such a crisis, and he knew how to flatter his vanity. "Lord Cochrane," he wrote in August 1825, "is looking very well after eight years of harassing and ungrateful service, and, I trust, will be the liberator of Greece. What a glorious title!" All his Radical friends were in the movement; even old Major Cartwright was dug out to provide one of his paper constitutions for the occasion. As usual, it began hopefully with a statement of "those principles of truth and morality, on which political and social order depend." How the Greek financiers on the London Committee must have laughed! In vain Cochrane's more realistic acquaintances warned him that the modern Greek had nothing in common with his famous ancestors; that the language used by their friends abroad was merely wind in the ears of a population of priests and peasants and pirates, of "counting-house Catilines, bankrupt merchants and intriguing adventurers." Before his death Byron had discovered the truth of all this for himself: "Whoever goes into Greece at present should do it as Mrs. Fry went into Newgate—not in the expectation of meeting with any especial indication of existing probity, but in the hope that time and better treatment will reclaim the present burglarious and larcenous tendencies, which have followed the General Gaol Delivery." And his companion, Trelawny, who was recovering on the island of Zante from wounds received in an attempt made on his life soon after Cochrane's arrival in Greece, adds: "The Greeks love money. Gold is their idol—gold is dearer to them than the bright eyes of their mistresses."

In political matters Cochrane was at the mercy of his friends. He could not but share their generous enthusiasm, however cruel his experience of such movements had already been. He was a professional crusader, and he had no desire or opportunity to re-enter the arid wastes of politics in a country still under the heel of a Tory administration. He was deeply in debt, and he had no other chance of earning a livelihood. This time he did at least embark with his eyes open: "My undertaking will outdo the adventures of Quixote," he told Burdett.

As with the Brazilians, he was particularly careful about the terms of his commission. The Philhellenes, who had succeeded in raising a loan on the London market as the result of the presence of a few adventurous capitalists on the Committee, could afford to be generous in their terms, though they spent two years negotiating with him. It was some time before he actually received his commission as admiral of the Greek navy at a salary of £57,000, to be paid in instalments, though he had originally stipulated that half the sum should be paid in advance. No sooner was this settled than he was persuaded to invest a large part of the sum in a Greek loan, with the surprising result that (according to Greville) he made £100,000 out of it.

On paper the force he was to command looked promising enough. £30,000 was set aside to provide for the building of six steam vessels in Britain and two 60-gun American frigates. The idea of employing such a force was originally that of Captain Abney Hastings, a Trafalgar veteran who was engaged in active service in Greek waters. Writing to Byron in 1823 he laid it down "as an axiom that Greece cannot obtain any decisive advantage over the Turks without a decided maritime superiority; for it is necessary to prevent them from relieving their fortresses and supplying their armies by sea" (which was exactly what Ibrahim was doing from Egypt). Such superiority, Hastings maintained, was only to be won by steamships of 200 tons burden, mounting two long 32-pounder guns fore and aft and a 68-pounder on each side.

These suggestions were evidently the basis of the memorandum submitted by Cochrane to the London Committee in November 1825.

"Required:

"Six steam vessels having each two guns in the bow and perhaps two in the stern not less than 68-pounder long guns.

"The bottoms of two old 74-gun ships, upper decks cut off and heavy cannon mounted on the lower deck.

"These vessels well manned appear to be sufficient to destroy the whole Turkish Naval power.

"Lord Cochrane will give any advice relative to the details that may be required to further the interests of Greece, so far as regards naval matters. But he cannot consistently subject his family to the loss of half of all he is entitled to for seven years' service in South America by offering his services as an Officer. Nor would he under any circumstances engage in the service of Greece as a Naval Commander of their present inefficient naval force.

"Should the Greeks, however, deem Lord Cochrane's services of sufficient importance to them, he will accept two-thirds of what he can show to be due to him in South America and never require the remainder until Greek funds be at par. And further he will serve without pay or other recompense save the proceeds of Captures made from the Enemy as is customary in such cases amongst all civilised nations."

The Committee, having agreed to this curious arrangement, undertook to set about building the fleet required. Had that fleet been built the revolution in naval armaments from sail to steam would have occurred far more speedily than was actually the case. Steamships had been used previously in warfare, for example by Cochrane's pupil, Captain Marryat, in Burma, but never on such a scale. As Lord Exmouth is reported to have said when he heard of the scheme: "Why, it's not only the Turkish fleet, but all the navies in the world, that you will be able to conquer with such craft as these." However, the building of the ships was Cochrane's first disappointment. The hulls were laid down by Brent and the high-pressure non-condensing engines built by Galloway, the talkative Radical engineer who had already failed him when he engined the *Rising Star*. The original contract was for four 50-h.p. steamer engines at a cost of £14,000; at the end of 1825 Galloway had received £23,840 and had not even got three engines ready. Hastings calls him "the most impudent liar I ever met with"; and Ricardo, the Philhellene banker, remarked when the first steamer was launched six months late: "Galloway is the evil genius that pursues us everywhere; his presumption is only equalled by his incompetency, whatever he has to do with us is miserably deficient; we do not think his misconduct has been intentional." On the other hand it is likely that it was so, because we know that, in the style of modern armament firms, he was working on a contract for Ibrahim at the same time.

Hastings did at last set sail in the *Perseverance* (later renamed the *Karteria*) in the summer of 1826, but Cochrane had already gone out to the Mediterranean in despair of her completion. The *Perseverance* was powered with an 84-h.p. engine, and armed with 45-pound mortars, and 68-pound guns. She was the only steamship which actually took part in operations in Greek waters. The *Enterprise*, which sailed early in 1827, arrived too late because she was forced to put into Plymouth for repairs, owing to a burst boiler and a rudder so small that it rendered the ship unmanageable. After the fighting was over Cochrane went out again in the *Mercury*, but he never actually fought a steamship. The remaining three steamships were never built. As for the American frigates, the business was equally mismanaged because the Greek agent fell into the hands of financial sharks (he was actually a Frenchman, not a Greek). One fine, well equipped frigate, the 60-gun *Hellas*, actually reached Greece before Cochrane did, but she cost more than the original sum allocated for two such ships.

While waiting for the fleet to be built, Hastings was able to give his new admiral some idea of the situation he would have to face when he reached the scene of operations. The Greek armies consisted of hordes of undisciplined bandits who had proved themselves guilty of more inhumanity than the Turks themselves. For the first part of the war they were nominally under the command of General Gordon, to whose staff the historian Finlay was attached. At the same time as Cochrane was given the command of the navy, Sir Richard Church was invited (possibly at Cochrane's suggestion) to replace Gordon, and though he had spent a lifetime training Neapolitan levies he failed to maintain discipline among the Greeks, with the result that he achieved even less than Gordon. As for the sailors, they were merely pirates. They invariably refused to fight unless there was material gain in view, and if there was the remotest chance of opposition they sheered off in search of weaker prey. However, under their own leaders Miaoulis and Kanares, patriots of a different pattern, they had achieved some success against the Turks. Of the former, Hastings reported that he was "a very dignified, worthy old man; possesses personal courage and decision, and is less intriguing than any Greek I know." Like Blanco Encelada, both of them magnanimously agreed to serve under Cochrane when he was appointed over their heads (even though Miaoulis had won the only Greek naval victory to date). As to the other leaders, Hastings's reports filled the new admiral with apprehension: "ignorant and dirty"; "drinks three bottles of rum a day"; "undistinguished, except by his colossal stature and ferocious countenance."

Cochrane was still in England waiting for his ships when he was warned that the Tory government intended to prosecute him under the Foreign Enlistment Act. In a hitherto unpublished letter to Burdett, dated 8 November 1825, he writes: "My life is rendered so inquiet by the constant fear of prosecution under the Foreign Enlistment Act which Brougham has given his opinion may be put in force against me, even for my services in Brazil, that I have resolved to place myself on the other side of the water without delay, and tomorrow morning I make the attempt by steamboat from the Tower." He and his wife first went to Boulogne; but they had been there only a few weeks when he was warned of a fresh danger, this time prosecution on account of the capture of a French brig in the Pacific. They escaped to Brussels where, he wrote, he was holding himself in readiness for departure for Greece as soon as the fleet was ready. But there was still no sign of the *Perseverance,* and ultimately Hastings, who had been left behind to superintend matters, bought a schooner called the *Unicorn* "to take out the great man." The Committee urged him to sail without delay—"our only desire is to rescue the millions of souls that are praying a thousand supplications that they may not fall victims to the despair which is only averted by the hope of your lordship's arrival." In May 1826 Cochrane sailed on his last crusade, "more uneasy," wrote his wife, "than I ever before knew him to be."

Off Dartmouth he was still hoping that Hastings in the *Perseverance* would catch him up, "for it would be the height of madness to place myself in the power of a set of savages without force to aid them or protect myself"; especially as he was finding it difficult to discipline the "pack of blackguards" shipped aboard the *Unicorn.* Arrived in the Mediterranean there was still no sign of news of the steamship. However, "I shall not relinquish my purpose without attempting more than I have ever yet done for a nation not my own."

At Marseilles the energetic head of the Swiss Committee, Dr. Gosse, took the initiative in buying him a corvette, the *Sauveur*, which he could take out to Greece to supplement his meagre force. Gosse's description of the tall, weather-beaten seaman who became his lifelong friend, is worth quoting: *"grand et d'une charpente osseuse, solide et sec, cependant peu corpulent. Cheveux rougeâtres, physionomie douce, quoique grave, d'une conversation agréable et nourrie."*

In March 1827, accompanied by Captain Thomas in the *Sauveur*, he reached Greek waters to find the *Hellas* waiting for him. As soon as her American crew turned her over to the Greeks, she was run aground by a mutinous crew; but she was a well equipped ship and Cochrane had no hesitation in hoisting his flag in her. Soon after, the *Perseverance* made a belated appearance, to be renamed the *Karteria* for the Greek service. Mention should also be made of the *Hydra* corvette, commanded by Crosbie, his old flag captain in the Chilean navy.

The new admiral had certainly taken some time to reach the scene of action. But he had good reasons for his delay, which Finlay ignores in his complaint that he "had been wandering about the Mediterranean in a fine English yacht!" The historian regarded the man who intended to be the saviour of Greece with a sober eye: "He was tall and commanding in person, lively and winning in manner, prompt in counsel, and daring but cool in action. Endowed by nature both with strength of character and military genius, versed in naval science both by study and experience, and acquainted with seamen in every clime and country, nothing but an untimely restlessness of disposition, and a too strongly expressed contempt for mediocrity and conventional rules, prevented his becoming one of Britain's naval heroes. Unfortunately, accident, and his eagerness to gain some desired object, engaged him more than once in enterprises which money rather than honour appeared to be the end he sought." The shadow of the *cause célèbre* of 1814 still came between Cochrane and anyone who met him for the first time. However, Finlay testifies to the moral importance of his arrival in Greece: "His influence became suddenly unbounded, and faction for a moment was silenced."

All was chaos when he arrived. Defeated at every point, the Greeks were on the verge of civil war amongst themselves. Missolonghi had lately fallen; Ibrahim controlled the Morea and was indeed at the gates of Athens, where General Fabvier (originally one of Napoleon's officers) with a thousand "patriots" still held out on the

Acropolis. "At this instant," writes Cochrane on the evening of his arrival, "the barbarian Turk is actually demolishing, by the shells which are now flying through the air, the scanty remains of the once magnificent temples." More dispiriting still was the open quarrel between the two Greek governments. Both factions immediately began to intrigue for the support of the newcomer, but for Cochrane unity of command was the first essential, and he began by shaming these men of words into a reconciliation. Having insisted on their joining in the foundation of a National Assembly, "his lordship expressed his regret that so many able and brave military officers as those he saw before him should occupy themselves with civil discussions in the present state of the country." With cutting effect he quoted Demosthenes to his audience: "If, Athenians, you will now, though you did not before, adopt the principle of every man being ready where he can and ought to give his services to the state, to give it without excuse, the wealthy to contribute, the able-bodied to enlist; in a word, if you will become your own masters, and cease expecting to do nothing himself, while his neighbour does everything for him, you will then, with the help of God, get back your own and punish the enemy." He concluded with an appeal to their natural cupidity by promising them another sack of Constantinople if only they would hold together.

Having enforced some semblance of political unity, Cochrane turned his attention to the military situation. By now his prestige was such that he found himself (not in the least to his regret) in the position of generalissimo in the Athens area, the more so because Church spent his time on board his yacht in retirement. Flushed with success, Cochrane's self-confidence was more buoyant than usual, but the situation demanded a cooler judgment than he was capable of. Fabvier was on the point of capitulation to a Turkish army of four times his strength, and it was an army which, though Cochrane did not know it, was in daily expectation of reinforcements. The messages from the beleaguered Acropolis became more and more urgent; food was running out and the garrison could not last much longer. Something had to be done quickly. Cochrane began with one of those addresses in the flamboyant style with which he had been so successful in South America. Raising a standard of his own devising, a blue and white flag with an owl in the centre, he shouted above the cheers which greeted his appearance in the camp: "Soldiers, whoever of you will lodge this flag on the summit of the Acropolis shall receive from me, as a reward for his bravery, a thousand dollars, and ten times that sum shall be my share of the recompense to the force that accompanies him!"

Loud cheers greeted the announcement, but nothing more. A chance encounter with the Turkish forces a few days later proved that the Greeks were capable of following a determined lead. Cochrane happened to be on shore at the time, and with no better weapon than a telescope he led his men in a charge which routed the enemy, cutting off a large force of Albanian levies within the walls of the St. Spiridion monastery, which was speedily reduced to a ruin by the fire of the *Perseverance* and the *Hellas*.

This local success was naturally exaggerated into a victory which roused Church to action. Without taking anyone's advice he concluded an armistice with the St. Spiridion force which would permit them to leave their refuge in safety. This ridiculous compact showed his complete ignorance of Greek psychology. The admiral was on board his flagship with General Gordon and George Finlay when the Albanians began to evacuate their position. "All those men will be murdered!" exclaimed Finlay as he watched the Greeks ominously gathering along the line of retreat. Cochrane turned to Gordon. "Do you hear what he says?" "I fear, my lord," replied the general, "it is true." Fifty yards outside the gate of the monastery the enemy were set upon, and of the two hundred and seventy men who started to run towards the Turkish lines, less than seventy reached safety. The remainder were shot down as they ran, stripped of their clothing, and the bandits who massacred them fought over the spoil.

By the beginning of May, Fabvier declared that he could hold out no longer. The Greek generals did nothing to help him. Sometimes they appeared to be on the point of advancing, but something invariably happened which made them change their plans. From the quarter-deck of the *Hellas* Cochrane watched these dilatory proceedings on the coastal plain with increasing impatience. Every day, sometimes every hour, he sent notes to Church demanding immediate action; the execrable handwriting of these messages, which are preserved in the British Museum, show what a fever of impatience he was in. "Pray let me know if the army *will* or *will not* advance." The present "dastardly gang" of officers will never do anything. Why not sack the lot and appoint fresh leaders? Finally he played the trump card which he had used to such great effect in South America: "I leave to-morrow, 1st, if the army will not march; 2nd, if 2,000 men do not embark and proceed direct to Athens; 3rd, if no other reasonable plan is adopted and be put into action before May 2."

Such behaviour shows that the admiral was usurping military powers to which he had no right. But Church never had the makings of a leader. He was not on the spot when his army did finally advance; his intelligence service was so faulty that he was not warned of the approach of large enemy cavalry reinforcements; his orders were contradictory; he showed no knowledge of the terrain over which the attack was made.

On May 6 the advance on Athens at last began. Each company insisted on building pill-boxes for themselves every few hundred yards. The result was that the element of surprise, on which Cochrane had insisted in his plan of a rapid advance across the plain under cover of darkness, was entirely lacking. The Turkish cavalry, which had arrived the previous night, fell on the Greeks on an open plain in broad daylight. The rout was instantaneous and complete. Cochrane, who was on shore with Dr. Gosse, was caught in the rush towards the sea as the enemy cavalry swept across the plain. Flying from the slaughter of the scimitars, hordes of Greek fugitives made a rush for the ships' boats. The admiral and the doctor were forced back to the beach, and, while Gosse held the painter of the picket boat, Cochrane waded out to seize the oars. Somehow they pushed off without being overset by the fugitives and Cochrane pulled hard for the flagship. Once on board, he trained the guns of the *Hellas* on the cavalry now hewing down the struggling mass at the water's edge. Only after an hour's bombardment did the Turkish horsemen withdraw.

It was the most calamitous defeat the Greek cause had suffered so far. What was left of an army of 15,000 men melted away in a few days. Nearly two thousand men had been cut down by the Turks, and the rest deserted as soon as opportunity provided. Fabvier was forced to surrender the last Greek garrison on the mainland.

With the fall of the Acropolis the situation was worse, far worse, than when Cochrane arrived at the beginning of the year.

In a despondent frame of mind he took the fleet to Poros to review what forces remained faithful to the cause. He had under his command the *Hellas* frigate, the *Sauveur* corvette, and a few Greek brigs manned by pirates, who apparently joined him because trade was slack at the moment. The result of this, his first naval review, was so farcical that it is a tribute to his determination that he did not resign on the spot. One flotilla refused to take station unless the crews were paid there and then, the seamen insolently reminding their commander-in-chief that he had sufficient funds on board the *Hellas* to meet their demands. Cochrane pointed out that so much had been paid out during the attempt to raise the siege of Athens that he could not give them more than a fortnight's wages. The "patriot" seamen spurned the offer and weighed without more ado in order to set off on piratical expeditions of a strictly private nature. Finlay describes the scene: "The afternoon was calm, the sun was descending to the mountains of Argolis, and the shadows of the rocks of Methana already darkened the waters, when brig after brig passed in succession under the stern of the *Hellas*, from whose lofty mast the flag of the High Admiral of Greece floated, unconscious of the disgraceful stain it was receiving, and in whose cabin sat the noble admiral steadily watching the scene."

Such was the proud seaman's first encounter with the Greek. Their seamen were worse, much worse, than anything encountered in South America. His letters are full of stories of their astounding inefficiency and insubordination. Their dark faces, long moustaches fiercely curled to a point, their hair down to their shoulders, voluminous blue cotton trousers bound at the waist with scarlet cummerbunds in which pistols and long knives were stuck, gave them the air of what indeed they really were—an undisciplined gang of pirates. By this date piracy and brigandage had become synonymous with patriotism. One of the chief bases was the Greek "naval" headquarters at Hydra, where the right to search was simply interpreted as the right to steal. Since the chief task of the British Mediterranean Fleet at that date was the suppression of piracy in the Levant, the position of anyone in command of the so-called Greek "navy" was distinctly anomalous. Indeed, the first lord, Melville, admitted that Codrington had been appointed commander-in-chief of that station largely because "he is a person who I have no doubt will *stand up* to Lord Cochrane, and compel him to keep within proper bounds."

The fearsome appearance of Cochrane's men belied their courage. On one occasion he was holding a magic-lantern show on the lower deck. Unwisely he threw on the screen a slide depicting a Turk cutting off the head of a Greek fugitive. The whole audience promptly bolted up the hatches, and some even jumped overboard in their terror, refusing to come on board again until the admiral had calmed their injured feelings. "The obstinate refusal of the Greek seamen to embark or perform the smallest service without being paid in advance, the contempt with which the elder portion of the seamen treated every endeavour to promote regularity and maintain silence in exercising the great guns and other evolutions, rendered their improvement hopeless. . . . The frequent mutinies or resistance to authority, and the numerous instances in which I have been obliged to return to port, or abstain from going to sea, are recorded in the logbook of the *Hellas,* together with the disgraceful conduct of the crew in stripping and robbing prisoners, and their want of coolness in the presence of an enemy exemplified by the firing of upwards of four hundred round shot at the corvette now named the *Hydra,* without hitting the hull of that vessel four times, although she was within a hundred yards of the *Hellas.*" No crew would sign on for more than a month's service, so that training of any kind was out of the question. Frequently the admiral had to maintain discipline by knocking down laggards with his own fists; nor did he ever dare to stir out of his cabin without a loaded pistol.

A few weeks after the review fiasco he was able to collect enough nondescript craft from the islands of the Aegean to sail south with the intention of attacking Ibrahim's fleet in the harbour of Alexandria. The strategic aim was commendable, for Alexandria was the source of all the supplies of the Turkish forces in Greece. As for tactics, if he could defeat a highly disciplined French force in a strong position as had been the case in the Aix Roads, he should have no difficulty in dispersing a heterogeneous assemblage of Egyptian ships. The force at his disposal, however, was hardly comparable. On June 16 the *Hellas,* accompanied by the *Sauveur,* fourteen armed brigs and eight fireships under the command of old Kanares, came in sight of the Egyptian fleet. For the hundredth time the admiral attempted to instil some offensive spirit into his recalcitrant crews. "Brave officers and seamen, one decisive blow and Greece is free. The port of Alexandria, the centre of all the evil that has befallen you, now contains within its narrow bounds numerous ships of war and a multitude of vessels laden with provisions, stores and troops intended to effect your total ruin. The wind is fair for us, and our enterprise is unsuspected. Brave fireship crews, resolve by one moment of active exertion to annihilate the power of the Satrap. Then shall the siege of Athens be raised in Egypt!"

In vain. Kanares was ordered to attack with his "brave fireship crews." Two ships obeyed him and succeeded in destroying a small man-of-war. There was a general movement of alarm in the roadstead. Now was the moment for an attack. But the Greek commanders had interpreted the movement as one of attack, not of confusion. Without paying the smallest attention to the signals flying from the peak of the flagship, they made for the open sea. Next day their admiral rounded up a few fugitives thirty miles out to sea, but the majority had made good their escape back home. On their return to a Greek port even the crew of the *Hellas* deserted in a body.

Cochrane was desperate. He tried to cover up the failure of his force in a grandiloquent letter to his employers: "Your Excellencies may rest assured that our visit to Alexandria will have a powerful effect in paralysing the equipment of an expedition." The result was actually the reverse. Only one miserable Egyptian vessel had been sunk. He had scotched the snake, not killed it. Ibrahim regarded the attack as an affront to his dignity and honour; he pressed on with all the more energy to fit out his invading force, and his fleet put to sea within a few weeks. Over a hundred Egyptian men-of-war reached Navarino in August, thereby destroying the hopes of the Great Powers that the Sultan would settle the Greek business on their own terms without further bloodshed.

It was clear to Cochrane that no such thing as a Greek navy could be made to exist. For the rest of the war he decided to confine his efforts to single-ship actions in home waters; even then only Captain Hastings in the *Karteria* steamship, and Captain Thomas in the *Sauveur* could be relied upon. Such activities were regarded by the government, and even more so by Admiral Codrington in command of the British Fleet based on the Ionian Isles, as merely piratical ventures, an imputation which made Cochrane all the more angry since his professed intention was the extirpation of just such pests. On more than one occasion he rounded up a Greek pirate and sent him ashore to be dealt with by the proper authorities. Prizes such as he himself had hoped to win were few indeed, two being the total during a three months' cruise off the western coasts. A sad falling-off for a man of his record! One of these was a corvette of twenty-eight guns captured near Navarino in August. It was his only real fight during his service in Greek waters. Though for once he was in command of a greatly superior force, the behaviour of his men was such that he had the greatest difficulty in securing the vessel: "The boys behaved pretty well; but the oldest and ugliest and fiercest-looking bravos of Hydra ran to the other side of the deck, roaring like bulls."

In September 1827 he was off Missolonghi making ineffective attempts to capture a fort. It was at this moment that the "untoward event" occurred which miraculously freed Greece at a time when her fortunes seemed hopeless. The Great Powers had long been worrying about the outcome of the revolt. Russia, France and Great Britain had finally reached an agreement that summer to achieve the independence of Greece while maintaining the nominal suzerainty of the Sultan. Cochrane's fiasco at Alexandria had ruined the hopes of a settlement, because it stirred Ibrahim to a more inhuman and truculent behaviour than before. The presence of Codrington's Allied fleet forced him, as well as the rebels, to accept a nominal armistice, the news of which never reached Cochrane and his captains on their cruise in the Gulf of Corinth.

At the time of this temporary settlement Cochrane appears to have been intending an attack on Albania. Codrington interpreted this as a threat to his base at the Ionian Isles, at that time under the British flag; consequently he placed his force in such a position that Cochrane could not carry out his plans, while Ibrahim could not pursue him from Navarino. Cochrane therefore cruised aimlessly south, leaving Hastings and Thomas to attack Turkish shipping in the Gulf of Corinth, which they did with excellent effect, the *Karteria* firing red-hot shot from her 68-pounders and entirely destroying the enemy ships. This brought Ibrahim out from Navarino; but a storm, and Codrington's threat of force if he did not return to port immediately, compelled him to put back again. Instead, a flying column was sent north overland to burn a few more miserable villages and enslave their inhabitants.

Codrington was in a serious dilemma. His orders were extremely equivocal, since on the one hand he had been told to cut Ibrahim's supply route and on the other to avoid any open conflict. Ultimately the duke of Clarence (at that time lord high admiral) and his own conscience urged him to "Go in, my dear Ned, and smash those bloody Turks." On October 20 he decided to enter Navarino Bay and demand an explanation from Ibrahim of his recent brutalities. The Allied fleet anchored in hostile silence alongside the crescent of Turkish ships. Nobody, least of all the commander-in-chief, knew what was going to happen next. A suspicious movement on the part of the

Turkish fireships brought a boat out from a British frigate. A musket-shot broke the stillness of the morning air, and the guns of both fleets went off of their own accord. Four hours later nothing was left of the Turkish fleet but a few blazing hulks.

The freedom of Greece was won by a single battle at sea, but not by the Greek navy. How little its first admiral knew of this far-reaching event is shown in a letter to Dr. Gosse dated October 28: "If you have heard the result of the battle of Navarino pray inform us, we are quite ignorant of everything but that a terrible fight did take place."

Now that their cause had triumphed, and Ibrahim was swept from the seas, the Greek ships degenerated into unashamed piracy. In vain the admiral tried to restrain the ships nominally under his command, but after Hastings's death in action he had no one to rely on. The *Enterprise,* the second of the steamships, made an appearance at the end of the year, but he could not get a crew to man her. Cochrane's position was, indeed, unendurable. The Allied commanders blamed him for piracies committed by ships flying the Greek flag. The Greeks deserted if he dared to put into port. In the end he told the head of the Greek Government that he could do nothing without more seamen at his disposal, and that he intended to raise them in England since they were not forthcoming in Greece. In January 1826 he suddenly left for London. There was an immediate outcry. Luriotis, of the London Committee, regarded his precipitate action as a breach of contract and demanded the return of the £37,000 granted to him when he first went out to Greece. Cochrane replied angrily that it was impossible to command a Greek navy since "there are no naval officers in Greece who are acquainted with the discipline of regular ships of war, the seamen will submit to no restraint, they will not enlist for more than one month, they will do nothing without being paid in advance." To a friend on the Paris Committee he was even more outspoken, declaring that the Greeks "are collectively the greatest cowards (not excepting the Brazilians) I have ever met with. Indeed, though styled commander-in-chief of the Greek naval forces I have, since the 12th of April last, when I hoisted my flag, been in truth under the control of wild and frantic savages, whose acts are guided by momentary impulses or heedless avidity to grasp some immediate pecuniary or petty advantage, regardless of any future benefit, however great, to their country or to themselves."

The Foreign Enlistment Act prevented him from recruiting the men he wanted, so at Dr. Gosse's urgent request he returned to

Greece once more in September, this time in the steamer *Mercury*. He found the situation in no way improved. Count Capodistrias had just been elected president, and his dislike of foreigners was well known. The fleet was still non-existent and the country still in a state of anarchy. On December 15 Cochrane wrote to Gosse: "Glad shall I be when the tops of these mountains sink beneath the horizon, and when new and agreeable objects shall obliterate the names of Mavrocordato, Tombazi and such double dealing knaves from my recollection." Five days later he struck his flag.

A dirty old coasting brig was lent him to return home in, the crew of which took every opportunity to insult their late commander. Fortunately the Russian admiral who had fought at Navarino took pity on him: "I am certain that Lord Cochrane must have suffered greatly from the treatment to which he has been exposed. In proof of my esteem I beg that he will send back to their kennels these miserable causes of his annoyance, and proceed to Malta in one of my corvettes."

Cochrane's last letter to Gosse is a pathetic admission of the results of the last of his quixotic enterprises: "Thank God we are both clear of a country in which there is no hope of amelioration for half a century to come."

$\rightthreetimes$

In His Own Cause

WHEN COCHRANE RETURNED from Greece he was fifty-three years old. He died in 1860 at the age of eighty-five. We have seen him as a crusader fighting in the cause of Reform, as well as in the cause of the liberation of oppressed peoples in America and Europe. In the long years of retirement he fought with equal vigour in his own cause to rehabilitate his honour and his fortunes.

The story is a complicated one of petitions, memorials, pamphlets, lawsuits and pertinacious propaganda to prove his own innocence. The central question, whether he was guilty or not of the Stock Exchange fraud in 1814, can probably never be satisfactorily determined at this date; it is one of those cases in which opinion is always bound to differ on account of the conflicting and incomplete nature of the evidence. No one will ever know how much was truth and how much perjury. Personally, I believe that he was innocent, but for reasons which are not of the sort acceptable in a court of law. His temperament certainly led him to gamble in the funds; but a man of his character would never stoop to criminal methods to do so, nor would he have been so grossly casual in the conduct of the crime had he been implicated. It is unbelievable that a man of his reputation for intelligent preparation of *coups de main* in war would have been so careless in the arrangements of that famous hoax, or would have acted as he did when it was discovered. But even if we grant that he was in some sense guilty, we cannot agree that he deserved the savage sentence inflicted on him. From a legal point of view the case was probably conducted with as much fairness as anyone had a right to expect at that date, but there was undoubtedly a great deal of political animosity in the severity of the punishment inflicted. Whatever the truth, Cochrane did ultimately succeed in convincing the public that he was as good as innocent, and hence that his claims for reinstatement to rank, honour and money was a reparation for the injustice he had suffered.

Crabb Robinson noted his pitiable appearance as he left the court on that terrible 21st of June: "When the sentence was passed he stood without colour in his face, his eye staring and without expression; and when he left the court it was with difficulty, as if he were stupefied."

The memory of that blow was with him until he died nearly half a century later. Scores of times before and afterwards he stood in danger of his life; but that was the one occasion on which his honour was assailed. At the time it looked as if the consequences were irreparable: he lost his name and honour; he was discharged from his profession; his decorations were stripped from him; he was ruined financially. The blow would have killed a lesser man; but, as we have seen, he fought on at home and abroad until the time should come for the last fight in his own defence.

As the political scene began to change from the period of the Tory repression to the more liberal epoch of the 'twenties he decided, on his return from Brazil, to petition the first lord for reinstatement of rank. The answer was a flat refusal. The memory of 1814 was still fresh in the minds of those in authority, and the Foreign Enlistment Act could not be flouted with impunity. "I apprehend," wrote Lord Melville, "that nothing but a free pardon from the Crown can now do away with the effect of the verdict"; and he added that he was not prepared to advise the king to grant such a pardon. We know to-day, from the testimony of Admiral Sir Byam Martin, how impossible such a step would have been. At a state banquet held at Portsmouth soon after the trial the Prince Regent (now George IV) addressed some sixty senior officers of all nationalities; there were also present the king of Prussia and Lord Melville (then, as now, first lord). "In emphatic words," reports Byam Martin, the Prince desired that Lord Cochrane's name should be struck off the Navy List, and that he should be stripped of his honour of the Bath, since His Highness would never permit a service of unblemished honour to be disgraced by Cochrane's continuance as a member. From what we know of Prinny's own character, this gratuitous insult before such distinguished representatives of foreign powers is a fine example of hypocrisy.

Three years later, in 1827, Cochrane returned to the attack. This time he petitioned the more sympathetic figure of the duke of Clarence, at that time lord high admiral, but on the advice of the duke of Wellington his petition was again refused. However, the Tory epoch was fast drawing to a close. In 1830 the duke became William IV, the "Sailor King"; Cochrane's friend Brougham became lord chancellor in the first Whig government; Parliamentary Reform, the cause he had for so long had at heart, was in the air. Greville met him at Florence that year and "told him I thought things would explode in England, which he concurred in, and seemed to like the idea of it, in which we differ, owing probably to the difference of our positions; he has nothing, and I everything, to lose by such an event. . . . It is a pity he ever got into a scrape; he is such a fine fellow, and so shrewd and good-humoured."

The times were auspicious. A cleverly written *Review of the Case of Lord Cochrane*, which sought to lay the blame on the solicitors for the conduct of the defence, was distributed to the king and his ministers by way of a memorial. Grey was impressed, but, as prime minister, bigger problems engulfed him at the moment. He wrote to Burdett, still Cochrane's chief ally: "You may be assured that I have this matter at heart; but I am very unwilling to have it brought into public notice at a moment when the bitter and hostile spirit which prevails in the party most opposed to the Government would be likely to seize upon it as a good question for annoyance."

In July 1831 the old earl of Dundonald died in poverty in Paris. Lady Dundonald, as Cochrane's wife now became, seized the opportunity of a visit to the new king at Brighton to throw herself at his feet and press the new earl's claim to reinstatement. No one could refuse such a gesture on the part of one whose beauty was still so much admired, and whose joyous laughter made her the best of companions. On 2 May 1832 a "free pardon" was granted. The proud Dundonald, as we must now call him, was not entirely satisfied, since a pardon is not the same thing as a reversal of a sentence. Nevertheless it allowed his name to reappear once more in the Navy List with the rank of rear-admiral on half-pay. Soon after he was gazetted Rear-Admiral of the Blue, and in that capacity attended a levee at which he was congratulated on all hands. It was his first appearance in Court society for nearly twenty years.

The outlook for his own future grew brighter with the change of the political climate, as unhappy memories faded with the darker past. In 1841 he was awarded a good service pension. In 1847 he was reinstated in the Order of the Bath as Knight Grand Cross (though his banner, which was recovered from an old curiosity shop, was not replaced in Henry VII's Chapel until a few days before his funeral).

There were some curious preliminaries to this decisive step of restoring him to his honours, which was tantamount to a reversal of the verdict. His friend Brougham informed him that he was not restored earlier because the late king (William IV) had objected to giving him back both his rank and the Bath at the same time. Moreover, in 1832, there had been a rumour that when his uncle, Cochrane Johnstone, heard in his exile abroad that his nephew had been pardoned, he took it as a reflection on his own guilt and threatened to produce damaging evidence of the latter's inculpation. Since nothing more was heard of this evidence, it is doubtful if the jealous old man ever possessed it. Furthermore, before restoring him to the Bath the views of most of the senior admirals in the Navy were sought by Lord Auckland, the first lord and a personal friend of Dundonald's family.

At last Dundonald felt that the days of the Regency, of St. Vincent, Mulgrave, Melville, and Ellenborough, and all those who had disapproved of him and his politics had passed away. As earl of Dundonald, with his Whig sympathies of long standing and his record of services unparalleled by any living seaman, he now had powerful friends—Lord John Russell, the marquis of Lansdowne, the duke of Hamilton, Lord Brougham, Lord Auckland, Douglas Jerrold of *Punch* and Delane of *The Times.* He was no longer ostracised at Court or at the Admiralty. The scene at the muster of all the Knights Grand Cross at Windsor, with Prince Albert as Grand Master of the Order, was symbolic of the change. Of all people, one of his sponsors was the son of Lord Ellenborough. The grandson of the famous old judge, who made it his business to continue the family vendetta a hundred years after its inception, thus comments on his father's behaviour on that occasion: "Taken by surprise, he may well have preferred to act as his sponsor to causing an unseemly squabble in, or almost in, the very presence of the Throne, and I do not see that any inference can well be drawn from his conduct." Possibly; but how much a man like Dundonald with a long memory must have relished the scene!

That was a great year for Dundonald. To crown it the following letter arrived from the first lord at the end of December:

> "I shall shortly have to name a commander-in-chief for the North American and West Indian stations. Will you accept the appointment? I shall feel it to be an honour and a pleasure to have named you for it; and I am satisfied that your nomination will be agreeable to her Majesty, as it will be to the country—and particularly to the Navy."

Next spring he sailed once more, as proud an admiral as ever trod the quarter-deck of a flagship.

Complicated monetary claims against all and sundry mark the next and less pleasing stage in his crusade in his own interest. Here we are on much less certain ground, on account of his wildly exaggerated figures. As a starting point we may consider the extraordinary bill of damages which he prints in his *Observations on Naval Affairs, including instances of Injustice experienced by the Author* (1847), a book which may be regarded as a preliminary draft for his autobiography.

Fines and legal expenses of the trial £5,000
Claim on the British Treasury for 18 years'
 half-pay. 4,000
Loss of legacy from his uncle Basil Cochrane, who
 was "wrought on in his dotage by the aspersions
 and insinuations of those around him" 40,000
"Similar arts were practised on the late Sir Robert
 Preston," resulting in the loss of Culross Abbey
 and estate 50,000
Claims on Chile 26,000
Claims on Brazil for the sequestration of
 estates, etc. 100,000

To which he would like to add £15,000 due for reimbursement for costs of scientific research work (admittedly of a voluntary character), which necessitated the sale of property to that value to creditors. Thus he arrives at the conclusion that he was fined not £1,000, as originally intended, but £240,000. However, he omits to mention the story (of which great play is made in another of his books) that the loyal electors of the city of Westminster made good the £1,000 fine by a penny collection. No wonder that those he regarded as his creditors for these fantastic totals denied their indebtedness.

Taking the Brazil claims first, it will be recalled that he left the service of that country in circumstances which his employers regarded as bordering on desertion. Moreover he left them to deal with a number of legal cases in which his seizure of ships and cargoes were contested by the neutrals involved. With the width of the Atlantic between debtor and creditor, and with the sequestration of his Maranham estates by way of retaliation, the Brazilian Government no doubt regarded the matter as closed. But the Dundonald family was singularly pertinacious where money was concerned. In 1858 appeared the *Narrative of Services in the Liberation of Chili, Peru and Brazil*, an uninspired work largely compiled by Dundonald's literary collaborator in his old age, G. B. Earp. Earp had just completed a *History of the Crimean War* in defence of Admiral Napier, whose conduct of the Baltic Campaign had been much criticised. He was an able pleader, and Dundonald was certainly wise to make use of his services at a time when his own memory was failing. By his will Earp was to receive ten per cent of all moneys extracted from British or foreign governments. That book, and still more the *Autobiography of a Seaman*, which appeared in the following years, was a great success in recalling the attention of the public to Dundonald's past services.

Earp's collaboration ended with the death of the 10th earl. Thereupon the 11th earl engaged a certain Mr. Scully to represent the family interests at Rio, for which he was promised twelve and a half percent of the proceeds. In the course of time the Brazilian Government paid £40,000 of the £100,000 originally claimed. Immediately the other claimants under the will demanded their share; but they had to go to law to get it. In 1878 Earp's heirs were granted £3,000 of the Brazilian payment and £500 of the back pay claims still to be described. At the same time Scully brought an action for £5,000. The earl tried to compromise and delayed payment. In the end he was compelled to pay £2,000.

It would appear that Brazil behaved handsomely in this matter, the more so when their Government paid the debt of honour at the accession of Edward VII. On that occasion a party of Brazilian sailors, along with Dundonald's grandson, paid an official visit to place a wreath on the grave of the old liberator.

The claims on the British Treasury for arrears of pay between the years 1814 and 1832 was a more difficult business. Since Dundonald was never chosen to represent the Scottish peers in the House of Lords, it was left to his friends in the Commons to argue the case. The precedent he had in mind was that of General Wilson, who was discharged from the Army for creating a disturbance at the funeral of Queen Caroline; when he was reinstated his back pay was granted to him. But it was not really a parallel case, for Wilson had never been found guilty of committing a crime. Hence the Dundonald claim rested largely on reversing the verdict passed in 1814.

Technically, this was never achieved. But the success of Dundonald's books went far to rehabilitate his character in the public eye. When he died it was generally felt that the last of the great seamen of the period of the French War had gone, and that he had been shabbily treated by his countrymen. The prominent position given him for his tomb in Westminster Abbey illustrates this. Seventeen years after his death, therefore, his son went down to the House of Commons with a copy of the *Autobiography of a Seaman* in one hand and a petition for payment of arrears of pay in the other. Wisely, he decided to fight on the grounds of sympathy and justice to the memory of a great sailor, rather than demand a re-trial of the Stock Exchange case. The Government declined to accede to his request, so the matter was raised in the House by friends of the family on 10 April 1877. Sir Robert Anstruther moved a petition "praying Her Majesty to be graciously pleased to complete the gracious act of Royal justice which restored the late Lord Dundonald to his rank and honour." He was supported by Lyon Playfair, later Lord Playfair the scientist, with whom Dundonald had deposited his Secret Plans, who said: "Let me read from his autograph will which I hold in my hand, the touching terms in which it is bequeathed. 'I leave exclusively to my grandson Douglas all the sums due to me by the British Government for my important services, as well as the sums of pay stopped (under perjured evidence) for the commission of a fraud on the Stock Exchange. Given under my trembling hand this 21st day of February 1860, the anniversary of my ruin.' "

Now this is an extraordinary statement, because the real will at Somerset House reads very differently. There is nothing in it about a "trembling hand" or "the anniversary of my ruin"; and there is a lot about the ten percent due to Earp. The first paragraph of the real will leaves all the moneys due from the Chilean and Brazilian Governments to be divided equally between his sons Thomas (born in 1814), Horace William Bernardo (born when he was a friend of Bernardo O'Higgins), Arthur Auckland Leopold Pedro (born when he was in the service of the Emperor Pedro), Ernest Grey Lambton Cochrane, excluding the percentage due to Earp. Next he bequeathed to his grandson Douglas, together with a percentage for Earp, "all the moneys due to me from the British Government for my important services. Also the amount due from the British Government of my back pay of which I was injuriously deprived during forced expulsion from the British Navy on perjured evidence which neither the Courts of Law nor the House of Commons would give me the opportunity of rebutting."

The Committee appointed to investigate the claim included, curiously enough, the names of Gurney (son of the prosecuting counsel in 1814) and Butt (a relative of the man in whose innocence Dundonald always believed). As soon as he heard that this Committee had been set up, Ellenborough's eldest surviving son intervened to see that no injustice was done to his parent by reversing the original verdict; at the same time he reprinted two articles from the *Law Magazine* of 1861 containing a document which goes some way to clearing the solicitors, whose conduct of the defence Cochrane had attacked. In consequence the Committee ignored the trial and evaded the obstacles raised by the Ellenborough family by recommending a "reparation," "the justice of which seems to follow by a natural inference from the steps that have been already taken." Their report was passed unanimously by the House, and a grant of £5,000 was made to the petitioner "in respect of the distinguished services of his grandfather." The amount, almost equalling the arrears claimed, was a most satisfactory token in the circumstances. But, as already mentioned, Earp's heirs had to go to law to get their £500 under the terms of the will.

There is another somewhat mysterious figure mentioned in the will—William Jackson, "my steady friend and former secretary"—who benefited to the amount of £100. Just as Earp was partly responsible for the later books which pass under Dundonald's name, so it is probable that Jackson had a finger in the earlier pamphlets. He seems to have entered Cochrane's service in 1811; he followed him out to South America, where he collected what was left of the admiral's papers after the earthquake at Quintero. Indeed he seems to have possessed himself of most of Cochrane's papers, for we find Earp writing to him for material, and again, when he was short of money, he told Dundonald's heir that he possessed over a thousand of the late earl's letters—"I think they would be cheap at a hundred pounds." All he got was £25. From what little is known of him he does not seem to have been a particularly estimable character. Lady Dundonald said of him: "I have always despised the man, and look upon him as the greatest enemy my husband had in life, and the ruin of his purse and character. Alas! Lord Cochrane had much more confidence in him than he deserved."

The Autobiography of a Seaman, which is thus the combined work of Dundonald, Earp, his "friend and literary coadjutor," and Jackson, who provided much of the material, appeared in two volumes in 1859 and 1860. It takes the story of his life to 1814, when he was thirty-nine. The two volumes of the *Narrative of Services in the Liberation of Chili, Peru and Brazil* had appeared two years earlier. Dundonald's son, with the assistance of H. R. Fox Bourne, continued the story from the time he went to Greece up to his death, in two more volumes which were published in 1869. A shorter, one-volume edition of these books was later issued by his grandson. The continued success of these books, together with Fortescue's brilliant little sketch in the *English Men of Action* series (a book which, though it admirably fulfils the aim of the series, does scant justice to his career as a politician or an inventor) appears to have roused the Ellenborough family to do something to redress the balance in favour of their ancestor. The old judge's grandson sought to do this by traducing Cochrane's name anew. A lawyer named Atlay was engaged to reassess the events of 1814 in *The Trial of Lord Cochrane,* an able piece of work in so far as it seeks to prove the assumption on which it is written—that Cochrane was guilty and that the trial was properly conducted. Lord Ellenborough's own *Guilt of Lord Cochrane in 1814* carried the vendetta a stage further in 1914—a centenary volume which, in order to "refute the attacks made on my grandfather," does not limit itself to the events of 1814 but submits Dundonald's whole career to most searching and prejudiced criticism.

Among other things, the *Autobiography of a Seaman* is here called "a fraud on the boyhood of England for over fifty years. It is not an autobiography, it was not even written by a seaman." And of the *Nar-*

rative of Services: "It was the first of a series of Earp-Jackson-Dundon-ald writings, which were written by a certain Mr. Earp, regardless of facts, dates and documents, for the purpose of supporting Lord Dundonald's money claims, of which Mr. Earp himself was to receive a substantial percentage if his writings met with the desired success."

They were certainly successful, but to call them fraudulent is the grossest exaggeration. There is nothing wrong in an old man, unaccustomed to literary work, engaging the services of someone to help him: Napier did it, and Lord Ellenborough himself employed Mr. Atlay. Dundonald made no secret of the help he received from Earp, since he expresses his gratitude to him in each of the prefaces for having "unravelled what, in the lapse of time, had become the almost inextricable confusion of my papers. That, however, has, with his assistance, been accomplished in such a way as to base upon original documents every incident contained in the work—the more important of these documents being adduced, so as to admit of neither doubt nor question." Earp later explained the method on which they worked: "My general practice in writing that book was to write it from his documents, not from his words, because I frequently found his memory fail of late years. I wrote it from his documents, and in general he made little if any alteration, he was quite content with it."

Strictly speaking, therefore, the book is not an autobiography. But if Earp held the pen, Dundonald revised and dictated most of the material. Naturally the volumes seek to give a sympathetic picture of the subject; as Earp told Jackson, "my object is to clear Lord Dundonald's character." Hence Dundonald's biographer must use the material with circumspection. Where so much political and personal prejudice is involved, where the subject himself is such an extraordinary amalgam of unselfishness and spitefulness, the biographer must make up his own mind where Cochrane was right and where he was wrong. In the *Autobiography,* of course, Cochrane is always right. He appears as an heroic figure compassed about with the meanest enemies.

Readers of this book will, it is hoped, realise how far from the truth that picture is. Cochrane was in many senses a great man; though not of unblemished integrity, he did fight the forces of corruption and obscurantism at a period when those forces predominated; he did live up to his fine maxim that "a British nobleman is a free man, and therefore has a right to assist any country endeavouring to re-establish the rights of aggrieved humanity," though at the same time he would not have been human if he had not tried to make something out of it. He invariably championed the cause of the under-dog, partly because he himself was a man with a grievance, partly because he genuinely strove for the democratic ideal of freedom. Being far from modest, he inevitably exaggerates his own importance in these crusades. But that is not to impugn the veracity of the book which passes under his name. The truth is that, in so far as his record eschews personalities, it is as reliable as any book can be which deals with such a wide range of facts, involving so many controversial episodes, both naval and political. But wherever money or personal prejudices are involved the reader will be wise to be on his guard. Dundonald was an extremely likeable character, and in many ways a most estimable one, but he was a man of violent prejudices, and it needs little critical sense to see that his portrait of St. Vincent, for example, is a travesty of the truth. There are many dull and many irritating passages in the *Autobiography of a Seaman;* many relevant facts are distorted or omitted; one has always to reckon with the ulterior aim with which the book was composed; but taken as a whole it fully deserves its fame as one of the most fascinating narratives of an extraordinary career ever written.

CHAPTER V

Last Years

I T IS INTERESTING to compare the portraits of Cochrane in his thirties by Stroehling and Allan Ramsay as a dashing young captain in a theatrical pose, with a photograph of the venerable patriarch in his eighty-fifth year. Dundonald's uniform of an Admiral of the Fleet, bedecked with orders and decorations and gold lace, seems to hang loosely on his shrunken frame; but the face is impressive, the eyes shrewd and full of vitality, the jaw determined. There is no trace of senility here: he was active and vigorous to the last.

Essentially a man of action, it is significant that he left the composition of his memoirs to the last years of his life. When he was not fighting, he was interesting himself in mechanical things, giving evidence of that insatiable curiosity which he inherited from his father. Not that he was anything of a scientist, but he had a mechanical aptitude for inventing and improving things. During the long period he lived in retirement after his return from Greece he had the opportunity to satisfy his ingenious turn of mind. A born reformer, every novelty had an attraction for him. His mind was always a generation ahead of those of his contemporaries whom he was apt to regard as supine conservatives. Hence the multitudinous variety of his inventions—from Turkish baths (by which he cured his friend Dr. Gosse of a fever in Greece) to smoke screens and a Thames Embankment.

The majority of his improvements were naturally connected with ships. One of the earliest was the construction of a convoy lamp to prevent the dispersal of ships in convoy and the consequent delays and dangers. The letter sending specifications of this was despatched to the Admiralty a few days after the Stock Exchange hoax occurred. Of course it was ignored, but he was able to win the £50 prize offered a few years later by entering his lamp under another person's name.

We have already seen something of his use of steamships in warfare. Like Symington and Fulton, he was far in advance of his time on this question, as can be seen from the fact that seven years after his *Rising Star* had reached the Pacific there were only three steamboats in the Navy, all of them engaged on the sort of work we see in Turner's *Fighting Téméraire* being towed to her last berth. There were sound reasons for the unpopularity of these early vessels: their paddles interfered with the mounting of guns broadside; they were vulnerable, dirty, noisy, expensive, and unreliable; but the future was inevitably theirs. Cochrane estimated that he spent some £15,000 on steamship improvements out of his own pocket. Contrast this with Lord Melville's views, first lord at the time the *Perseverance* was being used to such effect in Greece: "Their Lordships feel it their bounden duty to discourage, to the utmost of their ability, the employment of steam vessels, as they consider that the introduction of steam is calculated to strike a fatal blow to the naval supremacy of the Empire."

That was the attitude Cochrane had to contend with at first. However, Melville's successor, Sir James Graham, knew better, and he did his best to help him. "It is impossible to over-estimate the paramount importance of steam in future naval operations," he told Dundonald in 1834, "and it is fortunate that you have directed so much of your attention to the subject." But the old indifference returned. Some sentences from a letter to the Admiralty in 1843 show how far ahead Dundonald was looking, and if the authorities had been quicker to take his advice the Navy would not have been caught in the early stages of the transition from sail to steam by the outbreak of the

Crimean War: "I believe that all our old vessels of war, save the class of 80-gun ships and a few first-rate and large frigates, are almost worthless; whilst our steam department is deficient in most of the properties which constitute effective vessels. No blockades worthy of the name can now be maintained by fleets of sailing ships." And again in 1847 (the year in which his *Observations on Naval Affairs* told the public much more to the same effect): "The timidity as to change caused many years to elapse after the commercial use of steam vessels before the naval department possessed even a tugboat.... Permanent blockades, my lord, are now quite out of the question; and so, in my opinion, are all our ordinary naval tactics. A couple of heavy line-of-battle ships suddenly fitted, on the outbreak of war, with adequate steam power, would decide the successful issue of a general action." However, he was not the only inventor to suffer from the dilatoriness of war departments: the familiar story continues from the days of Coles' epoch-making turret guns to the days of tanks and aircraft. One of Dundonald's contemporaries gave it as his experience that "generally speaking, if it is a matter connected with ship building or fitting, it is submitted to the Surveyor of the Navy, and, in common language, he pooh-poohs it.... I very much question whether you will find one single instance in which an inventor has gone to the Surveyor's office and received an acknowledgment of his invention having been good."

The *Rising Star* of 1818, a full-rigged sailing vessel with auxiliary steam powered by two 45-h.p. engines and a retracting internal paddle (similar to Symington's *Charlotte Dundas*), was his earliest experiment. This was the mysterious contraption described by Captain Bissell (probably the Lieutenant Bissell of the Aix Roads explosion vessel) to Farington the artist. He told him that Cochrane was building for his own amusement at a cost of £20,000 a 500-ton vessel which "had oars to be worked by *steam* in calm weather, for which purpose he has put 200 chaldrons of coal in her. The oars do not appear at the *side of the vessel* but pass through the *bottom*, and for security iron plates are laid over the lower part of the ship. When the oars are worked the consumption of coals will be four chaldrons in twenty-four hours."

In 1834 Dundonald produced one of the first rotary engines, the advantages of which over the reciprocating type he describes in a pamphlet now in the British Museum. When used in H.M.S. *Firefly* it was not entirely successful, but a standard Victorian work on the subject describes it as "the most perfect engine of the class that has yet been projected." In 1843 he patented a new type of propeller in which the blades, instead of being set at right angles with the shaft, formed an angle with it to correct the centrifugal action of the screw. The first naval vessel fitted with a screw, the *Rattler*, was built that year, and in her famous tug-of-war with the *Alecto* paddle steamer two years later proved to everyone's satisfaction that the days of the screw-propelled warship had dawned. Dundonald also appreciated the importance of streamlining in the design of the hull: he proposed to build a frigate in which there should be "the uniform delineation of parabolic curves, forming a series of lines presenting the least resistance in the submerged portion of ships and vessels."

This was the *Janus* paddle steamer, which an enlightened Admiralty consented to build on his specifications. She was launched in 1845 and incorporated most of his improvements, including four boilers in which tubes were substituted for flat flues. There is a model of her engines in the Science Museum, the power being produced by four tubular boilers with three furnaces each; we are told that the pressure rarely exceeded 30 lbs. Unfortunately the displacement of the frigate was miscalculated (Dundonald, of course, suggested sabotage) and she was found to lie much deeper in the water than had been expected, so that her low freeboard—like that of the ill-fated *Monitor*—made her a dangerous vessel in rough weather.

These experiments were interrupted by his appointment to the American station. He sailed in the *Wellesley,* one of the old type of line-of-battle ship, accompanied by the *Scourge* steam vessel. It is a curious illustration of that transitional period in naval architecture that it was his practice to get the *Scourge* to tow the *Wellesley* in calm weather, while the *Wellesley* took the *Scourge* in tow when the wind was favourable.

Just before his death one of the recurrent French war scares (this time due to the great advances in naval architecture made by Napoleon III) gave him the opportunity of renewing his advice on naval strategy in words which were quoted with great effect in a debate on the policy of fixed fortifications for national defence. Having experienced the weakness of such methods at places like Valdivia and Callao, he was at all times a convincing opponent of the policy of fixed defences. So at the end of his account of his Secret Plans in his autobiography he attacked the Maginot Line attitude of a group of his contemporaries in words which should never be forgotten by those responsible for our defence methods:

"Immovable stations of defence, as a protection against invasion, are not only costly and of doubtful utility, but a reliance on them is, in my mind, an indication of a declining state. It is little short of imbecility to suppose that because we erect great imposing fortifications an enemy will come to them when he can operate elsewhere without the slightest regard to them; and the more so as the common experience of warfare will tell him, that numerous fortifications are in the highest degree national weakness, by splitting into detail the army which ought to be in the field against him, but who are compelled to remain and take care of their fortifications. Yet half the sum required for fortifications as defences in time of war would suffice to place the Navy in a condition of affording far more effectual protection. There is no security equal to that which may be obtained by putting it out of the power of the enemy to execute hostile intentions."

Another project which he canvassed in his last years—that of a "mosquito fleet"—points forward to the days of motor torpedo-boats and gunboats. It is based on the sound principle that in an offensive weapon it is fire power that counts, a principle on which the "all-big-gun" dreadnoughts were later built. "Give me," he used to say, "a fast small steamer, with a heavy long-range gun in the bow, and another in the hold to fall back upon, and I would not hesitate to attack the largest ship afloat." "As large a gun as possible in a vessel as small and swift as possible, and as many of them as you can put upon the sea" was his ideal.

He died a few months after the *Warrior* was launched, the ship which produced a revolution in naval architecture because she ushered in the age of the ironclads. The last of Brunel's epoch-making series of ships, the *Great Eastern*, the first of the Atlantic leviathans, had been built only two years previously. So Dundonald's name may stand among the pioneers of the modern steamship, along with those of Symington and Fulton, Pettit Smith and Ericsson—that band of pioneers on both sides of the Atlantic who were richer in expectation than achievement.

He followed more closely in his father's footsteps with his numerous patents for the use of tar. At first his work was as little appreciated as the old earl's had been. A type of preservative, for instance, which he recommended for woodwork proved a failure because the public disliked the smell. But his visit to the Trinidad Pitch Lake while on the West Indies station revived his interest. He describes it as three miles wide, and at that date given up as useless for commercial purposes. He himself saw a great future for its products in their "application to the pavements of London and other cities." On his return he patented a number of uses of bitumen, such as that of a surface mixture and a method of coating and insulating pipes, etc. While he was still at sea he tried to use bitumen mixed with coal as fuel for the *Scourge*. Ten years later Anthony Trollope visited the great Pitch Lake "of which that indefatigable old hero, Lord Dundonald, tried hard to make wax candles, and oil for burning. The oils and candles he did make, but not, I fear, the money which should be consequent on their fabrication. I have no doubt, however, that we shall all have wax candles from thence, for Lord Dundonald is one of those men who are born to do great deeds of which others shall reap the advantages. One of these days his name will be duly honoured for his conquests as well as for his candles."

DUNDONALD SAILED for Halifax as commander-in-chief of the North American and West Indies station in the spring of 1848. A peace-time cruise such as this was not much to the liking of his aggressive temperament, but he must have felt a considerable pride in hoisting his pennant after so many vicissitudes, and he certainly made a thorough inspection of his command. The period was one during which imperial feeling was at a low ebb, when colonies were regarded as millstones about the neck of the mother country, which was advancing by great strides into the era of Free Trade. Dundonald's keen eye discerned the disastrous consequences of this attitude. After his death a brief account of what he saw and felt was published under the clumsy title of *Notes on the Mineralogy, Government and Condition of the British West Indies and North American Maritime Colonies*. Before that, in letters to *The Times*, he had attempted to rouse the conscience of his countrymen to what was happening on the other side of the Atlantic. He had already pointed out the strategic importance of the Falkland Islands, which had been abandoned as useless, in consequence of which they were resettled. The nation reaped the reward of his foresight in 1914 and again at the beginning of the last war, when the *Graf Spee* could never have been cornered if the Falklands had not been our fuelling base in the South Atlantic.

He discerned the same policy of drift in the North Atlantic. "In Newfoundland there is no income whatsoever derived from the soil—no mines in activity—no capitalist having interest from his funds—no foreign trade or trade at all, except the articles of mere necessary consumption, with the exception of fish," and even this occupation was rapidly falling into the hands of the French and the Americans. In Nova Scotia no effort was made to exploit the coal measures, a matter of the first importance in view of the needs of the fleet on the other side of the Atlantic in the coming age of steam.

The condition of the West Indies was worse, because the emancipation of the slaves and the policy of Free Trade had ruined planters and negroes alike, the latter being reduced to a state of poverty and idleness which was worse than their condition as slaves. He was shocked by the destitution, dirt, and unhealthiness of the islands: "So long as our North American possessions [and by that he meant all our colonies] shall continue attached to the British Crown, their interests ought not to be surrendered to the view of the presumed interests of Great Britain, but considered as part of the whole, even if maintained at the cost of some slight sacrifice." The recent colonial development grants show that we have only just begun to learn the lesson he taught a hundred years ago.

Of all our possessions out there he found Jamaica the worst—"negroes in rags, lying about the streets of Kingston; the gaols full; the Port is destitute of shipping, the wharves abandoned and the store houses empty." He concluded his visit with a letter in his old style to the mayor, a copy of which he forwarded to the Admiralty to urge them to do something about the state of the naval barracks and hospitals: "Never have I seen a place so disgustingly filthy, or which could give so bad an opinion to foreigners of British Colonial Administration, as the town of Port Royal."

On his return he found events moving towards war with Russia. Two fleets would have to be employed, one in the Baltic and one in the Black Sea. After so many years of peace it was a difficult matter to choose suitable commanders. The mechanical process of promotion by seniority (which he himself had attacked) brought to the top men whose sole qualification for command was their advanced age. How the command of the Baltic went by default to Sir Charles Napier (and even he was nearly seventy) is pathetically clear from a letter from Sir James Graham to the Queen. The two senior admirals on the active list were Lord Dundonald and Sir William Parker. The latter's health was failing; as for the former, he "is seventy-nine years of age, and though his energies and faculties are unbroken, and with his accustomed courage he volunteers for the service, yet on the whole there is reason to apprehend that he might deeply commit the force under his command in some desperate enterprise, where the chances of success would not counteract the risk of failure and of the fatal consequences which might ensue. Age has not abated the adventurous spirit of this gallant officer, which no authority could restrain; and being uncontrollable it might lead to unfortunate results. The Cabinet, on the most careful review of the entire question, decided that the appointment of Lord Dundonald was not expedient."

What a tribute to Dundonald's vitality! But even he realised that he was too old for the post. One of his own midshipmen, Houston Stewart, was now an admiral in the Black Sea. "Believe me," he told Napier, "that I sympathise with you, but do not envy the exalted position in which you have been placed, knowing that my remaining energies are incapable of effecting objects which you have already accomplished." Unfortunately, Napier failed to accomplish anything at all. Greville voiced the general feeling that his appointment was a mistake, and that, though Dundonald was too old, he was certainly "a far abler man."

As we have seen in recounting the story of his Secret Plans (see page 105), the gallant old man did not consider himself too old for a subordinate position in which he could supervise their use against the fortifications of Cronstadt and Sebastopol. He bombarded the Admiralty with requests to seize the opportunity of trying them out, and we can imagine with what impatience he witnessed the sluggish and indecisive naval operations of that war, not to mention the incredible inefficiency of the Army authorities. We cannot tell whether his plans would have succeeded, but of course he continued till his death supremely confident in their efficacy.

A final step in the reinstatement of his fame and character came shortly before his death, when the prince consort invited him to become the Navy's representative amongst the Elder Brethren of Trinity House. In reply Dundonald said: "I shall ever look forward with anxiety to prove my devotion and gratitude to her most gracious Majesty for the signal acts of justice and favour, and to your Royal Highness for this highly appreciated mark of your consideration."

The wheel had come full circle. The rebel of half a century before, the sea wolf whose aggressive temperament made him so many enemies, the cantankerous demagogue who bitterly criticised what had for so long been taken for granted, the unconventional adventurer whom the rulers of those days covered with contumely, had become one whom the Crown loaded with honours and whose services were rewarded by a succession of governments. He himself described the moral of his chequered career in terms in which the old sense of grievance still echoes: "That they who, in political matters, propose to themselves a strict and rigid adherence to the truth of their convictions, irrespective of personal consequences, must expect obloquy rather than reward; and they who obstinately pursue their professional duty in the face of routine and official prejudice, may think themselves lucky if they escape persecution." Unfortunately he and the Admiralty never agreed on the interpretation of the words "professional duty." Nevertheless he had the satisfaction of admitting that he had lived to see the adoption of the very principles for which he had fought, and the consolation of knowing that his devotion to a "noble profession" had not gone unrecognised. His remarkable career surely justifies his hope that he left "no unworthy legacy to my country."

At the time of his death he was living at the house of his eldest son in Kensington. It was here that he died peacefully on 31 October 1860, only a few months after the publication of the last volume of his autobiography.

His family were given the choice of a funeral at St. Paul's or the Abbey. They chose the latter on account of the old warrior's long connection with the City of Westminster. Admiral Seymour, his successor in the *Pallas* and his supporter in the Aix Roads; Admiral Grenfell, his second in command in South America; the Brazilian Minister; Captain Schomberg, the naval biographer; Lord Brougham, for fifty years his friend and ally, were among the pall-bearers and mourners. He was borne to his resting-place by the very door through which his banner had been ignominiously kicked half a century before. His conspicuous tombstone is to be found in the nave near the grave of the Unknown Warrior. Inscribed on it are the following words:

HERE RESTS IN HIS 85TH YEAR
THOMAS COCHRANE
10TH EARL OF DUNDONALD
BARON COCHRANE OF DUNDONALD
OF PAISLEY AND OF OCHILTREE
IN THE PEERAGE OF SCOTLAND
MARQUIS OF MARANHAM IN THE
EMPIRE OF BRAZIL
G.C.B. AND ADMIRAL OF THE FLEET
WHO BY THE CONFIDENCE WHICH HIS GENIUS
HIS SCIENCE AND EXTRAORDINARY DARING
INSPIRED BY HIS HEROIC EXERTIONS IN THE
CAUSE OF FREEDOM AND HIS SPLENDID
SERVICES ALIKE TO HIS OWN COUNTRY
GREECE BRAZIL CHILI AND PERU
ACHIEVED A NAME ILLUSTRIOUS THROUGHOUT
THE WORLD FOR COURAGE PATRIOTISM
AND CHIVALRY
BORN DEC. 14, 1775   DIED OCT. 31, 1860

BIBLIOGRAPHY

GENERAL

Works by Dundonald—
Autobiography of a Seaman (2 vols., 1859, 1860).
Narrative of Services in Chili, Peru and Brazil (2 vols., 1858).
Life of Thomas Cochrane, 10th Earl of Dundonald (2 vols., 1869), by 11th Earl of
   Dundonald and H. R. Fox Bourne.
Observations on Naval Affairs (1847).
*Notes on the Mineralogy, etc., of the British West Indies and North American
   Colonies* (1861).
Letter to Lord Ellenborough (1814).

BIOGRAPHIES

J. W. Fortescue, *Dundonald (English Men of Action Series)* (1906).
E. G. Twitchett, *Life of a Seaman* (1931).
"Taffrail," *Men o' War* (1929).

PART I

CHAPTER I.—**The Captain of the** *Speedy*
A. and N. Clow, in *Economic History Review*, XII, 1942.
R. Devereux, *J. L. Macadam* (1936), 42.
W. H. Smyth, *Capt. Beaver, His Life and Services* (1829).

CHAPTER II.—**The Cruise of the** *Speedy*
Naval Chronicle, III, 307; VI, 320; XXII, 5, 7.
James, *Naval History of Great Britain,* III, 96–108.
J. Ross, *Life of Saumarez* (2 vols., 1838).
Letters of St. Vincent, Navy Records Soc., I, 183, 191.

CHAPTER III.—**The First Quarrel**
J. S. Tucker, *Memoirs of the Earl of St. Vincent* (1844).
E. P. Brenton, *Life of Lord St. Vincent.*
Letters of St. Vincent, Navy Records Soc., I, 222, 348, 353; II, 194, 337,
    344, 431.
Letters of Admiral Markham, Navy Records Soc., 153, 366, 369.
Letters of Byam Martin, Navy Records Soc. (1901), Introduction.

CHAPTER IV.—**The Golden** *Pallas*
Hist. MSS. Com., 10th Report, IX, 552.
Naval Chronicle, xiii, 243, 315, 329, 358.

CHAPTER V.—**The Cruise of the** *Imperieuse*
Public Record Office, Adm. 37/1457 (Muster Book).
Public Record Office, Adm. 51/2462 (Captain's Log).
James, *Naval History,* vol. iv.
Naval Chronicle, xvii, 167; xxii, 285; xxxii, 201.
Christopher Lloyd, *Captain Marryat and the Old Navy* (1939).
F. Marryat (Mrs. Ross Church), *Life and Letters of Capt. Marryat*
    (1872), i.
E. P. Brenton, *Naval History,* iv, 25.
Crawford, *Reminiscences of a Naval Officer* (1851), i, 60.
H. W. Richmond, *Essay and Studies of English Association* (1944).

CHAPTER VI.—**The Battle in the Aix Roads**
Public Record Office, Adm. 57/2462 (Captain's Log).
James, *Naval History,* iv.
Christopher Lloyd, *Captain Marryat and the Old Navy* (1939).
Lady Chatterton, *Memorial of Admiral Lord Gambier* (1861), ii.
Naval Chronicle, xxi, xxii, *passim.*
W. Richardson, *A Mariner of England* (1908).
Letters of Byam Martin, Navy Records Soc. (1901), iii, 308, 329.

CHAPTER VII.—**The Court Martial**
Lady Chatterton, *Memorial of Admiral Lord Gambier* (1861), ii.
Naval Chronicle, vol. xxii (includes shorthand minutes by
    W. B. Gurney).
Annual Register, 1809.

PART II

CHAPTER I.—**The Cause of Reform**
W. Cobbett, in *Political Register,* ix, 968, 970, 971.
G. D. H. Cole, *Life of Cobbett* (1925), 113, 117.
M. Roberts, *The Whig Party* (1939), 187.
Graham Wallas, *Life of Francis Place* (1898).
Place MSS., British Museum, 27, 850; 27, 838; 27, 840.
F. Horner, *Memoirs* (2 vols., 1843).
M. W. Patterson, *Sir F. Burdett and his Times* (2 vols., 1931).
Life and Correspondence of Major Cartwright, ed. by his Niece (2 vols., 1826).
Memoirs of Henry Hunt, ed. Huish (1836), ii, 391.
Crabb Robinson, *On Books and Writers,* ed. Morley (1938), i, 61.

CHAPTER II.—**Prize Courts and Secret Plans**
Naval Chronicle, xvii, 66; xxv, 299; xxx, 129–34.
Letters of St. Vincent, Navy Records Soc., ii, 33, 446–68.
Lieut. P. W. Brock, in *Mariner's Mirror,* April 1930.
Panmure Papers (1908), i, 340.
W. Churchill, *World Crisis,* ii, 81.
12th Earl of Dundonald, *My Army Life* (1926), 331.
C. N. Parkinson, *Life of Exmouth* (1937), 393.
Public Record Office Adm. 1/5632.

CHAPTER III.—**The Stock Exchange Trial**
Trial of Lord Cochrane and Others, shorthand notes by W. B. Gurney, 1814.
The Trial of Lord Cochrane before Lord Ellenborough, J. B. Atlay (1897).
The Law Magazine, 1861 (reprinted as review of the *Autobiography of a Seaman,* by H. Spencer Law, 1877).
De Berenger, *The Noble Stockjobber* (1816).
E. D. Law, *The Guilt of Lord Cochrane* (1914).
A. Mackenrot, *Secret Memoirs of A. Cochrane Johnstone,* etc. (1814).
Lord Campbell, *Lives of the Chief Justices.*
Lord Brougham, *Statesmen of George III* (1839).
W. Cobbett, in *Political Register,* July 1814.
House of Lords Committee for Privileges on motion of Earl of Dundonald, 1861, 1862.

CHAPTER IV.—**In the Wilderness**
W. Cobbett, in *Political Register,* August 1816.
S. Bamford, *Passages in the Life of a Radical* (1844), i.
R. Coupland, *William Wilberforce* (1923).
The Times, 12 July 1814.
Creevey Papers, ed. Maxwell (1905), 203.
Farington Diary, ed. Greig (1928), vii, 223.

Part III

CHAPTER I.—**The Liberation of Chile and Peru**

W. B. Stevenson, *Historical and Descriptive Narrative of 20 Years' Residence in S. America* (3 vols., 1825).

Lady Calcott (Mrs. Maria Graham), *Journal of a Residence in Chili* (1824).

J. Miers, *Travels in Chili and the Plate* (2 vols, 1826).

General W. Miller, *Memoirs* (2 vols., 1829).

Basil Hall, *Journal on the Coast of Chili,* etc. (1824), i.

CHAPTER II.—**In the Service of Brazil**

J. Miers, *Travels in Chili and the Plate* (2 vols., 1826).

General W. Miller, *Memoirs* (2 vols., 1829).

Lady Calcott (Mrs. Maria Graham), *Journal of a Residence in Chili* (1824).

A. Caldeclough, *Travels in S. America* (2 vols., 1825).

CHAPTER III.—**The Greek War of Independence**

Finlay, *History of the Greek Revolution,* ii.

M. W. Patterson, *Life of Sir F. Burdett,* i, 348.

R. H. Galloway, *Refutation of Calumnious Statements* (1871).

K. Luriottis, *Correspondence entre deux Philhellènes, le docteur Gosse et l'amiral Cochrane* (1919).

S. Lane Poole, "Sir R. Church," *English Historical Review,* 1890.

British Museum, Letters from Cochrane to Church, Hobhouse, Burdett, etc.; Auckland MSS. 34, 459; Add. MSS. 36, 461; 36, 464; Place MSS. 36, 544.

Piracy in the Levant, ed. Pitcairn Jones. Navy Records Soc., 1934.

Jurien de la Gravière, *La Station du Levant* (1876), ii, 58, 103.

Historical Manuscripts Commission Reports, Bathurst MSS., 613 (Melville to Bathurst).

CHAPTER IV.—**In His Own Cause**

Crabb Robinson, *Diary,* ed. Sadler (1869), i, 432.

Letters of Byam Martin, Navy Records Soc. (1901), iii, 198.

Greville, *Journal,* ed. Reeve (1875), i, 301.

Greville, *Diary,* ed. Enfield (1883), i, 149.

M. W. Patterson, *Life of Sir F. Burdett,* i, 355.

Lord Ellenborough, *The Guilt of Lord Cochrane in 1814* (1914).

Times Law Reports, 1878.

Hansard, 10 April 1877.

CHAPTER V.—**Last Years**

Farington Diary, ed. Greig (1928), viii, 184.

British Museum MSS, 38, 781.

Hansard, April–June, 1855; 4 April and 19 May 1862.

F. Boyson, *The Falkland Islands,* 106.

C. S. Parker, *Life of Sir J. Graham* (1907), ii, 228.

H. Noel Williams, *Life of Sir C. Napier* (1917), 333.

Greville, *Memoirs,* ed. Strachey and Fulford, vii, 16.

INDEX

Aix Roads, Battle of, 36, 55 ff.
Alexandria, 179
Algeciras, Battle of, 23
Allemand, Adm., 55, 77
Ancon, 149, 154
Anstruther, Sir R., 191
Atalante, 99
Athens, 174–8
Atlay, J. B., 190
Auckland, Lord, 187
Autobiography of a Seaman, 189, 192–4

Bacon, Lord, 11
Bahia, 160–2
Bamford, S., 131, 137
Barfleur, 13
Basque Roads, *see* Aix Roads
Beaver, Lt., 14
Berenger, R. de (alias du Bourg), 116 ff.
Best, Serjeant, 120, 122
Blanco Encelada, Adm., 143, 144
Bolivar, S., 141, 157
Bradshaw, Cavendish, 85

Brenton, E. P., 40
Brenton, Sir J., 17, 24, 40, 103
Brougham, Hon. Lord, 67, 130, 186, 187, 203
Burdett, Sir F., 76, 83, 90–6, 120, 128–37, 169, 173, 186
Butt, H. G., 116 ff., 191
Byron, Lord, 168, 169

Caesar, 65
Calcutta, 59, 63, 65
Caledonia, 60, 63
Callao, 145, 148, 149
Calpe, 23
Campbell, Lord, 128
Canning, G., 93
Castlereagh, Lord, 129
Cartwright, Major, 93, 94, 130, 169
Caulfield, E., 44
Church, Sir R., 172, 175, 176–7
Churchill, Winston, 113
Clarence, Duke of, *see* William IV
Clarendon, Earl of, 67

Cobbett, Henry, 42, 144
Cobbett, William, 84, 85–6, 96, 100, 121, 128, 130, 136
Cochrane
Archibald (brother) 15, 17, 21
Adm. Sir Alexander (uncle), 12, 28, 30, 117
Basil (uncle), 131, 188
Hon. Basil (brother), 11, 59
Lady Cochrane, Countess of Dundonald (*née* Barnes), 131, 186
Archibald, 9th Earl of Dundonald (father), 8–10, 28, 130
Thomas, 11th Earl (son), 189, 190
Douglas, 12th Earl (grandson), 113
THOMAS, LORD COCHRANE, 10th EARL OF DUNDONALD Character and appearance, 7, 83, 98, 145, 173, 184, 193, 203. Joins Navy, 12. Court-martialled, 14. Appointed to *Speedy*, 15. Captured, 23. Promoted captain, 27. Appointed to *Arab*, 31, to *Pallas*, 33, to *Imperieuse*, 38. At Rosas, 49. At Aix Roads, 55. Gambier's court martial, 70. Resigns from Navy, 79. M.P. for Honiton, 84; for Westminster, 89. Besieged in Piccadilly, 95. Goes to Malta, 103. Secret Plans, 105, 202. Stock Exchange fraud, 116. Dismissed from Navy and House of Commons, 128. Westminster election 1814, 130. Order of Bath, 68, 131, 187. Marriage, 131. Escapes from prison, 132–3. Fined, 134. Admiral of Chile, 141. Valdivia, 146. Cuts out *Esmeralda*, 149. Admiral of Brazil, 159. Attacks convoy, 162. Returns to England, 166. Admiral of Greece, 170. Becomes 10th Earl, 186. Rear-Admiral, 187. Reinstatement claims, 188. Books, 188, 192. Will, 190–91. Inventions, 195–6. Crimean War, 201–2. Death, 203.
Codrington, Adm. Sir E., 178–82
Collingwood, Adm., C., 44, 52
Congreve, Sir W., 56, 107, 146

Conrad, J., 39
Continental System, 45
Conway, 152
Creevey, T., 127
Crimean War, 108, 201–2
Croker, J. W., 120, 128
Crosbie, Capt., 144, 151, 154–60, 174
Curtis, Sir R., 71

Dalrymple, Sir J., 8
Dartmoor prison, 37
Davy, Sir H., 9
Desaix, 22–3
Dockyards, 27, 101, 105
Douglas, Marquis of, 30
Duncan, Hon. Capt., 77
Dundonald family, *see* Cochrane

Earp, G. B., 189–93
Ebrington, Lord, 129
Eldon, 1st Earl, 105, 127
El Gamo, 19
Ellenborough, Lord, 96, 121–9, 134, 187, 192, 193
Enterprise, 172, 182
Esmeralda, 149
Etna, 60–5
Excellent, 49
Exmouth, Adm. Lord E., 107, 171

Fabvier, General, 174, 176
Falkland islands, 201
Faraday, M., 110–11
Finlay, G., 172–7
Firefly, 197
Fortescue, J. W., 192
Fortifications, 198
Freyre, General, 158

Gale Jones, Citizen, 95–6
Galloway, R. H., 171
Gambier, Adm. Lord, 55 ff.
Genereux, 15
Gillray, J., 88
Glascock, Capt., 98
Gordon, General, 172, 176

Gosse, Dr., 174, 177, 182
Graham, Mrs. (Lady Calcott), 143, 156, 159
Graham, Sir J., 108, 111, 202
Grenfell, Adm., 160, 163, 203
Greville, C. C. F., 186, 202
Grey, C., 2nd Earl, 130, 186
Guise, Capt., 144, 148, 151
Gurney, W., 121, 124, 191
Guthrie, Dr., 17, 42

Hall, Capt. Basil, 149, 152, 155
Hamilton, Duke of, 32
Hampden Club, 94
Hankey, Lord, 113
Hannibal, 24
Hardy, Commodore, 155
Harvey, Adm. Sir E., 56
Hastings, Capt. A., 170–3, 180
Haswell, Lieut., 35
Hazlitt, W., 88
Hellas, 172–8
Henty, G. W., 144
Hind, 12
Hipper, Adm. Von, 40
Hone, W., 135
Honiton, 84–7
Hood, Adm. Sir S., 90
Horner, F., 88
Hunt, "Orator," 92–5

Ibrahim Pasha, 169, 179, 180–2
Imperieuse, 41 ff.

Jackson, W., 191–3
Jamaica, 201
Janus, 198
Jeffrey, Lord F., 88
Jerrold, D., 187
Johnstone, Cochrane, 116 ff., 129, 187
Julie, 52, 103

Kanares, Adm., 172, 179
Kangaroo, 21
Karteria (Perseverance), 172–6
Keith, Adm. Lord, 13, 14, 15, 22, 28, 31, 107

Kent, Duke of, 136
Keppel, Hon. H., 169
Kingfisher, 36–7
King George, 46, 102
Kitchener, Lord, 113

La Fortuna, 34
Larmour, Jack, 12
Lavie, Lawyer, 75, 120
Le Blanc, L. C. J., 125, 126
Lima, see Callao
Linois, Adm., 22

Macadam, J. L., 9
Maitland, Capt., 71
Malta, 46, 102–3
Mapleton, Lt. D., 34, 41
Maranham, 160–6
Markham, Adm. J., 30, 100, 101
Marryat, Capt. F., 38 ff., 59, 171
Martin, Adm. Sir Byam, 109, 185
Maudeslay, H., 142
Mediator, 59, 60–2
Mehemet Ali, 169
Melville, H. Dundas, Viscount, 32, 85, 178, 185, 196
Mercury, 172, 183
Miaoulis, Adm., 172
Miers, John, 143
Miller, General W., 144 ff.
Minerva, 37
Mitford, Mary Russell, 97
More, Hannah, 77
Mosquito fleet, 199
Mulgrave, Earl of, 54, 55, 70
Murdoch, W., 10

Napier, Adm. Sir C., 189, 202
Napier, Hon. W., 42
Napoleon I, 58, 77, 129
Narrative of Services, 189, 192
Navarino, 180–2
Neale, Sir H., 67
Nelson, Adm. Lord, 14
Newfoundland, 201
Notes on Mineralogy, etc., 200

Observations on Naval Affairs, 188
Ocean, 62
O'Higgins, Bernardo, 141
Order of the Bath, 68, 187

Pallas, 33 ff., 65
Pallière, Capt., 23
Palmerston, Lord, 30, 111, 112
Panmure, Lord Maule, Earl of Dal-
    housie, 105, 112
Parker, Lt., 17, 20, 29
Parker, Adm. Sir W., 109, 202
Parliamentary Reform, 83 ff., 137
Paull, James, 90, 92
Pedro I, of Brazil, 159, 160, 165
Pedro Primiero, 161
Perseverance, see *Karteria*
Piranga, 166
Place, Francis, 90–5, 128, 157
Playfair, Prof. Lord, 113, 190
Plymouth Corporation, 33
Political Register, see Cobbett
Popham, Adm. Sir Home, 55
Prize courts and Prize money, 101 ff.
Propaganda leaflets, 36
Proteau, Capt., 62
Prueba, 155
Pulling, Capt. C., 21

Quintero, 156–9

Rattler, 198
Ricardo, D., 172
Richardson, Gunner, 59, 65
Rising Star (or *Rising Sun),* 142, 167,
    171, 197
Robinson, H. Crabb, 185
Rockets, 56, 146
Rosas, Trinidad Castle, 49 ff.

St. Vincent, J. Jervis, Earl of, 13, 14,
    26–32, 36, 93, 100
San Martin, General, 141 ff.
Saumarez, Adm. Sir J., 23
Savannah, 142
Scarlett, Lord Abinger, 120
Scott, Sir W., 167

Scourge, 198
Scully, Mr., 189
Seymour, Adm. G., 37, 65, 75, 203
Sheridan, R. Brinsley, 90, 91–2, 130
Spartan, 48
Speedy, 7, 16 ff.
Spry, Capt., 144, 148, 154
Steamships, 171, 196. And *see Janus,*
    etc.
Stevenson, W. B., 149
Stewart, Adm. W. Houston, 42, 202
Stopford, Adm. Sir R., 65
Strategic ideas, 40, 53, 196–9

Tapageuse, 35
Tar, use of, 9, 200
Thetis, 13
Thomas, Capt., 174, 180
Thornborough, Adm. Sir E., 35
Tonnant, 117
Trelawny, E. J., 169
Trinidad, Pitch Lake, 200
Trinity House, 203
Trollope, A., 200
Turkish baths, 196

Valdivia, 146
Vidal, Ensign, 147

Walcheren, 77, 95, 105
Warrior, 199
Wellesley, 198
Wellesley family, 105
Wellington, Duke of, 107, 186
West, Capt., 49
Westminster elections, 88–90, 130
Whitbread, S., 89
Wilberforce, W., 76, 137
Wilkinson, Capt., 144
William IV, 186
Wilson, General Sir R., 190
Winsor, F. A., 10
Wood, Sir C., 111

Young, Adm. Sir W., 35, 42, 71–3, 107

Zenteno, Minister of Marine, 142, 148

ABOUT THE EDITORS

The Heart of Oak Sea Classics book series is edited by DEAN KING, author of *A Sea of Words: A Lexicon and Companion for Patrick O'Brian's Seafaring Tales* (Henry Holt, 1995; second edition, 1997) and *Harbors and High Seas: An Atlas and Geographical Guide to the Aubrey-Maturin Novels of Patrick O'Brian* (Holt, 1996), and editor, with John B. Hattendorf, of *Every Man Will Do His Duty: An Anthology of Firsthand Accounts from the Age of Nelson, 1793–1815* (Holt, 1997).

Comments on or suggestions for the Heart of Oak Sea Classics series can be sent to Dean King c/o Henry Holt & Co., 115 West 18th St., New York, NY 10011 or E-mailed to him at DeanHKing@aol.com.

The series' scholarly advisors are JOHN B. HATTENDORF, Ernest J. King Professor of Maritime History at the U.S. Naval War College, and CHRISTOPHER MCKEE, Samuel R. and Marie-Louise Rosenthal Professor and Librarian of the College, Grinnell College, author of, most recently, *A Gentlemanly and Honorable Profession: the Creation of the U.S. Naval Officer Corps, 1794–1815* (Naval Institute Press, 1991).